Earth and Spirit

Medicinal Plants and Healing Lore

from Puerto Rico

María Benedetti

VERDE LUZ

This book is available in Spanish as *¡Hasta los baños te curan!*
Remedios caseros y mucho más de Puerto Rico

Published by
VERDE LUZ
HC-1 Buzón 6361
Orocovis, Puerto Rico 00720-9706
Tel: (787) 867-5561

para Puerto Rico, pasado, presente y futuro

Acknowledgments

This book has been written in gratitude to the people of Puerto Rico who, along with their knowledge, shared food, shelter, warmth, music and laughter with me along the way:

Edwin Aguayo, Rosa Ligia Alvarez, Petra Angleró, Mikhail Antoun, María Cruz Avilés, Félix Nicolás Beato, Beba, Alma and Roberto Cabán, la familia Carrer, Ana Clausells de Costoso, Carmen Colón de Jorge, Carlos Alberto Costoso, Pepe Chávez, Delia, Eusebio Díaz Díaz, Cecilia Fernández, Angel González, Ricardo Osvaldo Guerrero, María Lagoa de González, Irenio López Mercado, Tomás Luzcampos, Freddy Martell, Eliot Monteverde, Carmen María Morales Serrano, Panky Negrón Maldonado, Esteban Núñez Meléndez, Alida and Edgardo Ortiz, Ramona Ortiz Santana, Casimira Osoris Fuentes, María Otero Collazo de Santiago, Altagracia Pagán, Rafaela Parrilla, Josefina Pizarro, Providencia Rivera, Luisa Flores Rovira, Kique and Tato Rodrígez Valentín, Carmen Rodríguez Vargas, Margarita Roque, Carmen Rupert, María Salgado, Cruz María Santiago, Eugenio Santiago Marrero, Julia Santiago, Marinilda Santini, Aida Sotomayor de Ramos, Brígida Sotomayor Vargas, Mercedes Sotomayor de Martell, Tai, Unmilo, Paula Valentín Mercado, Vanessa, Brunilda Vargas Muñiz, Camila Vargas viuda de Sotomayor, Inés Vargas Muñiz, Primi Socorro Vargas, Carmen Vega, Victor, Yari.

Also, I offer sincere thanks to the following people for volunteering their editorial and moral support, for believing in the value of this project, and for, in many was, helping me to bring it to fruition:

María del Perpetuo Socorro (mami), who read every interview in English and in Spanish, helped with difficult transcriptions, and whose love, music and ongoing support over 34 years made this book possible,

José Manuel Torres Santiago, who shares his love for and pride in his culture through classes, writing and public talks, and whose knowledge inspired my commitment to this project,

Jaime Antonio Estades Roque, who said, "Go! I know a few people there who will be glad to talk with you . . .",

Pedro Acevedo Rodríguez, for checking my botanical references,

Elmer Sánchez, for verifying congruence between taped and written material,

Kenneth Gumbs, for sharing his encyclopedic knowledge about Afro-caribbean music and religions,

Judith Vélez, for help with two difficult transcriptions,

Kal Wagenheim and *Olga Jiménez de Wagenheim*, for making important editorial suggestions,

Melchia Crowne, for ongoing and essential wisdom and support,

Susun S. Weed, for her workshops, classes and writings since 1978, and

Librada Sotomayor Fernández, for her stories, cooking lessons and love.

Finally, my deepest thanks to the circle of wholeness, the roads that opened, my protectors and guides, the music, the dreams, the plants, and very especially, the trees . . . who give of themselves so that we may read books.

Contents

ACKNOWLEDGMENTS

PERSONAL FOREWORD
A Tradition of Earth and Spirit   ix

THE INTERVIEWS

1 **The Medicine of Yesterday, Today**   **1**
Paula Valentín Mercado and Tato Rodríguez Valentín
of Las Marías

2 **Doña Petra's Favorite Remedies**   **13**
Petra Angleró Ortiz of Maricao and Mayagüez

3 **Midwife and Bonesetter of Orocovis**   **21**
María Cruz Avilés

4 **Herb Women of Mayagüez**   **33**
Brunilda Vargas Muñiz, Primi Socorro Vargas
and Brígida Sotomayor Vargas

5 **Two Spirit Healers of Loíza**   **57**
doña Casimira and doña Bolina

6 **A Humble Medicine of Earth and Spirit**   **77**
Cruz María Santiago of Morovis

7 Beauticians and Neighbors of Carolina   **89**
Ana Clausells de Costoso, Josefina Pizarro,
María Salgado, Julia Santiago and Monín Santana

8 Planting with the Moon in Caguas   *105*
Francisco (Panky) Negrón Maldonado

9 Living on the Land   *113*
Cheo and Bárbara Rodríguez of Orocovis

10 Healing with Plants for Sixty Years   129
María Otero Collazo and Eugenio Santiago Marrero
of Mayagüez and Morovis

EPILOGUE
Passing It On   **159**

PRACTICAL REFERENCES

Medicinal Plants and Folklore at a Glance   *171*
How to Prepare the Remedies
Contributors
A Practical Reference of Botanical and Spiritual Folklore

Medicinal Plants by Name and Family   **219**
Two Plant Identification Indices Organized Alphabetically
by Spanish and English Folk Names

Spanish and Puerto Rican Words and Terms   **245**
A Glossary

INDEX

Océano Atlántico

Mar Caribe

ISLA DE CULEBRA

ISLA DE VIEQUES

PUERTO RICO
Cortesía del Banco Gubernamental de Fomento de Puerto Rico.

A Tradition of Earth and Spirit

personal foreword

This book offers a glimpse of the tradition of popular medicine and related practices alive in Puerto Rico during the late 1980s: a system of mutual support and healing carried out by people close to their cultural roots.

This tradition of healing has arisen from real need, observation, experience and respect, both for the individuals in need of healing, and for the environment that provides the tools and catalysts for that healing. And it survives because — on many levels and in many ways — it works.

* * *

The process of working on this book has allowed me to explore and bring together two important aspects of my life: my love of nature and natural healing ways, and my Puerto Rican heritage which, too small a part of my childhood, I have begun to reclaim as an adult.

My grandmother's grandmother, Monserrate de Rivera, was a midwife in Mayagüez, Puerto Rico. Two generations later, my grandmother's sister, Librada Sotomayor Fernández, was an *espiritista** in the same town. She knew the medicinal plants, counseled people according to her access to the spirit world, and healed children with stomach disorders through a type of spiritual massage known as *santiguo*. It was Librada, my familial link in

**See glossary on page 241 for definitions of italicized words in Spanish.*

New York with the old ways of Puerto Rico, who told me about the value of rue *(la ruda)*** for "female problems" and taught me how to make a proper *sancocho* or tropical stew, *"como Dios manda."* As I prepare now to move to her homeland, I thank her and my grandmother for reminding me of and connecting me to such a venerable tradition of earth and spirit.

* * *

When I was eight, I began working with diet and other natural methods of healing to treat serious allergies. Thanks to my nature-loving father, my city-based childhood and adolescence were rich in rural experiences, and early on I fell in love with the natural world. When I was 17, I moved to the Catskill Mountain countryside of New York where, between college classes, I spent as much time as I could in the woods, hills, orchards and fields exploring my spirituality and learning about plants. During eleven years of country living, I studied herbalism and shared information and experiences with friends involved with forms of medicine that not only cure disease but also nourish and strengthen. I worked with sound and color, a diet of whole foods, and wild plants that grew in my surroundings.

Why wild plants? For starters, most pesticides used routinely on cultivated plants kill off not only insects (and people, if we're not careful) but also beneficial bacteria, fungi and other microorganisms in the soil. These microorganisms normally break down the elements of the earth and make them available to plants. Without these microorganisms and the chain of life that supports them, plants can not receive minerals from the soil, and are thus made dependent — almost exclusively — upon the nitrogen, phosphorus and potash that are added to the earth in the form of commercial fertilizers.

** *All plants are fully identified on pages 219-244. To search by Spanish folk names, see pages 219-230; to search by English folk names, see pages 231-244.*

Nitrogen, phosphorus and potash may help plants to grow big and fast, but in terms of nourishment, such plants can't compete with their wild and organically grown counterparts which — under good conditions — ingest a wide range of minerals from non-contaminated soil.

Since we've evolved as a species eating and healing with wild plants for thousands upon thousands of years, using wild plants also affirms our connection with our ancestors, and thus with the traditions that sustain and define us as a people . . . and as natural beings.

Finally, communion with the world of wild plants — using wild plants as food and medicine — is an ideal path to health maintenance, strengthening and healing. For plants are a direct connection to the life force within and surrounding us all. This life force imbues the plants (and us!) with the power to transform and thus, to heal.

Of course, as I learned from my mother and grandmother, the most effective medicine is often based on more than plant-related knowledge.

When I was growing up in Queens, New York, *abuelita* came often to care for my brother and me while my mother worked. And for 15 years, every single Wednesday, abuela cooked for us: *arroz con pollo, pollo guisado con papas,* mouth-watering *rellenos de papa,* unforgettable *pasteles* and, once or twice a year, *arroz con coco:* coconut rice pudding, island style, with raisins, ginger, cinnamon and bright, whole cloves. The ritual of eating this Puerto Rican soul food kept us sitting at the table for hours, savoring, remembering, laughing, arguing, planning, singing. On Wednesdays half the block smelled like *abuela's* food, and our kitchen became a rollicking center of sharing and celebration.

Abuela's most memorable gift to us may have been physical nourishment, but she was also there for my brother and me when we were sick. She healed us as she rocked us on her lap, offered us teas of chamomile flowers, told us stories about childhood hardships in Puerto Rico and tried desperately to teach us to iron. It was through *abuela* that I first became conscious of the relationship between love and the exercise of arduous quotidian chores (her way was always the long way, the slow way) and between healing and nourishment, always through love.

We are all healers. For when we cook with love for one another, dance, sing and play music that moves us, use home remedies based on plants and other natural resources from our surroundings, ask for information from our dreams, pray or meditate, offer massages and act intuitively on hundreds of other levels to create and restore harmony and keep ourselves (and/or others) healthy, we are practicing medicine ways shared by traditional peoples all over the world.

Although certain people have always been recognized as having the "gift" of healing, traditional folk medicine is generally accessible to all. That is, regardless of economic and educational backgrounds, everyone can learn to use some useful, natural healing techniques. The work of most traditional healers is based upon nourishment on physical, emotional and spiritual levels, and upon an ability to transform through this nourishment. Few are specialists. Many work "full time" in other, unrelated fields. These factors contribute to traditional folk medicine's invisibility but make it no less valuable.

Since the dawn of human society, traditional healers have worked in myriad ways to support the health and integrity of individuals, families and entire communities, while helping to maintain a balanced relationship between people and their environment. Even today, traditional folk healers tend to 80% of the world's entire population.[1] And all over the world, the practices of

---

[1] From *The Hidden Power of Plants,* WGBH Educational Foundation, NOVA series, Public Television 1987.

traditional midwives and healers — from shamans to bonesetters — are being validated through science.

Traditional peoples from Africa to Greenland, from Tibet to the Americas have always recognized and made use of psychological and spiritual influences in medicine. During the last 25 years or so, post-industrial science has assured us that yes, our own bodies can be stimulated by certain psychological states to produce the chemicals we need to feel and get better when we are depressed or ill. And the investigations have only just begun.

Meanwhile, plants used by traditional healers and midwives worldwide (ranging from garlic to the fungus ergot) are being recognized and taken more and more seriously as valuable crude drugs and/or sources of essential oils and alkaloids, which serve as the basis of pharmaceutical preparations. In fact, several pharmaceutical companies are taking part in special research programs with the aim of finding drugs to treat cancer, AIDS and herpes[2]. These programs involve working closely with traditional medical practitioners who have been using plants for generations, and who have established empirical evidence of success.

---

[2]According to the Herb Research Foundation's journal, titled *Herbalgram* (#11, winter '87), during 1987 The National Cancer Institute awarded five-year contracts to The New York Botanical Garden, The Missouri Botanical Garden, and the University of Illinois. ($627,000 will be spent on plants from South America; $654,000 on plants fromAfrica; and $1.4 million on plants from Southeast Asia.) The New York Botanical Garden will collect about 1,500 specimens from Latin American tropical forests, especially those used medicinally by indigenous populations. The plants will be tested in extract form for anti-tumour activity.

Anti herpes and anti-AIDS substances are also being pursued in the same way with great interest. Plus, a natural insecticide is currently being sought to fight against the mosquito *Aedis egyptiae*, responsible for the spread of dengue and malaria.

In general, connections with folklore guarantee a high probability of finding active substances. Also, as evidenced in this volume, traditional healers are likely to find not just one, but several uses for each plant, while the academically trained pharmacologist tends to investigate isolated compounds of a "complex, crude drug specimen" (plant), in search of one specific activity to counteract one particular health condition or narrowly related problems.

Several contributors to *Earth and Spirit* use plants whose value has not been proven by the scientific establishment. There are many reasons for this. For instance, when science tests plants for their value as drugs, "non-active" constituents such as glucosides, chlorophyll and nutritive factors are ignored. In most cases, only alkaloids — which have the most dramatically observable biological effects — are sought, measured and tested. [3]

While this approach has yielded many life saving drugs, it

---

[3]The process of isolating individual "active" constituents is described by Dr. Oswald Guerrero of the Department of Pharmaceutical Science at the University of Puerto Rico in Río Piedras:

"First, the plant must be collected and dried; we're not interested in the water content of the plant, and dried plants take up far less space than fresh ones. (There are special drying ovens which allow for the process to take place slowly.) Once they're dried, we powder the plant material and make extracts of the plant using solvents such as ethanol. The ethanol extracts most of the plant's components. We then evaporate the alcohol and we're left with an extract of the plant. This extract includes the plant's constituents in a small volume, which makes it very easy to work with.

"Next, the extract is given to the pharmacologist or to the microbiologist, the scientist who can help us to determine if the plant has the activity we're looking for: diuretic, anti-diabetic, etc. (The pharmacologist might use animals or micro-organisms to do the testing.)

"Then we divide the extract into two solvents, which have a different polarity, and using a process called chromatography, we separate the fractions or individual components of the extract even more. When we present these fractions to the pharmacologist again, s/he'll be able to tell us exactly which part is active and we separate that fraction from the others."

ignores the factors of *nourishment* (wild plants are extremely high in vitamins and minerals in a form that is optimally received and utilized by the body), *the tonifying effect* of plants taken over a long period of time, *the often surprising synergistic effects of combining plant substances,* and the *psychological-spiritual aspect of working with local plants and a trusted, loving healer.* Of course, this last aspect of healing, although impossible to measure or prove by objective means, is recognized and valued to varying degrees in every culture.

Through generations of experience and empirical testing, the people of Puerto Rico have made some astute and extremely important observations in terms of plant classification. For instance, the designation of medicinal plants as "hot" or "cool" in their activity roughly corresponds to two scientific categories, denoting the presence and absence of alkaloids, chemical substances that cause marked physiological changes.

According to the Puerto Rican pharmacognosist, Dr. Esteban Núñez Meléndez, most "hot" plants taste bitter. Containing alkaloids, their use should be controlled according to the knowledge of experienced herbal medicine practitioners. Many produce side effects. "Cool" or "cooling" plants are mostly nourishing and strengthening or tonifying, and refreshing. Many are diuretic. They can be taken on a regular basis, and are not bitter. "For this reason," he explains, "you'll note that 'hot' herbs are recommended for acute conditions, including fevers, while 'cooling' herbs may be taken all the time."

* * *

Personally, I can attest to the efficacy of many of the remedies described in this work. Aloe *(la sábila)* for bronchial complaints, burns and constipation, wild balsam apple *(el cundeamor)* for skin problems, chicken bone or pigeon broth for chronic fatigue, rue and broad leaf coriander *(el recao)* for menstrual irregularity, and herbal baths for physical and spiritual renewal are among them.

Meanwhile, modern computer studies validate the tremendous knowledge and foresight demonstrated by traditional farmers throughout the world, proving that practices like composting and planting according to the moon's phases not only offer us superior nourishment, but also contribute greatly to the health of our environment.

Rich in practical knowledge and wisdom, this island nation's earth-based medicine tradition represents a tremendous contribution to the contemporary science of healing, and to Puerto Rican and Caribbean culture.

I hope that this small body of work will spark interest in the passing on of more and more information by word of mouth, songs, writings, and the growing practice of what we may still remember.

María Dolores Hajosy Benedetti
September 1988

The Medicine of Yesterday, Today

Paula Valentín Mercado
and
Tato Rodríguez Valentín
of Las Marías

elder   *el saúco*

Paula Valentín Mercado

Tato Rodríguez Valentín sun-dries freshly picked coffee beans.

The Medicine of Yesterday, Today

Paula Valentín Mercado
and
Tato Rodríguez Valentín
of Las Marías

My meeting with doña Paula took me by surprise. I had stopped the car just outside of Las Marías to photograph her home, bordered by orange and coffee trees, banana plants and an interesting variety of medicinal herbs.

As I approached, I inhaled the welcoming smell of a wood fire, and suddenly faced doña Paula as she trudged up the hill behind her house, wiping the sweat from her forehead with a well-worn handkerchief.

"What are you looking for?"

"I was hoping I could take a picture of your beautiful herbs. I'm interested in medicinal plants."

"Well plants are my medicine! Pills make me feel horrible, so I use the plants, and I grow them right here."

"I'd love to hear about how you use herbs."

"At your service. But let's go inside and have something cool to drink first. Do you like pineapple juice?"

That's how it started.

I stayed for two days and two nights with doña Paula and her sons, eating rice with fresh pigeon peas (gandules) just picked off the bush, knocking papayas and oranges (chinas) off the trees, climbing the nearby hills, separating small pebbles from the sun-dried coffee

3

beans, watching a mountain sunrise and a 7 AM livestock sale, touring the road to Arecibo and all points in between, asking questions about plants and traditional agricultural practices, roaming the farm, drinking spring water from impromptu cups made from wide, green malanga leaves, and collecting leaves, stems, roots and flower specimens for my book of pressed, medicinal plants. All this in the warm and familiar spirit of rural Puerto Rican hospitality.

Doña Paula raised six sons without moving even a mile away from her father's farm, where she grew up. In her life she's seen many rural paths become paved roads, and many of her old neighbors have chosen urban life. But in rural Las Marías, the land is still a source of livelihood for many, and a source of pride for all.

Paula: I'm 71 years old, and I was born right below, at the lower edge of the farm here. My parents were simple *jíbaros*, and they worked hard, cultivating the land.

In those days, we all worked at embroidery and washed clothes for people; but most of all, we harvested coffee. And believe me, it wasn't easy. Back then, a 28-pound measure (*almúd*) was worth 15 cents! Anyway, that's how we grew up, always working. There were eleven of us kids.

They built a school nearby when I was ten years old. In order to get there, I had to cross the river and walk along roads that were really just mud paths. I made it through the third grade when I was 14. Then I started working full-time on the farm and at a neighbor's house.

M: What do you like most about living in the country?

Paula: I love the plants and the animals. I've always raised cows and chickens, for instance. We have 18 chickens, a bunch of chicks, and three baby roosters that have just begun to crow. We also have cows and calves, and they provide fertilizer for the plants. Country life is so satisfying!

M: I was attracted to your home by the medicinal plants growing outside. Would you please tell me about some of them?

Paula: Well, I have *la paletaria*. *Paletaria* tea is cooling and very good for children when they get heat rash and other skin irritations. *Paletaria* tea is also good for bladder problems, especially when someone has difficulty urinating. It's very cooling.

A strong tea of rue *(la ruda)* is also good for painful urination and bladder problems but, like fennel *(el hinojo)*, it's most well known for women's monthly cramps and related conditions.

Here we have lemon balm *(el toronjil)* and Caribbean spearmint *(la yerba buena)*. They're both very good for the stomach. If you're nauseous and vomiting, you just need a good tea of the two combined. I'll tell you, that lemon balm is the best thing in the world! But if there's none around, you can also use sour orange leaves *(las hojas del naranjo)*.

M: Do you use these remedies frequently?

Paula: Whenever I need them. The plants are my medicine! Look, there's an important medicinal plant, black nightshade *(la mata de gallina)*. It makes a good tea mixed with Caribbean vervain *(la verbena)* for fever. Black nightshade and *paletaria* grow all over the place! And look over there; that spineless *tuna* cactus is great chopped up and boiled for a while. It's nourishing and it's also good for stomach problems.

I had some beautiful lemon verbena *(la yerba Luisa)* and marjoram *(la mejorana)* too, but once I had to leave home to care for my grandson for a few days, and when I returned, people had come by and they'd taken the plants that were just budding. You see, people today just don't know how to work with plants. For example, few people know that lemon verbena should only be picked during the cool of the morning.

We walk toward the back yard, which offers a view of the mountainous, green countryside below and beyond us.

Paula: These are our coffee trees. I plant coffee, I harvest it, I dry it, I toast it over a wood fire, grind it up and then I boil and drink it. And I love it! I have cans of coffee waiting to be toasted, but I only do that work in the cool of the morning. Otherwise I get a terrible headache.

Doña Paula points to an old fashioned, outdoor cooking hearth.

M: You don't see too many of these any more! The smouldering fire wood smells wonderful.

Paula: Yes, here I toast my coffee and cook up starchy vegetables *(las viandas)* and beans. I also prepare food for the pigs here. I use my outdoor stove for the most difficult cooking chores. When you came along, I was cooking beans for dinner.

M: How did you learn about medicinal plants?

Paula: From my mother. When I was a child, we never bought medicines. We always used the plants from the earth. Whenever we got sick, *mamá* made remedies from whatever was growing. She used sour orange leaves and elder *(el saúco)* a lot, for instance. And I still use them. You just boil up the beautiful white elder flower with some orange leaves and ginger *(el jengibre)*. That tea takes away your cold. We used to make that and many other medicines from boiled plants. We call those teas *guarapos*. We usually added honey, which is the best thing in the world!

For colds and congestion, we also used *guarapos* of *el poleo*.

M: And for fevers?

Paula: I mentioned a mixture of Caribbean vervain with black nightshade, but you can also combine black nightshade with common plantain *(el llantén)*. Lemon grass *(el limoncillo)* also lowers fever. My mother used to peel and mash up lemon grass root, and then boil it up with anise seeds *(el anís)*. We'd drink that tea hot, and no matter how high the fever was, lemon grass tea with anise seeds always lowered it.

M: Lemon grass has such a beautiful fragrance!

Paula: And it's so useful! You can even brush your teeth with the root. You make a little packet with it and just rub it over your gums as if it were a toothbrush. It freshens up the breath and makes your mouth feel great!

But before I get off the subject of fever, you can also take sour orange leaves and add *poleo* and yellow trumpet leaves *(el saúco amarillo)*. That *guarapo* cools the fever and gets rid of even the worst cough in the world!

For fever and headache, we always used *la salvia*. For a simple headache, we might just tie warmed-up leaves on to our forehead and temples with a handkerchief. For fever, we would stick *salvia* leaves to the soles of our feet with camphor ointment *(el alcanfor)*, and stick more leaves onto our foreheads.

In the U.S. you probably don't see too many of these home remedies, but here we grew up harvesting coffee and planting native fruits and vegetables. We were always enduring the heat of the midday sun, and we got tremendous headaches. That's why we used the *salvia* leaves so often.

I get headaches nowadays too, but it's from high blood pressure.

M: How do you treat high blood pressure?

Paula: When passion fruit *(la parcha)* is in season, I drink the juice. I've also heard that papaya lowers the blood pressure, but I've never tried it. I'll tell you one thing though, papaya mixed with grated coconut and boiled up with sugar makes one phenomenal desert!

M: Are there some activities that seem to affect your blood pressure?

Paula: My headaches seem to be related to what I eat, and red meat seems to make them worse. When I have chamomile *(la manzanilla),* I use it and it helps me, but not only for headaches! It's also good for the stomach and for body aches and fever. Yes, chamomile helps me a lot! Here in Las Marías, the chamomile plant flowers in December; by January it's already dry. I save the flowers that come in December for making my teas all year long, because it's the best thing in the world! And you know, they sell chamomile flowers in drug stores and even the fancy stores too, nowadays!

If my headache is really bad, I put my feet in a big bucket of hot water. Then I put a bag of ice on my head or around my neck. That treatment also lowers the blood pressure when I feel it's gone all the way up.

When I get to feeling nervous or anxious, I make a tea of sour orange leaves, and that helps a lot.

M: Have you ever sold any of the herbs you grow here?

Paula: No, but when people come looking for medicinal plants, I offer them the remedies they need. In fact, just the other day a doctor from town came looking for some aloe *(la sábila)*. A child had been badly burned, and aloe is the best thing in the world for burns. First the doctor came, then the next day his wife came by, and finally, they sent a little boy to get some more!

M: Do you know of any other uses for the aloe plant?

Paula: It's very good if someone has chest pains, and there are many ways of preparing it. My father used it a lot. First we'd peel it, cut it up, and put it in a jug of water. Then we'd leave it outside during the night, *al sereno*. During the day, he'd drink it. My father also used to get sore throat and coughs, and he swore by aloe for those conditions too.

I'm always in the sun and I use aloe when my skin gets dried out and burned. I simply cut it and pass the inside gel over my skin as if it were a lotion. It's tremendous for the skin, really.

You know, when my father's kidney pains started in, we used to cut the fat leaves of the spineless *tuna* cactus into two flat slices. Then we cooked them among the coals for a while, and when they'd cooled off, we'd place them on his lower back and cover that poultice with a towel. That helped him a lot.

I show doña Paula the pressed plants I've been collecting.

Paula: Here you have *la ipecacuana*. It's very good for coughs, and it can be used by children and grownups alike. You simply boil up some new leaves with Caribbean spearmint or lemon balm or marjoram leaves. It really gets rid of phlegm!

The castor bean plant *(la higuereta)* is used for making poultices. We used to heat up the leaf, chop it up, mix it with belladonna ointment and apply it as a wrap for swollen ankles.

9

It was good for any kind of inflammation, including for the cows, after giving birth.

They don't sell belladonna ointment in Las Marías any more, but my mother used it a lot. It was great when someone had a toothache or other swellings of the mouth, even mumps!

And when someone suffered from arthritic joints, we rubbed the grease of a guinea hen on the joints as if it were an ointment. My girl, there are so many home remedies!

M: I've heard that *el cundeamor* is used for getting rid of skin fungus.

Paula: If you have a problem with itching, you simply boil it up and take a bath in it. The castor bean plant can be used in the same way, actually.

We go inside to separate stray pebbles from the dried coffee, and Tato, her eldest son, arrives. I show him my book of plant specimens, and spontaneously, the conversation resumes.

Tato: The boiled root of *el moriviví* cured my brother when he had an infected molar. He swished around mouthfuls of that tea and the pain subsided completely. It worked right away, and his tooth hasn't bothered him since then at all. And that same remedy — repeated over time — can even be used to make a bad tooth fall out!

Then there's *el guaco*, which grows just about everywhere. A bath of *guaco* is good for open sores, cuts and many other conditions. It kills germs. In fact, there's a saying, when someone is beyond all help, "Not even *el guaco* can save you!" It's a plant you can trust.

Paula: You know, I prepare ginger with hot milk at night when we have cold weather, and we *do* have cold weather in the mountains here. You simply mash up the ginger and boil it in a little bit of water for ten to fifteen minutes. Then you mix that tea with hot milk and add sugar to taste. Delicious!

Ginger is tremendously warming, whether you take it internally or use it as a poultice. When my father suffered from leg cramps, my mother prepared bitter ginger *(el jengibre amargo)* this way: First she would roast it among the live coals. When it got soft, she'd take it out and let it cool. Then she'd mash it up and put it in some *alcoholado* for rubs. She used two or three handfuls of ginger per liter of *alcoholado*, which got stronger with time. Those ginger rubs really worked for him!

Tato: Ginger is also great for stomach cramps, or when you're just feeling weak. It stimulates the circulation. And we've always used it for therapeutic baths.

M: Can you describe one of those baths?

Tato: First you find the plants you want to use: avocado leaves *(el aguacate)*, Caribbean vervain, castor bean leaves, *el higuillo oloroso, la rompecota, el sacabuche,* ginger root, a little bit of everything. We use about three handfuls for five gallons of water, boiling the plants for a good half hour so that their medicinal qualities can be transferred to the water.

Paula: Then, when that liquid is no longer too hot, wash up, strain the bath water, get into the shower, and then you have someone pour that bath over your entire body. The running stream of water takes away body pains and other bad feelings.

Tato: After the bath, you can't rinse yourself off or anything, because you don't want to dilute the benefits of the plants. The best thing about these herbal baths is that they wash away both physical and mental complaints.

If someone has a fever, the same type of bath will help to lower it.

M: Tato, do you have a favorite plant?

Tato: Absolutely! The elder! For me it's the plant with most beautiful flower in the world, and I've done a lot of traveling, seen a lot of flowers. I also admire it for its subtle fragrance.

M: I've enjoyed elder flowers as a food, fried up in batter like fritters. The berries are also wonderful. And the root of the elder tree is known around the world as a universal remedy. It's probably one of the most important medicinal plants available today.

Tato: I've used it for colds and fever, but you can drink teas of the flowers and leaves even if you're not sick. It's a beautiful plant!

Paula: Well, that's how it was, the medicine of yesterday. It worked for us then, and for some of us, it still does!

Doña Petra's Favorite Remedies

Petra Angleró Ortiz
of Maricao and Mayagüez

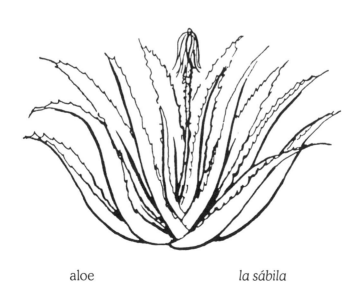

aloe   *la sábila*

Petra Angleró Ortiz poses with a treasured aloe plant.

Doña Petra's Favorite Remedies

Petra Angleró Ortiz
of Maricao and Mayagüez

I met doña Petra Angleró Ortiz in La Plaza de Colón of Mayagüez during a nocturnal Holy Week procession. My cousin Mercedes had told me: "Petra knows about plants that heal," and she was right. Doña Petra lives in a modern retirement condominium, where she participates in several community activities. She also serves as a member of the Legion of Mary, caring for the aged and infirm. Although she lives in the city, she stays close to the natural world through her house plants (aloe, violets, the "lucky chucho" or snake plant) and even through the presence of neighborly reinitas, small songbirds who drop in through her sunny balcony to snack on the sugar she leaves for them in her living room. She says her eyes are "bad," but from her sixth floor apartment, she pointed out little plants in the lot below that I couldn't distinguish even with my 20/20 vision. "It must be my affinity for them," she explained smiling.

Petra: I was born in Maricao, and that's where my mother, Felícita Ortiz, taught me all about plants. In those days, when we had asthma attacks, she would go out to the backyard to cut some elder *(el saúco)*. Then she'd mash up the stems to extract the juice. For every two tablespoons of that juice, she would mix a teaspoon of cooking oil and a pinch of salt. We took it as often as she told us to, and within two or three days, good bye, asthma!

In those days, everyone recognized the value of the plants, but look out that window. They just chopped down the biggest bay rum *(la malagueta)* tree around! Nowadays people just don't take plants seriously. I don't know what they must be thinking. What could be more important than nature and the medicine that comes from nature?

M: I've been thinking a lot about the times when people didn't have access to hospitals as they do now. How did the people of Maricao deal with a broken arm or leg?

Petra: When I was growing up, we used a plant called Madeira vine *(la suelda consuelda)*. We heated the leaves over a bit of steam, chopped them up, and mixed them in a little bowl with warm cooking oil. After the bone had been set, we put that Madeira vine poultice all over the affected area and covered it with gauze or other fabric. We would leave it for about two days before changing it, and it helped a lot. It was also very effective when used for sprains.

M: Have you used many plant-based poultices?

Petra: Sure! I've made many the way I just described, and I've made them by simply placing a leaf covered with ointment on top of the affected area and holding it on with a wrap of some kind. You can also mash a leaf up to extract its liquid, and put that liquid on top of the bruise or burn or whatever it is. It depends on the problem you want to treat.

I prepare my own medicated camphor ointment *(el alcanfor)* to use with plant poultices. It's refreshing, it eases the pain, and it opens up the pores so that the medicine of the plant can penetrate better.

First I mash up two little blocks of camphor until they're just powder. Then I melt a five-ounce jar of Vaseline in a little saucepan on a low flame. When the Vaseline is liquid, I add the powdered camphor and stir until it's well dissolved. I let it cool a little and then I spoon it all back into the same Vaseline jar.

When I want to apply a leaf poultice, I place the leaf or leaves on the skin, and then apply the medicated ointment over the leaf. It softens the leaf and helps it to give up its medicine. I've used a lot of leaf poultices, and they help a great deal.

I've made plenty of poultices using *la baquiña!* And speaking of *la baquiña,* now I'm going to tell you a story.

I was taking some pills that the doctor prescribed recently, and they caused an irritation in the urinary tract. During that time, I had a lovely dream that I was picking the leaves of *la baquiña*, a plant that grows in cool, shady places.

The very next day I went to see a friend, and she had lots of *la baquiña* at her place. I told her, "What a coincidence! Last night I dreamed about la baquiña, and here it is!" She offered me some, and I boiled up enough to fill a couple of bottles. And it cured me of the irritation I'd been feeling. *La baquiña* is good for the entire urinary system. It even gets rid of kidney stones!

But won't you have something to eat, my child?

M: No thank you, doña Petra. I'm full. But, I'm very interested in remedies used as food, remedies that nourish the body.

Petra: The best remedy for a woman who has just given birth is what we call the calabash *(la higüera)* or white gourd medicine. During birth, the uterus goes through a lot, and may even get displaced. The white gourd medicine nourishes and tonifies the womb at a time when it needs support. With this remedy and a good rest, the mother will always be fine.

M: Do you cook up the gourd?

Petra: No, it's a type of tisane, so it's not cooked at all.

The traditional way of making it is this: First, bore a hole in one end of a large, unripe, white calabash and pour into that hole as many whole cloves *(clavos dulces)*, anise seeds *(el anís)* and anise stars *(el anís de estrella)* as fit into one's hand. Then, seal and bury the gourd for a couple of days until a liquid forms inside. The spices keep it from spoiling, but it does ferment a bit.

If you want to be more modern, you can make the same medicine by scooping out all of the gourd's flesh and seeds, putting it all in a glass bowl, adding the spices and leaving it in the refrigerator for a few days.

Any way it's prepared, she should take about a cup a day, liquid and solid, for about nine days straight, always at room temperature. And during that time she should rest. In fact, if she wants to preserve her womb, she shouldn't do any heavy work at all for a full 40 days! Today so many modern women go back to work just a couple of weeks after giving birth.

M: A lot has changed!

Petra: Yes, but women still boil up the paper-like peel and the ends of a couple of heads of garlic *(el ajo)* to treat menstrual pains. And even now, if you have a growth of fungus on your skin, the best remedy is a bottle of *el cundeamor*. Simply fill a bottle with the chopped-up, fresh plant, and cover it all with three parts cooking oil or mineral oil and one part rubbing alcohol. Then leave it for a few days so that the medicinal qualities and the color of the plant can seep into the liquid. Apply it to the affected area as often as needed. *El cundeamor* heals! And I guarantee it, because I've used it to cure my son's condition with it, once and for all!

M: And it's so easy to prepare!

Petra: It's only easy if *el cundeamor* is growing in your neighborhood. Thank goodness, it's easy to find lemons around here. I practically cured myself of arthritis using lemons. And I was almost in a wheelchair!

M: Tell me how you did it!

Petra: I read about this remedy in a book, and let me tell you, it worked for me. You start out drinking the juice of one lemon *(el limón)* in a bit of water, without sugar or anything. The next day, you drink the juice of two lemons in water. The next day, you drink the juice of three, and so on, until you drink the juice of 30 lemons in one day. Then you start reducing the number until you're down to one again. It's a two month process.

M: I guess so many sour lemons send the arthritis running!

Petra: *(laughter)* Now I just drink the juice of one or two lemons a day, and I'm nearly free of arthritis, thank God.

M: Amen! Doña Petra, I'm sitting here admiring your beautiful aloe plant *(la sábila)*. Do you use aloe as medicine?

Petra: Come and see what I have in the refrigerator, so you can learn something new. With this aloe compound, I've relieved my grandson's asthma several times. Used to be he couldn't even sleep; he'd be coughing all the time. And his poor mother, running to the doctor at all hours of the night. That's when I started preparing him my aloe compound. But taste the raw aloe first.

M: It smells like stale, old underarm sweat! And it tastes *extremely* bitter!

Petra: That's right! Now taste my aloe compound. Most of the liquid you see here is from the aloe, which I'm letting steep with honey and spices . . . and rum.

M: Mmmmm! It tastes like cloves! Spicy . . . almost hot, and it's lost its bitterness. Delicious! What's the recipe?

Petra: Just peel two large aloe leaves, cut the inner gelatin into cubes, and place them in a quart-size glass or ceramic jar. (The aloe should fill 1/3 of the jar.) Then add nearly ½ cup of spices including star anise, whole cloves and cinnamon sticks *(la canela)* and a full cup of honey. Top it off with rum to preserve it. Without the rum, you'd have to refrigerate it, or mold would grow in it. But I think the rum enhances the flavor too! *(laughter)* And it will keep forever! I wait three or four weeks before taking it, a tablespoon at a time, liquid and solid combined. Because the aloe takes on a good flavor!

M: Yesterday I interviewed three people, and after each interview I was offered a full meal. I ate so much that this morning my stomach was a little edgy. I couldn't even eat breakfast! But your aloe compound seems to be helping already.

Petra: Of course! Besides treating asthma, coughs and colds, this remedy is great for digestion, too. Look around for a little jar in that cabinet and take some with you. May it serve you well, and may God bless you for me.

Midwife and Bonesetter
of Orocovis

María Cruz Avilés

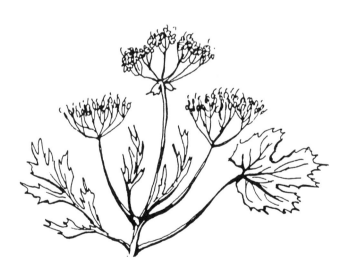

anise   *el anís de semilla*

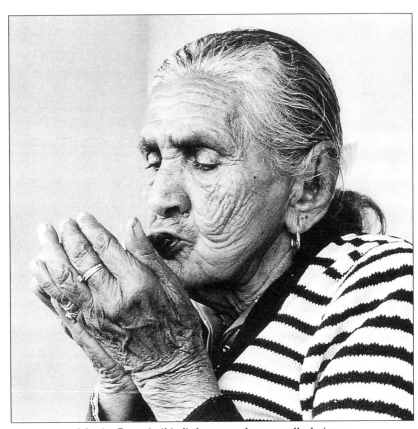

María Cruz Avilés lights up a home-rolled cigar.

Midwife and Bonesetter of Orocovis

María Cruz Avilés

I arrived in Orocovis one Sunday in May of 1987, just in time to enjoy the town's annual farm festival. Enjoying the privilege of being surrounded by people who love the land, I began to ask adults of all ages about traditional healers in the area. Almost everyone mentioned doña María Cruz Avilés.

"She helps the women give birth."

"She sets broken bones."

"She gives healing rubs."

"She must be almost 100 years old by now!"

"Everybody knows her!"

"She was my midwife."

"If you pull a muscle, she can help you."

"If you break your arm . . . "

"She helped deliver every child in my family!"

The festival was small but generous, and I gathered free samples of cacao, young tree saplings, and locally grown fruit. There was excitement in the air, partly because later than night, Andrés Jiménez (el Jíbaro), Orocovis' own internationally famous troubadour, would perform. With eight hours to wait before the concert, I was guided to the road to Las Alturas, a housing project about two miles out of town.

Doña María greeted me as if she'd known me all my life. First we planted the saplings, then she squirreled away the cacao, offered

23

me some fresh, home-roasted coffee, and we sat down to a talk that rambled on for hours. Here's a short excerpt of our exchange, which was interrupted by several side conversations, a photo album session, and a wonderful supper of chicken and rice delivered by a neighbor.

María: A lifetime is a long time! I'm 88 years old, and I've almost always worked as a midwife. I caught my first baby when I was 13, but I didn't keep on working at that time. When I was 18, I married a 40-year old man. That's when it really began. I had 17 children, and I had them all by myself.

M: No one helped you to give birth?

María: No one. No one ever helped me, nor has anyone seen my private parts! I've never been admitted to a hospital. When I felt the pains coming, the old man would go into town to shop or do other errands. Then I would put wood on the stove to heat up the irons* and give birth alone. It wasn't easy, but I did what I had to do. Seventeen children!

M: What position did you get into to give birth so many times?

María: Come into my room, and I'll show you. When I felt the labor pains, I'd get down on my knees and hold on to the bedpost here, shaking my belly all the while.

M: Is that the position you have other women get into to give birth?

*In doña María's time, just before birthing, several irons were heated among live coals. These were used to heat cotton wraps, which were placed over the womb area in order to lessen the pain and hasten delivery.

María: No. I have the others lie down on their backs because that's how they want to do it.

M: Tell me about your work as a midwife.

María: Let's say you've come to me for help. If you've never given birth before, the first thing I do is check to see if you're wide enough for a baby to come out of you. If I see that you're not, I'll tell you: "When you feel the first labor pains, go straight to the hospital so that they'll be able to do a Caesarean on you."

I also check your belly to see if the child is positioned to come out head first or by its bottom, in a breech position.

M: And if it's positioned to come out breech?

María: Then I rub and rub and rub and rub and rub your belly. If the baby's little head is here on top, I massage you so that it ends up down here at the bottom.

Let's say you come to me four months pregnant, and I see that you're going to have twins. I'll prepare you so that they'll both come out head first, just right.

When my granddaughter was four months along in her pregnancy, she came by for one of my massages. The baby was upside down, but I didn't say anything to her about it. I just told her to stop by every once in a while so I could massage her. When she was ready to deliver, I put three sheets and two pillows on the floor, she lay down, and the baby came out perfect.

M: What if I haven't come to see you so soon in my pregnancy? What if I am nine months pregnant, and the baby is in a breech position?

María: I'd tell you to go to the doctor, because I can't change a baby's position so late in the pregnancy. For that, I have to start working with you from the fourth month on.

I'm going to tell you something . . . . I can tell by the color of the mother's nipples if the child will be a boy or a girl!

M: How did you learn all this?

María: After giving birth to 17 children all by myself? I guess I should know something about it! *(laughter)*

Listen, my first child was born when I'd only been married eight months. He was a seven monther. So I know better when they tell me that a child weighing four or five pounds or more has been in the making for only seven months. No one can fool me! And I'll tell you something else. I've never performed any of those dirty operations. Never, never, never! I'm not that kind of woman!

M: Have you had good luck with the babies you've helped to deliver?

María: Honey, I've never lost a mother, and my only stillborn child was a poor little thing with two heads. No other baby has died in childbirth with me.

M: More or less, how many births have you attended?

María: Don't even ask! One of my daughters has six children, but that's nothing. All of the others have ten, up to 16. And that's just my own family! How many births have I attended? I could never count them. I've been working for so many years, and working constantly! Children are born easily with me, thank God.

Once my daughter Blanca said she wanted to give birth in

town, although she'd already had four with me at home, with no complications at all. I told her: "If you want to go to town, let's go!" So we went into town with her husband and all, and as soon as we got her to the hospital, she gave birth. There was no need for her to be hospitalized, but she was. All the nurses asked me: "What's going on here, doña María?" So I had to explain that my daughter had wanted to give birth in town. But her husband said: "Listen, from here on in, no child of mine is going to be born in town!" *(laughter)*

She had more after that.

M: At your place?

María: Yes indeed. It's much, much better at home.

Thanks to God and the Virgin Mary, I've never had any real problems with the births I've helped along. Nowadays, women get pregnant and they go to the hospital and the hospital gives them milk. But it's a cold kind of milk! And they walk around all day, up and down with store-bought milk so that their babies can drink out of bottles. Well, I'd never give that milk to my own! I brought up my children on breast milk. I never gave them a bottle, never in my life. Never, never, never! And now, you see so much of that junk.

M: Today, even in the United States, where so much of that store-bought milk formula is manufactured, doctors recognize that breast milk protects babies best from infection and disease. I've also read that the muscle tone in the mouths of children who breast feed is much better than in those who nurse from bottles. Breast feeding is pretty common in the U.S. now.

María: Well, I should hope so!

27

M: So let's say that I've come to you because I'm in labor. I'm going to give birth now. What will you do?

María: I'll stay here with you. Every time you have a pain, I'll give you a rub with a special ointment and a strong tea of anise seeds *(el anís)* with the leaves of coffee senna *(la hidionda chiquita)*. That tea helps to eliminate gas, and if there's pain, it relieves the pain as well.

But maybe you're not pregnant, my child. Maybe you've come for a special massage because your leg or foot is injured or out of place. I make those kinds of adjustments too. I rub the area with a special alcoholated lotion *(alcoholado)* fortified with lots of fresh plants.

M: Like bay rum *(la malagueta)*?

María: Bay rum, nutmeg *(la nemoscá)* and other plants. Love, no matter how bad your headache or fever may be, just give yourself a rub with my lotion, and your headache will disappear!

Or maybe you've come because your leg is in really bad shape. Maybe you even think it's broken! In that case I begin to massage you with my alcoholated lotion. I'll be able to tell if it is really broken or just out of joint, and I'll make the adjustments you need, little by little.

M: What if someone has a terrible pain in the kidneys? What do you do then?

María: I rub with something warming like udder balm, and later I give *el santiguo,* a special massage blessing, in the sign of the cross.

M: How did you learn to give that kind of blessing?

María: I learned from Leo Negrón's father, in Pelleja, where I grew up. He taught *me* instead of teaching his own son, when we were youngsters. The truth is, you can only teach three people during your entire lifetime.

M: Have you already taught your three people?

María: Of course! Many years ago! I can't teach you or anyone else now.

M: But you're still helping people with those massages of yours, aren't you?

María: Yes! When someone's leg is badly injured or when someone falls and breaks an arm, I fix them up. And I've never left anyone lame or disabled. Not one person in all my years!

We pause to greet a neighbor who calls to us from the street, and after a lovely exchange, we resume our conversation.

M: I see a few medicinal plants here in your garden.

María: I've always used fragrant geranium tea *(el geranio oloroso)* or sour orange leaf tea *(las hojas del naranjo)* for flu. And the broadleaf coriander *(el recao)* here is good with garlic *(el ajo)*, onion *(la cebolla)* and sweet pepper *(el pimiento)* as a *sofrito* base for cooking just about everything.

M: Do you have any home remedies that aren't made from plants?

María: I have a remedy that will break anyone of the rum-drinking habit. First you have to catch a dozen *flinches*, those

29

white bugs that are always jumping on the surface of streams and rivers. Dry the *flinches*, then toast them over a low flame until they turn reddish, and leave them for eight days in a bottle of rum. Strain the contents of that bottle into an empty one. Then make a gift of that bottle to the person with the drinking problem. Well, that person will get a tremendous case of diarrhea and nausea, but she will thank you for it because she'll never touch a drop of rum again!

I tried it on my granddaughter, and she's never had another drink. Yes, she left that habit behind for the rest of her life, and it's a good thing! Because if she'd continued, she'd be dead by now. Her first husband even left her because of her drinking! But now she's married again, and she doesn't touch the stuff.

After sharing a good laugh, I prepare to go off to town. The next day, we continued our dialogue on the front porch of doña María's home, where she rolled a thick, loose cigar of freshly cured tobacco.

María: I used to sell tobacco, but now I buy a yard, already cured, for a dollar, and I roll my own cigars.

M: It smells strong.

María: That's how I like it. Strong! Try it.

She hands me the cigar and, timidly, I inhale. What a hit!

M: Not bad! And I bet it's good for the circulation. I feel my whole body heating up.

María: Naturally!

We sit silently, smoking.

M: When I went into your room before, I noticed that you'd lit a bunch of candles. Would you tell me something about your spiritual practice?

María: I give all the money I receive for my work to the Catholic church, and they bring me communion three times a month. And yes, my child, I light candles every single night, to pray with. My candles are for the Virgin Mary, for the saints, for the dead, for the souls. If you're my friend and you die, I light a candle for your soul. And I never sleep until the candles go out. Sometimes I light five or six, sometimes more. Because at times, the dead need our prayers more than the living!

M: Doña María, it's been such an honor to talk with you . . .

María: You're still writing things down? You understand, of course, that I never went to school, and I never even learned to read or write. Not a word!

M: But you offer a tremendous service to all the people who need you.

María: That's true! Everyone knows me, and they all come to see me. People from the bank, from the drug store, even the police! Once a policeman came here for a healing rub, but he took off his police jacket before he came inside. He knew I could help him, but he didn't want anyone else to see him coming here to my place. Imagine that! Just imagine! *(laughter)*

Herb Women of Mayagüez

Brunilda Vargas Muñiz,
Primi Socorro Vargas
and
Brígida Sotomayor Vargas

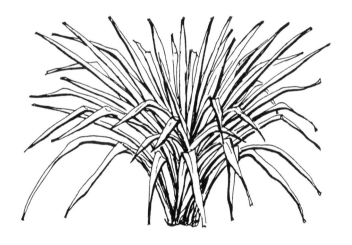

lemon grass   *el limoncillo*

Bruni steam-softens banana leaves to be used for wrapping pasteles.

Primi Socorro Vargas

Brígida poses with jagua *fruit.*

Herb Women of Mayagüez

Brunilda Vargas Muñiz,
Primi Socorro Vargas
and
Brígida Sotomayor Vargas

*Brunilda Vargas Muñiz and Primi Socorro Vargas live in the
outskirts of Mayagüez on adjoining plots of land. Their homes are
surrounded by fat plantain (plátanos) and banana plants (guineos),
mango, avocado and breadfruit trees (mangóes, aguacates and
panas), pigeon peas (gandules) and a surprising diversity of
medicinal herbs.*

*Bruni, grandmother of two, works in town as cooking
supervisor at a community program for senior citizens. There,
because of her knowledge of medicinal plants, she is affectionately
known as "la yerbetera," the herb woman.*

*Primi Socorro is a licensed beautician with a remarkable gift for
sharing her knowledge about the traditions passed on to her from her
grandparents.*

*Both women are proud of their heritage, and knowledgeable
about traditional agriculture and healing. Inventive and resourceful,
they know how to make do with little, and their generosity abounds.
Besides teaching me about the plants on their land, they helped me to
organize a book of pressed plants, and taught me too cook from
scratch (that means chopping down and softening the banana
leaves!) the most exquisite* pasteles *I have ever tasted, plus* arroz con
dulce *and* dulce de coco *on an old fashioned wood fire seasoned
with lots of earthy humor.*

Bruni: I was born in 1929, and I'm proud to say that I grew up in the countryside of Puerto Rico, land of cassava *(la yuca)*, the singing *coquí,* and everything that's good to eat.

There were seven kids in the family, and we all worked the land and harvested breadfruit, sugar cane *(la caña)*, *jobos,* guava fruit *(la guayaba)*, tamarind *(el tamarindo)*, bananas and much more. We kids were responsible for feeding the animals and we carried water to them in big buckets from the stream. We had pigs, cows, chickens, roosters, rabbits, goats, and more. So after school, we had lots of work to do. I made it through the eighth grade.

If we were stung or bitten by an insect, we would place some raw, crushed garlic *(el ajo)* on the bite so that it wouldn't swell up. If we got cut, we chopped up a leaf of Madeira vine *(la suelda consuelda)*, mixed it with cooking oil, and stuck it on the wound as a poultice. That helped it to heal quickly.

For muscle aches, we used baths of Caribbean mugwort *(la altamisa), el higuillo oloroso, la vara prieta, el tártago,* and bay rum *(la malagueta)*. You always felt like new after one of those baths!

If a woman was about to give birth, we offered her teas of nutmeg *(la nemoscá)* and belly wraps soaked in analgesic ointments like *"belladonna"* or *Triaca,* or "ointment of the air" for the pain. After the birth, she had to drink lots of chicken broth with burnt bread.

For ringworm, we applied pumpkin resin mixed in equal parts with the crushed leaves of the ringworm tree *(el talantro)*.

Arrowroot *(la maranta)* was a favorite with every mother because dried and grated fine, it made an excellent powder for burns and skin eruptions, especially for children. It even helped women who were temporarily sterile due to a condition we used to call "congested tubes". Those women would boil up the grated arrowroot tubers, mash them into gruel, and eat it by the tablespoonfuls. We had remedies for everything!

And of course, we all enjoyed making serving spoons, cups for drinking coffee and bowls for washing rice and shelling pigeon peas from gourds of *la higüera* tree.

For all of these reasons and many more, I'm proud of my Puerto Rico. I learned how to be a real *campesina* here, and that's what I'll be for as long as I live.

M: Would you tell me a bit about the land that you live on now?

Bruni: I was born and raised here, and I've never roamed any further than San Juan, because Puerto Rico is my home, and I like it. I inherited this plot of land from my father, and I plant every kind of seed that finds its way into my hands. Thanks to God, I have very good luck with the plants.

Lately I've been planting a lot of medicinal herbs: Caribbean spearmint *(la yerba buena)*, lemon balm *(el toronjil)*, *la malá blanca*, a little of everything. But we've had a drought this year, and in the long run, chlorinated water just burns the plants and weakens them. Then the ants come, and they're done for. So my harvest is small.

M: How did you learn about medicinal plants?

Bruni: My mother loved to make medicinal teas. She made a tea or *guarapo* for everything.

M: How is a traditional *guarapo* made?

Bruni: First, you take about a handful of the root or leaf or flower of the plant or plants you need. Then you wash it all very well. When it's clean, you add it all to a few cups of boiling water, then you lower the flame and cover the saucepan. After ten or 15 minutes of simmering, the water will turn deep green. When it has a good color, you turn off the flame and let it cool, still covered. All *guarapos* should be drunk warm in the evening. During the daytime they can be taken cold, instead of water, without sugar or anything else added.

M: Was making *guarapos* your mother's specialty?

Bruni: My mother could prepare just about anything. She used to make lots of *menorativas*, medicinal teas made from seven eight, up to ten or more different herbs. Usually, these mixtures are used to help clear out the lungs and bronchial passages.

I'm going to tell you a story, not because I'm proud of myself, but because I'm proud of the tradition handed down to me from my mother. They would say to her: "Fix me a *guarapo*," and she would always comply. Well, I'm the same way. At work they even call me *"la yerbetera,"* the herb woman! *(laughter)*

The other day, my supervisor said: "Hey, Bruni, my mother is really sick. She has a terrible fever with ashtma attacks and a bad cough. Can you make her a little remedy?" So I took a small handful of *cohitre blanco*, a chopped up "leaf" of spineless *tuna* cactus, some Caribbean spearmint leaves and chamomile or feverfew flowers *(la manzanilla)*, a small handful of *paletaria*, two juicy aloe leaves *(la sábila)*, and finally, a small handful of basil *(la albahaca blanca)* which is very good for chest colds. Then I washed everything and boiled it up all together, covered, for about 20 minutes in a half-gallon of water.

M: Where did you get that recipe?

Bruni: I learned it from my mother. I haven't forgotten a thing she taught me. And the next day, my supervisor came up to me and said: "Congratulations, Bruni. My mother was really suffering before she took that remedy you made her. But she's feeling much better now!"

Her mother also called to thank me, saying that before she took the remedy she could hardly breathe. She actually thought she'd have to be hospitalized. "I took two cups with honey," she said, "and I began to feel better right away."

Then when I went to work the next week, my supervisor said: "Bruni, please make me more of that remedy. Last week's supply is all gone."

So I made this one a little stronger. I added some ginger *(el jengibre)* and some *poleo* for the cough and hoarseness, and it cured her completely! She was very happy with that recipe.

M: Do you know of a simpler remedy for a bad cold or flu?

Bruni: For a flu or a bad cold with fever, the simplest and best thing is a guarapo of *la gran señora*, which is extremely bitter. Like *el botón de cadete*, it will always cut a fever. Later I'll show you some lemon grass *(el limoncillo)*, which also cuts fevers. Lemon grass is delicious, too, and blends well with bitter herbs.

M: What about the elderly people you work with? Do you ever get a chance to try your remedies out on them?

Bruni: I use one plant for almost all of their digestive complaints. A tea of Caribbean vervain *(la verbena)* with lemon *(el limón)* seems to do them good no matter what problems they may have, from chronic stomach ache to diarrhea. And it grows right there beside the building!

M: Besides *guarapos* and *menorativas*, what are some other ways you use herbs?

Bruni: In baths! For baths, I use aromatic plants, many of which, like *la campana* and *la vara prieta* are normally not taken internally (although teas of *la vara prieta* can be taken for parasites).

For a healing bath, you first get all soaped up, and you use the bath water you've prepared to rinse the soap off your entire body. After letting the bath water run over the body, you wrap the person up in warm clothes and blankets so that he can sweat a lot. The very process of sweating helps to eliminate the illness. I learned that from my parents.

I also use plants directly on the skin as poultices. Whenever people got badly cut, they'd go to see my mother because she had a plant called *la malá*, which stops the bleeding. She had a lot of godchildren, whose mothers loved and respected her a lot. They'd say: "Go see your godmother. She has *la malá*." First Mom would mash up the stalks of the plant and tie them on to the cut. Once the bleeding stopped, she would apply another medicine, like Humphrey's Udder Balm or belladonna ointment. By the way, belladonna ointment is also great for headaches. Or she would use the liquid gas we used to use in our lanterns.

M: You mean kerosene?

Bruni: It was something like kerosene, but we called it gas. After letting the lantern burn during the evening, we would simply drip the cool, "burned gas" into the open flesh, and it would cure cuts and wounds of any size. We used it a lot for the animals especially, because besides speeding up the healing process, it kept the flies out of their wounds.

For internal bleeding or an internal infection, what we call *el tabardillo*, we would cook up one big "leaf" of the *tuna* cactus with a handful of raw corn *(el maíz)* in a liter of water, and then drink it as if it were regular drinking water or juice. It's very cooling, very healing.

M: Did you ever use sheep tallow *(el sebo de Flandes)* as medicine?

Bruni: Not medicinally, but we did use it when our shoes were too tight. My father used to go into town to buy us shoes, but he just guessed our sizes! When he got home, we each took the shoes that fit us best. We really needed *el sebo de Flandes* to keep from getting terrible blisters and callouses!

M: Many women I know suffer from infections of the reproductive system. Up north, we use antiseptic herbs, from garlic to myrrh and goldenseal as internal washes. Here in Puerto Rico, how do you treat that kind of infection?

Bruni: I don't know about serious infections, but for menstrual difficulties, we've always prepared *guarapos* of chamomile, because although it is not quite "hot," it is a warming herb. Most often, we'd mix it with Caribbean spearmint and black nightshade *(la mata de gallina)*. To that decoction, you can also add some well washed and chopped-up *tuna* cactus, which is cooling, and take it as a beverage throughout the day as if it were water.

M: I've heard a lot about hot and cooling plants here in Puerto Rico, and you've mentioned that *tuna* cactus is cooling, while chamomile has warming qualities. Can you talk more about that?

Bruni: There are cooling plants, which are basically refreshing, like mallow *(la malva)*, *tuna* cactus, lemon balm, Caribbean spearmint, *la paletaria*, peppermint *(la menta)*, black nightshade and *el cohitre blanco*. They are all really good for when you have a condition of heat, in the stomach, for instance.

M: And the heating herbs?

Bruni: Some of the "hot" herbs are *el poleo*, ginger, *la gran señora, el botón de cadete* . . . And aloe is a hot herb. If you cut open a stalk of it and add some of its liquid to a tea and serve it, you'll see how warming it is. It's very good for chest pains or if you ever have a bad cold with a cough.

Chamomile, which is basically warm, is also very effective for mixed conditions. You might have a fever within, while feeling cold on the outside; or you may feel cool, but unable to eat, a symptom of overheating. That's when chamomile is especially good, along with something cooling like *el cohitre blanco*. That sort of remedy corresponds with both the heat and cold of the condition.

M: What about muscle sprains and dislocated joints? How did your mom treat that sort of condition?

Bruni: Most often in those cases, my mother gave alcohol or ammonia rubs so that the joints would remain supple and easy to move later on. She also made bandages out of fabric soaked in the same liquids. When a finger was twisted or swollen, we gave it pretty much the same treatment.

My mother's heating rubs were great! And they were very important because we almost never wore shoes, except to go into town, and the soles of our feet would get pretty darn cold! One of the heating liquids she used to rub us with was called *Aguarrás*, which was also good for getting rid of fleas, lice, ticks and other pests from the house. She used to mix it with undiluted ammonia solution and mop the house with it. It worked!

M: I've heard some people mention using ammonia solution for toothaches. How did you treat that type of problem?

Bruni: If the toothache was really bad, we might pull the tooth!

M: Didn't it bleed terribly, then?

Bruni: If it did, my mother would simply say: "Go to the kitchen and bring me two grains of salt." Because in those days, we used sea salt, in grains. Then she'd crush up that salt and place it where the tooth had been. And that's where it would stay (without rinsing) for a while. Salt cleanses, and also cuts the bleeding fast.

M: But doesn't it burn?

Bruni: At first it burns a little in the open wound, but you can take it for a while, and then it stops hurting.

If it bleeds heavily, you can use the leaf buds of *la salvia*. You simply wash, chew and hold them in place on the gum itself. In a short time the blood coagulates and the pain subsides.

M: Bruni, perhaps you can tell me about your own experience as a grandmother. What herbs and natural medicines do you use most often at home nowadays?

Bruni: Nowadays, very few people believe in what their grandmothers and grandfathers have to say. My daughter prefers to run to the hospital without even trying my home remedies. That's the way it is with my grandchildren, so what can I do?

But I use a great deal of witch hazel solution *(Agua Maravilla)* myself. It says here on the label that you shouldn't drink it, but I add it to several preparations. I added two tablespoons along with some honey to the half-gallon *menorativa* I made for my supervisor's mother, after I had boiled the whole tea up. Witch hazel solution is very good for colds when there's lots of phlegm in the chest.

43

M: That's probably because the witch hazel plant is very astringent. Up north, midwives use witch hazel bark to stop hemorrhaging!

Bruni: I've never seen that plant, but if we go outside we'll get to look at some of the plants that are growing here right now.

Outside, we are joined by Primi Socorro Vargas, roosters, dogs, children, and the enticing smells of crushed leaves, seeds, stems, flowers, roots and mangos. In an atmosphere of joyful noise, fresh air and good humor, Primi Socorro introduces herself:

Primi: I was the first of eight children, born of humble parents in 1944. My father was a farmer; my mother, a seamstress. But I grew up with my grandparents.

My grandfather loved to work the land. He really enjoyed cultivating sugar cane, coffee *(el café)*, ñame and other root vegetables, oranges *(chinas)*, plantains and all the other island products we love. My grandmother enjoyed planting fruit trees and medicinal plants. For every illness or accident, she had a home remedy growing right in our back yard.

I grew up in the country, and from the time I was three years old, I ran around the mountains chasing after the chickens, cows and pigs, eating mangos, bananas and oranges off the trees. As I grew up I learned to love and cultivate the land as well. I also learned to use home remedies for all kinds of conditions.

For instance, we wrapped bumps and bruises with rags soaked in cold, salt water. If the skin swelled and blackened without going down after two or three days, we would wrap the area in rags soaked with very hot salt water to break up the coagulated blood and bring down the swelling.

If you had a bloody wound, perhaps from having stepped on a nail, we would apply wood ashes mixed with roasted and well ground, dry coffee, wrapped up in rags.

And coffee was also good if someone had a migraine headache. First, we would heat up (with steam) enough *salvia* leaves to cover her entire forehead and the temples. Then we'd add a paste of roasted coffee and cooking oil on top of the leaves, place them on her forehead and wrap them all up with a towel. After lying down for a few hours with that bandage poultice, that person would feel tremendous relief.

Bruni: Look here! For diabetes, you can take guarapos of pigeon pea leaf buds or almond tree leaves *(el almendro)*. You just drink that tea as if you were drinking water, cold from the refrigerator during the day, and warmed up at night.

M: Are you saying that if I have diabetes, drinking those teas will cure me so that I can eat whatever I want?

Bruni: No, but if you drink those teas instead of soda and sweet juices, you'll see that when you go to the doctor, the level of sugar in your blood will have gone down quite a bit. And your doctor will suggest that you keep drinking them.

Primi: Look! This is *la paletaria;* it's very cooling. When you have a stomach ache, you take some *paletaria* tea and your discomfort simply vanishes.

And here is *la gran señora*. It's one plant that really dries a condition up. My grandmother used to make me teas of *la gran señora* when I had a cold with fever.

M: (I taste *la gran señora*.) *Ave María!* That's the bitterest plant I've ever tasted. Ahhhhrgh. It's almost unbearable!

Bruni: It's very bitter, and while a guarapo of *la gran señora* lowers fever, it's a powerful "hot" or heating plant.

Here we have Caribbean spearmint which, mixed with chamomile, is very good for stomach aches. You can add *la paletaria,* too.

Primi: If you have lots of one particular herb, it's good to make a simple brew. You can make a simple *guarapo* of chamomile if you have a lot of it, or of Caribbean spearmint, for a bad stomach. Of course, adding *la paletaria* will make it even more refreshing.

Bruni: Speaking of refreshing, here we have spineless *tuna* cactus and lots of black nightshade. Both are very cooling, and they're both good mixed with *la paletaria* when you have kidney pains. Just boil up a "leaf" of the spineless *tuna* cactus, a little handful of *la paletaria* and another little handful of black nightshade in a liter of water for 20 to 25 minutes. That's a refreshing and very healthful beverage!

Primi: And here is some broadleaf coriander *(el culantro del monte)*!

M: I've used that plant for menstrual cramps. It worked great!

Primi: Here we use it mostly in cooking. It's delicious with peppers, tomatoes, garlic, oregano and coriander leaf *(el cilantrillo)*, all mixed together and added to food.

Bruni: Let me see now if I can pull up a piece of sweet, Puerto Rican ginger *(el jengibre dulce)*. It's smaller than the commercial ginger, and better tasting. For making medicine, you have to wash it really well, take off the little hairs on the skin, mash it up a bit, and put it in water until it boils. It's spicy, hot! And besides using it in guarapos, it's also good when you're making sweet coconut rice *(arroz con dulce)*!

Primi: I'd go so far as to say that without sweet ginger, there can *be* no sweet coconut rice! *(laughter)*

Bruni: Here is what's left of my *malá* plant. Looks like the lizards have been eating it.

M: It's fleshy! It looks a bit like a miniature, rounded aloe plant.

Brígida Sotomayor Vargas approaches and, hearing us mention one of her favorite plants, stays to share with us.

Brígida: Aloe gelatin — and its juice — is great for cleaning out phlegm from the chest, and it works like a miracle on burns!

Primi: It also takes away spots and blemishes on the skin.

A small mango falls on my head amidst much laughter.

M: Do mangos have any medicinal value?

Primi: Absolutely! They're great for getting calories and vitamins into the whole body. *(laughter)*
And here's another fruit, *la jagua,* which makes a tremendous remedy for high blood pressure. You just cut it in pieces, put it in a jarful of water in the refrigerator, and then after a day or so, drink the water. It's a delicious refreshment, like *el maví.* It doesn't even need sugar!

M: I recognize common plantain herb *(el llantén)* from the north, where it grows even in big cities.

Primi: We use it here for stomach ulcers. The best way to prepare it is by juicing it. Just toss a couple of handfuls of fresh plantain leaf into the blender with a cup of water. And you can add some black nightshade. The two juices together make the best ulcer remedy.

Bruni: You can also add plantain leaves to *guarapos* and *menorativas* when you have chest pain.

M: It's astringent, I know. And the chlorophyll in the plant is very cleansing. Up north, we use common plantain herb for bee stings, insect bites, minor cuts and burns, even if we've touched poison ivy. We just chew up the leaves and apply that green mass, saliva and all, directly on the skin as a poultice. If the problem is on a small area of the body, like a finger or toe, you can even use a large, whole leaf to tie the little poultice on. It's a sort of universal bandage.

Brígida: And they say it's effective taken as a tea, even in cases of cancer!

M: Bruni, would you say that common plantain herb is a cooling plant or a heating one?

Bruni: I'd say it has the qualities of both. It cuts pain and it cuts fever, something like chamomile.
　　Here we have a sour orange tree *(el naranjo)*. The leaves are good boiled up in tea for a chest cold . . .

Brígida: And for emotional upsets and nervous conditions! When you need to calm down, a tea of sour orange leaves is tranquilizing.

Primi: Not only that, but the same, calming leaves give a wonderful flavor to food. And sour orange leaves are great for making "social teas" to enjoy with friends. Orange leaf tea is simply delicious, especially with a little bit of honey or sugar.

Bruni: Here's rue *(la ruda)*. It's good for women's pains and problems.

M: In large quantities it can cause abortion, but most women I've talked with use it in small doses for menstrual discomfort.

Bruni: That's right. And this is *la bruja*, which is good for earaches. You warm up the leaf, then crush it and soak up the juice with a little wad of cotton. Then you put the cotton in your ear while it's still warm, and as the liquid from the cotton seeps into the inner ear, the pain goes away.

M: And what's this little tree's name?

Bruni: That's *el tártago*, good for all sorts of enchantments! *(laughter)*

Brígida: People who work with the spirit world often plant these little trees in front of their homes for protection . . . and because *el tártago* has lots of value as a medicinal plant . . .

Primi: But not only that! See this resin? It gets rid rid of corns and callouses. Just rub it on with cotton as often as you can.

Bruni: Yes, and when kids want to play with bubbles, here they are! *(She blows some of the* tártago *sap off the end of a pine needle, and soap-like bubbles begin to surround her along with lots of laughter.) Now* you're learning something useful here, María!

Primi: Here we have *la vara prieta*. Its leaves, combined with *el cariaquillo* and mango leaves, makes a bath to remove all negative energies. Plants like *el sacabuche* and *la santa María* are also used. Basically, it's a psychological thing. The herb woman prescribes this kind of warm bath, and people feel better. Of couse, it might have something to do with the faith they have in the plants . . . and in the herb woman!

Bruni: It might also have to do with the fact that the same bath is also good for muscle aches and rheumatism!

M: Up north, we have plants that are like soap. They foam and remove dirt to some extent. Do you have any soapy plants like that here?

Bruni: When someone has dandruff, we apply aloe as if it were shampoo, just the juice as it comes out of the stem, raw.

Primi: And if your child happens to have head lice, you can boil up the vines of *el cundeamor* until the water turns green. Then you use it as if it were a shampoo, but you have to leave it on the kid's head for a good 15 or 20 minutes afterwards. Repeat the treatment twice during a week or so to kill all the eggs and larvae. *El cundeamor* kills lice and it's great for the scalp. And remember, you're talking with a beautician. I know all about hair!

M: As a beautician, can you talk about some of the plants you use for cosmetic purposes?

Primi: Ripe avocado makes a good head massage for dry hair, and it's excellent for dry skin. You can just rub it into your skin or into your scalp and hair, and leave it for about 20 minutes of so before washing or shampooing.

I also use coconut oil *(el coco)* when people start losing their hair. I rub it in and give a good scalp massage daily. It really stimulates hair growth!

And coconut water is the best thing for the kidneys. It's very soothing. So is *la baquiña cerrada*. It has a round leaf, and is excellent for treating kidney stones.

Brígida: *Juana la blanca* is also used in teas for kidney stones but I've heard that it's dangerous to use on a long-term basis. It supposedly damages the liver.

Primi: All I know is that it gives you lots of gas!

Bruni: Here we have white amaranth *(el blero),* another cooling herb. It makes a good tea for heating conditions, especially for the kidneys, when there is infection. Served cold, it's quite refreshing, and similar to *el cohitre blanco* in its effect.

M: It tastes like a kitchen vegetable!

Bruni: Of course! It is a vegetable! Something like purslane *(la verdolaga).* White amaranth, *el cohitre blanco* and purslane are all cooling, and that's how they heal.

M: In New York, cream of purslane soup is considered a real delicacy. And raw purslane is also quite popular in salads.

Primi: It makes a calming, nourishing tea, too.

M: That's good to know, because I like to drink nourishing teas every day.

Primi: Well, the cooling herbs we've mentioned: *el cohitre blanco,* white amaranth, purslane, *la paletaria,* and black nightshade would all be perfect.

Now, if you want to stimulate the circulation, you might try ginger tea. It's really warming.

Bruni: Here's annato *(el achiote)*, which is also good for the circulation. We use the leaves for hot baths when someone has muscle spasms. It really helps. And the seeds themselves are used to give color to food, especially to stewed rice . . . and *pasteles!*

Primi: Here is the moon plant *(la campana)*, which is used primarily for baths. Lately though, people have used it as a narcotic! And it's no toy! Some young people who've used it have actually suffered permanent brain damage. Years later, they're still walking around like zombies!

Bruni: It's a terrible waste, and a great loss. Now people go around ripping the moon plant out of the earth because they're afraid it might be used to do harm. But the moon plant has always been an important medicinal plant, especially for women.

M: And I've had the privilege of smelling its beautiful flower after dark. It's one of the most magnetic fragrances I've ever known!

And speaking of "fragrances," have you women ever used valerian *(la valeriana)*?

Primi: Of course! For my nerves. When I was little I went through a stage of being super nervous all the time. My grandmother finally went to the drug store and bought some valerian root. She boiled it up for me, and after taking just three *guarapos,* I was just fine. I bless that plant!

M: Maybe you got cured so fast because you just couldn't bear the smell! *(laughter)* I usually prepare valerian in alcohol as a tincture so that I can use just a small amount. It has such a strong, disagreeable smell and flavor! Didn't it bother you?

Primi: I didn't mind the flavor at all! I drank it right down, without sugar or any sweetener, even. That's the best way to get to know your plants, after all. *(Many nods of agreement.)*

Bruni: This flower here is called the fairy rose *(la rosa cienhojas)*. It makes a very good eye wash for conjunctivitis. Just leave half a dozen fairy roses in water over night, *al sereno*, and use that water to rinse the eyes with throughout the next day.

Primi: Look! That's mallow, another cooling plant. It makes a great tea for the kidneys, and when your skin erupts in boils or little cysts, it's an excellent poultice. Just wash the area with the water you've boiled the leaf in, then place the boiled leaf on top of the cyst. Strain and drink the water, even! Mallow water douches are also good for inflammation of the uterus.

And *la tuatúa* is another great plant for cysts or boils. If you have an external cyst that isn't opening up, you can put a steam-heated leaf of *la tuatúa* on top of it, and leave it there until it bursts open. And I'm speaking from experience. That's how I got rid of a horrible cyst the size of a hen's egg. And what a place to have a cyst! I saw stars every time I sat down.

M: Tell us the story!

Primi: I remember it as if it were yesterday, but actually, it was years ago, on New Year's Eve. The only way I could bear the pain was to spread my legs so far apart that one was heading for Maricao and the other for San Germán.* My grandfather had just died a little while before that, and I prayed to him, asking that he might illuminate my mind. "What can I do to cure this cyst?" I asked him.

Then I got the idea of using *la tuatúa*, and Bruni went and got me some leaves. First I boiled up some of the leaves, and while that water was cooling down a bit, I warmed and softened up another leaf by passing it back and forth over some steam. Then I washed the area with the warm "tea" I'd made, and put the softened leaf over the cyst, covered with a little oil in order to keep it stuck to my skin. *La tuatúa* is a "drawing" plant. It draws out to the surface whatever is causing the problem inside. So round about midnight, the cyst burst open and I got rid of blood, pus, everything that was inside. All the excesses of my system seemed to be located in that one place.

M: How did you deal with the open wound after that?

Primi: I boiled up some more tuatúa leaves, and with that "tea," I rinsed the area well. Finally, I applied an antibiotic cream the doctor had recommended, but it was *la tuatúa* that cured me! I'd had that cyst for more than two weeks, and the doctor had said he'd have to operate by January 2 if it hadn't burst by then. Imagine living with the pain of a surgical wound in that place! So at last it did burst open and left only a tiny scar, thanks to God and the Virgin Mary . . . and my grandfather! And I have witnesses!

Bruni: I don't know if you know a plant known as *la maya*. My grandmother used it when she wanted to coagulate milk to make cheese. It looks something like a pineapple plant, with tiny thorns and a little yellow fruit in the center. You add that little fruit to milk, and it sours quickly.

Primi: Of course, lemon coagulates milk too, and it's very good for the skin as well. It cuts right through oil and pimples, plus it helps in the digestion of shellfish and other heavy, greasy foods. And lemonade is the most refreshing drink in the world when you're uncomfortably warm.

Brígida: Not to mention for arthritis! I take pure lemon juice every morning, and it has really helped me a lot.

M: What about home remedies that aren't plants? One of the older women I interviewed mentioned that a child's urine poured over the forehead of a person suffering from fever, would lower the fever! I'd never heard of that remedy before.

Primi: That's a real old fashioned treatment! It's also used in massages when you have a cramp in your leg or foot. I must confess, I've never tried it myself, but my grandmother used it a great deal, and she swore by it!

Brígida: There's another good remedy for leg cramps. We always rubbed corn silk into the cramped area, and it worked!

Primi: You know, my uncle always used to say that urine could also be used if a bee or wasp stung you. That somehow it killed the pain. He would mix it with a little bit of earth and make a little poultice.

M: Urine also works to lessen the pain of a jelly fish sting. It seems that its ammonia content neutralizes the poison.

Primi: Raw garlic is also really good for the pain of insect and animal bites and stings, and it's antiseptic!

Brígida: Even the medical doctors are now saying that taken internally, garlic lowers the blood pressure.

Primi: Look at Bruni chewing breadfruit gum! *(laughter)*

Bruni: When I was a child trailing after my father on the farm, he'd tell me: "I'm going to go and cut the breadfruit tree so that tomorrow you'll have some chewing gum." And the next morning, I'd go to the tree to get my chewing gum. You can chew and chew and chew the sap.

M: What does it taste like?

All: Like breadfruit!

Primi: Which reminds me . . . It's time to cook dinner! Who wants breadfruit with *bacalao*?

Two Spirit Healers of Loíza

doña Casimira
and
doña Bolina

common plantain   *el llantén*

doña Bolina

doña Casimira

doña Bolina's principal altar

Two Spirit Healers of Loíza

doña Casimira
and
doña Bolina

The village of Loíza is an important center of Afro-Caribbean culture in Puerto Rico. Like many coastal towns, it supported a thriving sugar cane industry for generations, which was worked initially by Black slaves. After slavery was abolished, Loíza was home to a large population of free African-Americans who, isolated from the main roads that connected to other towns, managed to preserve many purely African and indigenous (Taíno) traditions.

Interested in medicinal plants, I went to Puerto Rico with the idea of meeting herbal medicine practitioners. And I found that in Loíza, most people who work with herbs to heal physical ailments are also involved in the mystical realm. The following edited interviews with two independent espiritistas (diviners and spiritual healers) of Loíza reflect the use of herbs as well as a variety of psycho-spiritual techniques for healing on many levels. Here, the world of plants and physical healing is integrally linked with spiritual renewal. And humanistic psychological counseling takes place in a context that affirms cultural values.

Although doña Bolina's pragmatism contrasts with doña Casimira's approach, both women recognize faith as the source of their inspiration and the secret of their success. Both women discovered their calling during childhood through religious visions, and both are especially devoted to — two different aspects of — the same saint. *Casimira works with the Infant of Prague, the Catholic patron saint of children, while Bolina works with Elegguá, an African expression*[1] *of the same spirit, the elderly yet childlike divinity or orisha charged with "opening the roads."*

Both spirit healers show a surprising ability to integrate ancient aspects of their tradition with modern perspectives and practices.

Doña Bolina is an initiate of the palo monte - palo mayombe[2] *and Yoruba traditions. She uses books such as Lydia Cabrera's literary and anthropological* El Monte *as a source of botanical information and prayer, and merges healing through faith with a sophisticated psycho-therapeutic outlook.*

Doña Casimira offers an expansive, ecumenical definition of God, while her allusion to plant symbology reflects the extent to which the ancient "word magic" of African and other indigenous traditions has been integrated into her practice.

Both women use a rich treasury of symbols ranging from candles to the saints themselves to represent certain kinds of thought and awareness. For both, the most important symbols recall the basic healing principles of faith, thanksgiving and love.

---

[1] During slavery, African people were forced to worship Christian saints. Thus, their own pantheon of spiritual beings was worshiped secretly. Each divinity was associated — and syncretized — with Christian saints according to the symbolism accrued to those saints in devotional works of art. For instance, Changó (a male deity or orisha associated with lightning) became Saint Barbara, whose visual representation always included a bolt of lightning, and so on. This example is taken from the Yoruba tradition known as Lucumí or — to non-initiates — santería.

[2] *Palo, palo monte* and *palo mayombe* are words used to describe the religion of the Bantu speaking people of the African Congolese civilization.

Meeting with doña Casimira

I waited in doña Casimira's parlor for about 20 minutes while she counseled a handsome, thirty-something lawyer, a long-time client and friend. He stayed to listen to our interview, which was interrupted several times by other clients who came by to leave offerings and other items to be used in Casimira's "works" for them in a separate little house in the back yard.

She made it clear that she was well known as an espiritista *not only on the island but in far away places as well. After listening to her talk about her work, seeing some evidence of her popularity (one client had come from 90 mountainous miles away to see her) and receiving a highly accurate personal reading, I knew I had found a gifted seer.*

Casimira: My work is spiritual work. It comes not from study or anything resembling study, but from the spiritual vision I receive through my thoughts. I also receive information from sources such as Tarot cards and the spiritual circles we *espiritistas* hold in order to call upon the powers of protection. Whatever I receive at these activities I then offer to the people who come to me. Most are looking for healing, for harmony, or for ways to increase and enhance their abilities.

I'm no doctor, but I can offer relief to people. Most often I help people with psychological problems, problems within a marriage, let's say. When people need some perspective, I help them to move ahead correctly. Sometimes people start abusing themselves with drugs or alcohol, and I help to re-orient them.

I work with the divine forces. If someone is on the wrong path, I tell him: "Look, according to my vision, it looks as if the following is going to happen." That person soon comes to me in tears, saying: "What you said would happen really happened!" That's because I receive help from those above. Some time may elapse, but everything the spirits tell me comes to pass.

M: Besides counseling people, what does your work involve?

Casimira: It depends upon what images and what information come to me through my visions and thoughts.

I use plants a great deal. For psychological problems, baths of Caribbean mugwort *(la altamisa),* aloe , Caribbean vervain *(la verbena)* and other symbolic plants help to cast off negative influences. So I may suggest specific baths according to need.

If someone comes to me with stomach problems, I offer a *santiguo,* a special massage anointing, which is done directly on that person's stomach in the form of the sign of the cross. Of course, the *santiguo* is always accompanied by special prayers. I might also offer that person medicinal teas for the stomach, such as a mixture of *la yerba buena, el poleo* and *guanábana* buds. These teas are traditionally given after a *santiguo.*

I've also dealt a great deal with skin problems, including a case of what had been called "incurable" eczema. That woman came all the way from Caguas to see me. I told her to apply the boiled leaves of the yellow trumpet tree *(el roble amarillo)* and to use a special soap. She came back within two weeks and her skin looked better than mine looks now!

M: Have you used plants to deal with life-threatening illness?

Casimira: Absolutely. My own son was at the San Jorge Clinic for a kidney operation not too long ago, and while he was there, the spirits told me: "He's going to be OK, and you won't have to go to the hospital; that would just be an added expense." And that was the truth. The treatment they wanted to give him at the hospital cost over $2,000! Then I received the "prescription" through my thoughts: common plantain herb *(el llantén)*, *la baquiña cerrada* and *Juana la blanca* boiled up together and strained, to be served with a coconut every morning. Well he endured some intense pain, but his kidney stones passed!

And not too long ago I treated a young woman with an advanced cancer. She couldn't have weighed too much more than 40 pounds. One look in her eyes, and you knew she was at death's door. Well, I received the means to help her. I told her to drink the boiled seeds of *el cundeamor* with shoots of *el anamú* and leaves of common plantain herb over a certain time period. With that medicine, she discharged everything she didn't need right out of her system. Now she's back to work at the food stamps division of Social Services, and she's just gorgeous. Plumper and better looking than the two of us combined!

You know, common plantain is recognized almost all over the world as a cancer remedy. The medicinal plants are a real aid for human health, but half the time we just ignore them.

In this country, people's knowledge about the healing plants goes back generations, because our grandparents and great grandparents took care of all kinds of health problems, naturally.

M: Are many Puerto Ricans turning back to the plants today?

Casimira: Yes, my child. I tell the doctors: "I know you don't believe in plants, but little by little you're losing your patients because more and more of them are choosing natural ways of healing." *Lots* of people are going to natural healers these days.

If you have a bad stomach ache, you boil up some peppermint *(la menta)* for a tea, you drink it up, and before you know it, you feel fine. Plants themselves are the best, the most effective and beautiful expression of medicine for human beings.

M: Earlier, you mentioned the use of "symbolic plants." Can you explain that term?

Casimira: It's something that comes down to us from our ancestors. I think people all over the world associate certain plants with symbolism. The world of the spirits corresponds with the world of plants, and the world of the mind — the world of words — also has its correspondence in the world of plants. So that peppermint *(la menta)* eases the mind *(la mente)*. *La salvia* helps one to be acquitted *(¡que se salve!)* when one is on trial. Common plantain *(el llantén)* is for a person who weeps *(llantée)*. That's one source of the symbolism, and there are others. For instance, the saints themselves each have their associations with certain plants. But we'll talk about that some other time.

M: You mentioned that you never studied in order to learn this type of work. So how *did* you learn about all of this?

Casimira: It all started for me when I got very sick as a child. I was seven years old, and for five days I was unconscious in my bed. It was a time when no one had money for anything. People made 40 cents for a whole day's work! Plants were the only medicine then, because even if you could afford to see a doctor, you could never afford to buy the pills or whatever he might prescribe. Children died with their stomachs all swollen from parasitic infestations. It was a sad life for so many people.

Well, my father was relatively well off. He had a large farm, and I had the privilege of going to school. By age seven I was already reading. But when the doctor came to see me, all he said was: "Make this girl a coffin. She's dying." Then, as I was hovering between life and death, God spoke to me. "Open your eyes," he said. "Look at me." And I saw the most beautiful handwriting with letters that said: "You are not going to die now. You will live a long life. I need you to do some important work." So I asked my mother to bring me some milk, which I drank, and the next day I started eating everything they put in front of me.

From then on, I started saying things like: "Mommy, so and so has a bad fever and she needs a good sweat tonight. They should put camphor compresses on the soles of her feet. "

Or if someone had diarrhea, I would receive the means to say: "He should be taking teas of basil *(la albahaca blanca)* with cashew husks *(el pajuil)* and *hicaco* fruit." God gave me the gift when I was seven years old.

That's why my favorite saint is the Infant of Prague. He has always worked miracles for me. He's the patron saint of children, and always helps when a child is sick or has other problems.

Anyway, my parents were uncomfortable with what I was doing, so they sent me to live with my aunts when I was nine. By the time I was twelve, I had started working for people, giving advice, telling them what was going to happen to them and which remedies they should take. Every bit of information I received through my thoughts and through my visions, I shared with the people who came to me. Then I decided to stop doing that work until I'd married and raised a child. But when my son was twelve, I began working again, and word began to spread. They've come all the way from Canada, from the Virgin Islands, and from New York to see me. All by word of mouth.

M: Can you talk about some of the important things you've learned during the years you've been working?

Casimira: I'm 74 years old, so they've been coming for more than 60 years. And in those years I've learned a few things about people, and about God.

I've seen lots of fighting and hostility among the churches here in Puerto Rico: the Pentecostals, the Evangelists, the Catholics. I remember that one day my mother said to me: "So and so can't go to heaven because they didn't offer a mass for his soul." And I said: "After someone has led a good life, you mean to tell me he can't go to heaven because some other people didn't pray for him?" That's when it became really evident to me that something was wrong. Because I felt, and I knew, that we can only be judged according to the greatest sacrament in life: Loving one's fellow human beings and treating them well.

People used to think that Catholicism was the only way to save people. But I say there's only one church, and all the rest are bastards. The church is God, the God of love who lives in the heart of every human being. If you help your fellow human beings, then you are living God's will. If you go to church every day, and then go home to live in ways that go against the sacrament of real love and caring for others, you betray God.

M: What qualities are most important in a person who wants to heal or otherwise help others?

Casimira: The most important quality and gift of every human being on earth is faith.

In all that you may do, you must call on God first. That's how favor is granted. When you open your hands and you have faith in God, He places His hand in yours. If you sincerely call upon God to help you in your work, then every time you put your hand on someone to heal, it will land in just the right spot. Your hands are blessed by God so that you can heal. Through your hands, the person receiving the healing can be blessed by God.

You can break through serious psychological problems and even someone's being bewitched if you do an anointing in the name of God. It's all faith, my love. Faith makes life happen. If you don't have faith, you can't do anything.

M: So you just lay your hands on the person . . .

Casimira: I simply place my hand on the person to bless her or him. That's one way of doing it. Or I might offer a santiguo healing, which is always accompanied by my own secret prayers. Prayers help with everything. If your head is all blocked up with negative thoughts or with other psychological problems, my hands on your temples and our silent prayers will open things up.

I also find that people need spiritual baths to cleanse themselves of negative energies and take in purity once again. When you are loaded down with problems, you're carrying around a tainted aura, an atmosphere that's not your own. Certain types of baths will help you to cleanse yourself and relax.

Every type of bath is different. For luck, you bathe in basil, Caribbean spearmint *(la yerba buena)* and marjoram *(la mejorana)*. To counteract spiritual problems or manipulation by others, bathe with *el poleo*, wormseed *(el pazote)* and *la salvia*.

M: Can you describe how a spiritual bath is prepared?

Casimira: First you boil the plants you'll be using, and let that water cool. Then, after bathing yourself with soap, let the plant bath flow over you from your head to your toes, over every part of your body. Then, without drying yourself off, you get out of the tub. You can't sit in the water, because the water has taken with it all the negativity that you don't want or need any longer.

There are baths for everything from muscle aches and arthritis to a broken heart. One thing all of the baths have in common is that they leave you feeling completely pure, and open to purity in your surroundings.

M: Is there something more you'd like to say to people about what you've learned over the years you've spent working as a healer and spiritual guide?

Casimira: The cosmos is charged with an atmosphere of great difficulty. It's an especially rough time for the world. This situation demands that people orient themselves through prayer, giving thanks and asking for positive visions. If you pray to receive insight for working through this era, you will receive visions to help you.

It is also very important that you live in a grateful way, always carrying with you a symbol of thanks in your thoughts. Those thanks, and your prayers, can break through any bitterness, any heaviness, any difficulty.

It all boils down to prayer, to sincerely searching for God, who offers protection, grace and power. Without God, the leaves on the trees do not flutter in the wind. Because God is nature, and nature is God, in every plant, in every flower, and in every positive thought! God is not present in negative thoughts.

When I hear people say: "Such and such a thing is going to happen, and how horrible!" I respond by saying: "What's the matter? Don't you have any faith?" Because if you do have faith, you will receive great blessings.

If you don't take the risk, if you don't shut your eyes and walk forward with faith in search of higher ground, you can not be charged with a real mission in life, and you'll never be prepared for your destiny.

One person comes to be born for one reason; another, for another reason. Fulfillment comes through the divine thoughts that put you on your path.

Meeting with doña Bolina

When I turned off the main street onto a slim dirt road, I saw low, gray clouds billowing from a tiny house. My escort shrugged: "That's the place," and left me about 15 yards away. Doña Bolina was performing a sahumerio *or psychic cleansing of her work space with the heady smoke of myrrh and other resins.*

She seemed glad to see me, and I was deeply moved by the variety and abundance of sacred images in her space. One wall was lined with a three-tiered altar of the mostly white-skinned Catholic saints (which, through a process of syncretization, have come to represent the African, mostly Yoruba divinities or orishas), flanked by an altar more clearly representative of the African orishas. A third altar supported busts of Indian figures, amulets and other symbols associated with the island's indigenous Taíno heritage. "I have them all," she said with pride, "because the Puerto Rican people are of African, Indian and Spanish descent. These are our roots."

Doña Bolina has built up her trade little by little while raising ten children to adulthood and working her way up for 27 years to the post of personnel supervisor at a nearby factory. "I don't have a formal education," she began. "I just went to the eighth grade. But I have been prepared spiritually . . . "

Bolina: When I was five or six years old I felt that the spirit world was talking to me, and I would answer. I saw several visions — apparitions of Christ and the Virgin Mary in many forms — but I didn't begin counseling people until I was 25. Even before I was initiated as a priestess, I recommended treatments, offering people spiritual therapy. I would suggest which saints to pray to, what kinds of baths to take, what plants to use.

Meanwhile, I got married and had 13 children. That was also part of my preparation. I've been through a lot in life.

M: Tell me about some of the saints represented on your altars.

Bolina: All these images of saints here reflect the essence of the divine beings. I work with God, and these figures represent aspects of God, so I treat them with a great deal of respect.

Working with the saints is a way of helping people make use of one of their greatest resources, their faith, in order to see and believe in their own strengths.

For instance, Saint Jacinto is the spirit of making peace. Saint Martin helps the poor. Elegguá takes many forms; here he is the Infant of Prague, guide and protector of all children. Saint James is a warrior. Saint Martha conquered the dragon, and helps people to be more assertive. She also helps couples to keep peace in their home. The woman who prays to Saint Martha brings the saint into her own heart in order to get along with her husband better. Saint Expedito is the patron of business and money. Saint Jude helps those who face difficult or impossible situations, and is the patron of all lawsuits. La Caridad del Cobre, the orisha Oshún, rules the waters that flow. Saint Barbara has two personalities, male and female. For six months of the year he is Changó, and during the other six months she is Barbara. The African Saint Barbara with the cut on her face aids the afflicted.

My Indian figures represent the spirits of our ancestral tribes. And my *madama* figure symbolizes the African religions, the spirit of those who dance to the drums, the spirit of those who work in my field of advice and consultations. I carry on with her work, and when there's a service, I play the drum and we dance in a spiritual way, just as the Congo people did, and still do.

M: Do you believe that everyone has a special relationship with one of the saints?

Bolina: Everyone has a spiritual guide who acts as a sort of an ideal self. For example, one day it occurs to you: "Today I should make a pan of sweet coconut rice." Don't let yourself get lazy! Don't say: "No, it's too much work." When your guide's voice tells you to do something, do it. You'll never regret it. Life is a chance for us to prepare ourselves on the spiritual and material planes. Our guides help us to do that.

My own special spiritual guide is the orisha Elegguá, who protects me and my children. I pray: "Elegguá, my spirit guide, you who know the roads of life, put my son on the correct path. Great African divinity, protect my son!" Then when I see that my prayers have been answered, I make an offering to Elegguá. I might put a dried coconut behind the door, or I may make a little amulet in the shape of one of Elegguá's implements. That symbol will help to develop my awareness of him and his protection, so I feel better in general. These practices clear your mind.

M: I notice quite a few cigars here. What do they mean to you?

Bolina: I smoke the cigars. As tobacco is a gift of the Indians, I honor these people with my tobacco. And with my coffee , I honor the Congo people of Africa.

M: Tell me more about what your work as a spiritual advisor. What methods do you use to help people effectively?

Bolina: First I'll say that faith is the essence of my work. It is the root of all I do. Because it's people's faith that heals them in the end. Everything I do comes through faith, and I have plenty of it.

I counsel people suffering from anxiety, people with

psychological problems. I help them through spiritual means. When they arrive, they see themselves surrounded by the saints, and they see that I am concentrating on this glass of water. I receive information from a spiritual source in order to see physical reality reflected in this glass of water.

If you come to see me, you'll see that as we talk, I'll begin scribbling on a piece of paper while the images come to me from the other world. My focusing on the water and writing helps the person to calm down, trust me, and concentrate better.

My response will depend upon what the person tells me and whatever other messages I receive about that person's needs in the cup of water. Let's say there is a psychological problem; I might say: "Someone has made a negative statement about you and you've accepted that statement. That's what's making you so anxious." Or perhaps there's a marital problem. Most likely I can help in that case too. Remember, I've been married for 42 years!

I've come to learn that if one is not relaxed, nothing will turn out right. So I create a relaxing atmosphere, and then I try to recommend that which will help my visitor to relax the most. Maybe that means sending her off to church to be still and pray. Or maybe it will mean prescribing a special bath of soothing herbs like Caribbean mugwort *(la altamisa)* and bitter orange leaves *(hojas de naranjo)*. Or maybe I'll suggest bathing in the ocean in order to cleanse the body and soul of all negativity.

I might recommend that my client drink special soothing teas like linden flower *(el tilo),* chamomile *(la manzanilla)* or orange leaves. If he can't sleep, I'll tell him to place a camphor pastille in a glass of water under his bed just before turning in for the night.

These remedies certainly can't hurt anyone, and if a problem is basically psychological, the very act of preparing a remedy with faith may be healing.

M: Do you have a pretty high rate of success?

Bolina: Oh yes! The remedies I offer almost always work. While I prescribe them, I'm affirming always: "Don't worry; God will take this trial away from you. It will pass." And I say it with total faith and a soothing voice so that they can really feel that passing.

M: What are the most common problems you've seen among people who've come to you for advice?

Bolina: So many people are traumatized by poverty. They always want what they can't have. They want what rich people have, what they see on television. Well, I've raised ten children to adulthood, and each one has a degree and a career. But when they were little, if I just had a little flour in the house, that's what we fried up for breakfast. If there was nothing nice to wear, they put on whatever there was. No complaints! So I base lots of my advice on this way of thinking . . . and always, on my faith.

Sometimes people feel so inferior, they think that other people have power over them. They believe that others are out to get them, that others are capable of bewitching them, of bending their will. They forget to have faith in themselves, in their own path. I help them to clarify what they want, and to say clearly: "I'm going to accomplish such and such a thing, and no one can stop me."

I also see marital problems and family problems, which come about through a lack of communication and understanding. When parents tell me that their children don't pay them any mind, I tell them to talk to their kids about their own lives. Talk with them about love and about sex, about alcohol and about drugs. And then listen to them! That's a way of opening communication up so there's more understanding within the family. Simple communicatino is a form of therapy in itself.

Another major problem I encounter is self-serving gossip that hurts people. That comes about when people get pleasure out of living their neighbors' lives instead of their own.

I always counsel people to stop looking at what others do and what others have, and to learn to live with their own lives; to accept their own lives.

M: Do you ever recommend that someone see a doctor or psychiatrist?

Bolina: Absolutely! I often send people to get help from medical professionals. Sometimes women come suffering from physical ailments, including reproductive problems. I send those women to see a doctor. And when people are too anxious to even listen to me, I recommend that they go to a psychologist or psychiatrist. But the high cost of going to the doctor is usually prohibitive.

Sometimes people go to the doctors first, and come to me later just to find that they get more relief through the spiritual healing, and through my work with the plants. Because, for the most part, people come to me feeling nervous and anxious and leave feeling calm and tranquil.

M: Tell me about the ways you use plants for spiritual healing.

Bolina: If you think you have something like bad energy following you around, I recommend that you take a bath of marjoram *(la mejorana)*, Caribbean spearmint *(la yerba buena)*, Florida water, or Caribbean mugwort *(la altamisa)*.

For a chronic problem like an allergy, I might have you boil a green papaya and drink the juice, or suggest that you drink lots of cooling teas, such as *la paletaria*, spineless *tuna* cactus, white amaranth *(el blero)* or purslane *(la verdolaga)*. Maybe I'll recommend that you eat lots of cooling fruits and vegetables.

If you have a cold, I'll say: "Boil up some star anise *(anís de estrella)* as a tea, add some honey and a few drops of lemon *(el limón).* Tomorrow you'll be a lot better." And lemon juice, so light and refreshing, is also good for certain types of headache.

For a cold in the body, a forehead wrap of coffee grounds will help, even if you have a migraine.

Now, if someone has a bad stomach ache, I'll probably say: "See a doctor," especially if I think it might be an ulcer. But if the doctor can't help, I'll suggest boiling up some black nightshade *(la yerba mora)* in milk, either alone or with common plantain leaves *(el llantén).* That should be taken on a regular basis.

If someone has eye trouble, I'll suggest that she mix some common plantain leaves with rue *(la ruda),* wash them well and place them in a clean glass of water to be left out *al sereno,* during the cool dampness of the night. That way, the plant's juices can be infused in that atmosphere. The next morning, after washing her eyes with that water, she'll feel much better. Of course, if the condition persists, I'll advise her to see an eye doctor too!

If someone complains of constipation, I suggest plenty of coconut water with lemon, a remedy from our African heritage.

If you feel very weak, I'll recommend that first you go to the doctor. But if the doctor's treatment doesn't help much, take a couple of fresh, raw eggs and make yourself a little eggnog with fresh milk, half an ounce of brandy or rum, and some brown sugar. I believe that an ounce of alcohol two or three times a week is good for the body. Everything is good in moderation!

M: Where did you learn about all of these remedies?

Bolina: I was trained as a priestess in the tradition of *palo monte,* which is a spiritual tradition that includes healing knowledge. And through the years I've tried many, many remedies which are part of the oral tradition here in Puerto Rico. I also use books on medicinal plants to guide me. For instance, Lydia Cabrera records that white amaranth is used to refresh and to do spiritual cleansings and renewals. It can even be used as a vegetable. Boiled, it helps the body to cleanse itself, and the leaves cooked for poultices are effective against tumors.

M: Do you know people who have used amaranth successfully to treat tumors?

Bolina: Yes, both as a poultice, and as a drink.

M: That's a powerful plant!

Bolina: But the mind is the most powerful thing. Look. This candle burning here can be seen as a means of calling someone to come to me through the five senses, the seven thoughts. It's actually a tool of thought transmission. I light it here at Saint Barbara's feet, and I tell the woman who waits for a call from her husband: "I lit the candle, and today he's going to call you." Sure enough, because she has that thought, he will call. Later she'll say that the results were my doing, but really, it was the power of her faith and of her thought.

M: Do you accept money for your work?

Bolina: The people who come to see me always leave a few dollars so I can continue with my work, and so I can buy my candles.

Candles don't mean much to most people, but to me, they symbolize that all-important faith and the bringing of light. I place a candle before each saint and that brings light to the spirit. Plus, they are beautiful.

A Humble Medicine of Earth and Spirit

Cruz María Santiago
of Morovis

stinging vine   *la pringamoza*

Cruz María Santiago

A Humble Medicine of Earth and Spirit

Cruz María Santiago
of Morovis

*Doña Cruz María is 73 years old, and lives with her husband
don Aurelio Santiago González in the outskirts of Morovis. She has
brought up twelve children, and has experienced the joy of seeing
them all married. At last count, there were nearly a dozen cows, 50
chickens and many medicinal plants sharing the Santiago farm.*

*Cruz María has the gift of making much out of little. She
prepares medicine from the wild plants that surround her, and she
heals herself and others using simple food stuffs such as lemon,
vinegar, salt and eggs. Always ready to help her neighbors, here she
offers readers a glimpse of her humble yet effective remedies, born of
earth and spirit, faith, and plenty of good humor.*

Cruz María: I was born here, I grew up here, and I'll die here.
The only way I'll leave this place is if they drag me, feet first.
Because I'm never leaving Morovis!

M: With twelve children and 73 years of experience, I'll bet you
know lots of home remedies. Would you tell me about some of
them?

Cruz María: I used to send the kids out to look for stinging vine (*la pringamoza*), which makes an excellent remedy for erysipelas, a terrible inflammation of the skin that burns like crazy.

You have to pick the vine leaves with gloves, because they sting. Then you cook some up in oil over a very low flame for five or ten minutes, until the oil turns green. Finally, you use a feather to paint the oil all over the inflamed area. And that little plant really works! I've used stinging vine to cure three of my kids when they had erysipelas. And I never had to take them to the doctor, even with the terrible fever that comes with that condition.

Plants are amazing! One time, my whole urinary tract felt sore. My kidneys were inflamed, and there was even blood in my urine. Well, I just happened to have three *prenetaria* plants growing behind the kitchen door. So I made a tea out of them mixed with a piece of spineless *tuna* cactus. That tea cured me! I drank it whenever I was thirsty, as if it were just plain water. And I've never had another urinary problem. *La prenetaria* is really medicine! I made a tea out of it that time, but you can also prepare it raw. You just wash it and add it to a jar of water and let it sit in your refrigerator. And you can drink as much of that tisane as you like.

M: It can't do any harm?

Cruz María: Harm? Never! There used to be a physician around here named Dr. Izquierdo. And whenever anyone had a kidney complaint, he prescribed *la prenetaria,* a plant that's always grown wild here!

One day, I was opening that gate over there, and I noticed that *la prenetaria* was really looking sparse. I said to God: "Look, with your help, I'm going to pull all of that poor *prenetaria* out of here and transplant it over there in the broadleaf coriander patch *(el recao)."* So that's what I did. And the plants have multiplied so now I have a little mountain of them growing, all I could ever need!

M: On the way in, I noticed a good sized *salvia* bush!

Cruz María: My mother always had a bandage of warm *salvia* leaves stuck to her forehead and temples with ointment because she roasted coffee beans, and that oily heat was very bad for her. It gave her terrible headaches, and *la salvia* helped her.

M: A few days ago, I stayed with a family in Las Marías, and the lady of the house, who also roasts coffee, suffers from terrible headaches as well.

Cruz María: Roasting coffee is simply dangerous! But *salvia* leaves, wrapped around the forehead like a bandage, make a good remedy for those headaches. And drinking *salvia* tea is very good for the throat, especially when you're hoarse. Or you can chew the leaf buds. *La salvia* is a good heating plant when one has a cold.

M: Did you plant this *salvia* bush?

Cruz María: Around here, no one plants it. The birds drop us off the seeds, thank God, and here it grows!

M: One of your neighbors told me that you have an excellent remedy for ringworm fungus.

Cruz María: I treat it with dumb cane *(el rábano cimarrón)*, the kind that doesn't have any white spots on the leaves. But you have to be careful because just a drop of that juice in your eyes will burn and can even blind you! You cut the burning quality by adding salt to the cane. Incredible, isn't it?

Just cut a six or eight-inch piece of dumb cane the long way, and put some salt into the cut. If you have large grains of salt, three or four grains will do, but you have to smash them up first. Then you leave it all outside overnight *al sereno*, so that it will absorb the cool, damp night air. During that time, the salt dissolves into the liquid from the cane, and in the morning you use a feather to paint the ringworm with that liquid. It burns a little but that's how ringworm is cured. No, I never took my kids to a doctor, not for any reason!

You know, at times I even cure myself with lemon *(el limón)*! I use lemon for gargles. Because when my throat is inflamed, the lemon's coolness helps a lot. Lemon is medicine!

Look, just last Monday I got out of bed and I couldn't swallow my own saliva. It was as if I had a ball in my throat. And imagining the worst, I said to myself: "Could this be a cancer? It must be a punishment . . . " But then I realized: "Wait a minute! It *can't* be a punishment because I haven't done anything wrong!"

So I went to the kitchen and squeezed some lemon juice into a cup with a little water and added some white vinegar and salt. Then, every once in a while I took the cup and gargled. I kept at it all through the night. The hot liquid cleansed and soothed my throat, and that problem didn't even last two days. It just disappeared, thank God.

And when the cows' teeth get loose, lemon juice tightens them right up. You squeeze all the juice and pulp out of a lemon and add some salt and sugar. Then you rub it along their gums, and don't give them water right away. Now if you don't have lemons around, you can use iodine. That's how I treat the cows. You see, they're chewing greens all the time, so they've always got to be pushing those jaws to work.

Just a little while ago, one of the cows had some loose teeth and she was getting skinny, fast. So I said to Quito: "Leave me alone with her. I'm going to give her some lemon." But the lemons had all been picked off the tree. So I went for the iodine, which I always have around. I passed that liquid iodine along her gums with a feather and I left it a while, because cows like the flavor. And that tightens their teeth right up.

My uncle used to prepare lemons for the cows by roasting them. After they exploded from the heat, he'd let them cool and then pass them, mixed with salt and sugar, all along the gums.

M: The good thing is that just about everyone has lemons at home or can buy them pretty cheaply.

Cruz María: Lemons, and salt too! There are times when I cut myself or something else will happen to me, and you'll see me with a little bit of salt water. I just wash myself with salt water, nothing more, and look! All these bumps I have here are from dealing with the chickens. I'm all marked up! And that's how I treat myself: with a little salt water.

Salt water even cured my grandson when that old dog — who is now hidden below there — bit him. You see, I have a bunch of cows over there, and we have a watering trough made of cement. Paco was fixing the trough because every morning after they're milked, the cows have to be able to drink their fill of water. Well, my grandson is never still, and he was running back and forth from the trough to the house here. During one of those trips, I think he must have hit the dog, or maybe he just tried to put his hand where he shouldn't have. Girl, that dog jumped on top of him, and suddenly I heard that boy yelling and that dog like a fury! I was washing dishes. Believe me, I threw down my dish towel fast! And when I got to where they were, the dog was still on top of him. I separated them, brought the boy up to the bathroom, and there I gave him a salt water bath.

That was Monday or Tuesday, and on Friday he was already better. Paco took him to the doctor, and the doctor said: "My God, how quickly you've healed!"

You know, that dog has bitten six people, but everyone he bites comes to me so I can wash them with salt water. And they're all just fine! *(laughter)*

M: What proportions of water and salt do you use?

Cruz María: Salt water for a bath or to drink means the saltiness of half a cup of water with a teaspoon or so of salt. I always taste the water to make sure it's salty enough, because it's the salt that's so medicinal.

The guys even use salt water when they castrate the pigs! After the operation, they wash 'em good with salt water so they don't get tetanus. Salt water is the best thing for so many conditions!

For the teeth! Look, the other day I went to the dentist so that he could pull a tooth. The next day I couldn't even touch my mouth. That whole side was all swollen up. I couldn't eat. My mouth began to twist to one side. And how I suffered at night! The next day I said to myself: "If I were a different kind of person, I'd go and form a labyrinth at the dentist's office!" Because nowadays people will sue for any little thing. But I'm not that kind of person. Then I said: "Wait just a minute!" And I took a little water with salt and I boiled it right up. I took a mouthful and kept it in my mouth for a good long while. And the next day, when I pressed the gum, a stream of pus came out, plus part of my molar that the dentist had left behind!

So thanks to God and the salt water, I got rid of that piece of tooth, the swelling went down, I went to bed, had a good night's sleep and the pain was gone. Just plain water with salt! Salt water is the best thing in the world.

M: Would you tell me more about some of the medicinal plants you use?

Cruz María: The broadleaf coriander I cultivate here is just for cooking, but some people use mouthfuls of a tea made from boiling the roots to help loosen a tooth for pulling.

And there's all sorts of black nightshade (*la mata de gallina*) growing around here wild. Sometimes people come to look for it here because when you have no control over your stomach — like when you've got a case of diarrhea caused by heat — there's nothing better than black nightshade with *sal de Eno* (a sodium bicarbonate-based digestive). If you eat something at night that affects you the next day, just boil up the black nightshade for tea, add the *sal de Eno* and drink it first thing in the morning on an empty stomach. Black nightshade is the best there is!

Once I got sick on a Monday. I didn't sleep that day nor that night, nor the next day or night. In fact it was Thursday when my husband, who was off to San Juan, said: "I'll leave the city early Friday afternoon so I can take you to the doctor." That's when I remembered the black nightshade, which doesn't cost a penny! I simmered some up until the water was dark green. Then I added the *sal de Eno* and I drank it, very strong. And that remedy cured me so well that nowadays I don't even remember what having a stomach ache is like!

At times, black nightshade disappears from where it's been growing, but right now, with all the rain that's fallen, you see it right alongside of you everywhere you walk. You prepare a planter with flowers or other plants, and black nightshade springs up right beside them.

Of course, the ideal thing is to have *la tautúa* growing around too, because black nightshade mixed with *la tautúa* makes for an even better medicine. You can also add it to enemas for children or they can take it as a tea. It's cooling and it settles the stomach when you're feeling a little "off."

And these tomato plants here are also medicinal!

M: You use the tomatoes themselves?

Cruz María: No. You heat the leaves and place them with some beef or sheep tallow *(el sebo de Flandes)* and egg yolk on boils so that they'll explode.

And that very same tallow is very good when you have swollen glands. You massage them with the tallow and they go down. One thing's for sure. If it doesn't cure you, you know it certainly hasn't done you any harm. People used to use tallow for mumps too, and for inflamed corns. Even for inflamed pimples on the face! They rubbed that tallow back and forth over the pimples, and they would disappear, little by little.

Another little story just occurred to me! My daughter Adelita, the one who lives in New York City, once had a boil under her arm that was this big *(joins her thumb and index finger to form an OK sign)*. Since it was located in her arm pit, she had to sleep with her arms above her head. My God, was that cyst ugly! And we didn't have the means to take her to the doctor. Then, suddenly, it came to me: a hen's egg!

I put the white aside, and using a piece of tissue paper, I painted that red boil with egg yolk. Beneath her, I put a couple of towels in case it exploded. And it did explode the next day! So I didn't have to take her to the doctor that time either. Cured by the yolk of a hen's egg!

M: Who taught you that remedy?

Cruz María: It was like a whim that just came to me. I guess the shape of the cyst itself suggested an egg.

M: Have you used egg yolk for any other conditions?

Cruz María: Of course! It's also good to make a punch with when someone has a bad chest cold. You beat a fresh egg white, and separately you beat the yolk. Then you heat them up together, but you have to keep beating them so that they don't cook! You add almond oil, brown sugar, cinnamon *(la canela)*, sweet ginger *(el jengibre dulce)*, cloves *(clavos dulces)*, anise *(el anís)*, all the warming spices you have around the house. Because they are *very* good for a cold and flu.

I don't know. It seems to me that nowadays people get worse colds and flu than before. People today seem to get sicker more often, too, although back then we weren't so conscious about hygiene as we are now.

You see, I had a big family and they grew up healthy and strong. I never took those kids to a doctor. If they had a cough, I gave them a rub with some warm Vicks and I made them some spiced eucalyptus *(el eucalipto)* or ginger tea. And they never got asthma or anything!

Well, that's about all I know, I guess. Anyway, I've got to get off to church now.

M: Seems to me you know a great deal. Thanks so much!

Cruz María: May God and the Virgin Mary bless and accompany you now and always.

Beauticians and Neighbors of Carolina

Ana Clausells de Costoso, Josefina Pizarro,
María Salgado,
Julia Santiago and Monín Santana

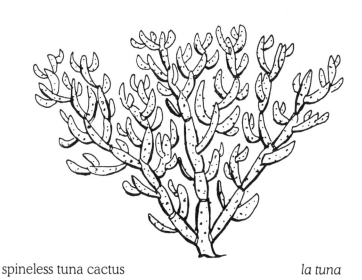

spineless tuna cactus   *la tuna*

Ana Clausells de Costoso shares a laugh with Julia Santiago.

Josefina Pizarro

Beauticians and Neighbors of Carolina

Ana Clausells de Costoso, Josefina Pizarro, María Salgado, Julia Santiago and Monín Santana

Ana Clausells de Costoso and Josefina Pizarro are housewives and mothers who also share the responsibilities of a beauty parlor at Ana's home, part of a peaceful community in Carolina. They speak from experience about plant-based beauty products as well as medicines.

Our interview flowed with the informality of a neighborly visit as one of their clients, María Salgado, and two very dear neighbors, Julia Santiago and Monín Santana, generously contributed their knowledge. The following conversation, which took place at both Ana's and Julia's homes, was punctuated by sips of Ana's delicious homemade tamarind ices, and the lively sound of doña Julia's roosters.

M: Doña Ana, your son Carlos Alberto told me that you use plants as medicine, cosmetics, and even to get rid of ticks!

Ana: Yes, we use *el poleo* for that. If there are ticks around, you put all the *poleo* that fits — leaves without stems — into a bucket of water. The stronger the better, but you don't boil it. You simply leave *el poleo* there to steep from one day to the next, and then you pour it in and around the dog house or wherever the ticks are. The water has a strong smell, and the ticks move on quickly.

María: *El poleo* is also good for a stomach ache! When something I've eaten disagrees with me, I go to the back yard and pick some *poleo* and some *guanábana* leaves for tea. The discomfort vanishes as soon as I drink it.

Ana: There were eight kids in my family, and when we had stomach aches, my mother used to give us a tea of budding mango leaves mixed with *guanábana* leaves. And it always worked! You see, since they're both cooling, they reduce the acid in your stomach.

Josefina: Not too long ago, everyone knew about medicinal plants. But along with progress, a lot of knowledge was forgotten. Suddenly now, with the come-back of naturism, the plants are being rediscovered. For example, everyone knows that aloe *(la sábila)* is good for a cough. You peel some thick aloe leaves, cut the inside gelatin up in pieces, put it in a bowl with a little witch hazel solution *(Agua Maravilla)* and some honey, and let it sit for a day or so, so that the plant's medicinal qualities are dissolved in the liquid. You take tablespoons of that mixture, and it loosens the phlegm from your chest.

Ana: One of my mother's favorite remedies for a cough was the papaya flower. Whenever I need it, I still boil it up myself and add honey. It's very effective.

María: *La malá* is also good for getting rid of phlegm from your lungs, especially for people who have asthma. You boil up two of the succulent leaves with a few anise stars *(el anís de estrella)* in a cup and a half of water for about fifteen minutes, and then you drink it. That gets rid of phlegm and blood too.

You know, I was born ill, and as a baby I was very sickly, and in a great deal of pain. My father thought I wouldn't last even a few weeks! He had me baptized right away so that I wouldn't die a "heathen" as they say; but my mother cured me with plants, and I never once went to a doctor when I was a child.

You know what they gave me when I had the measles? Love vine *(el afilerillo)*. It has a little white flower, and it grows up to 50 feet high. My mother prepared cooling drinks of love vine, which took away the burning heat that coursed through me. Thanks to mamá, I was cured of the measles within one week.

Josefina: When I had the measles, my mother gave me boiled milk with raisins. For that condition of inner heat, it was a good cooling remedy. It drew the measles right out of me, fast.

Other times, my mom would put raw rice in water and leave it there for an hour or more. Now it's coming back to me! She'd give us rice water for stomach ache and for diarrhea. But it was a different kind of rice in those days; the grains were very long.

M: The hulls of brown rice and other whole grains are loaded with water-soluble B vitamins, which tonify both the intestinal tract and the nervous system.

Josefina: It's amazing how much our mothers knew, just through their experience!

Ana: My mother used rice water for her skin. She would let raw rice sit in a little bit of water, then grind it up to make a paste. In fact, we all made facial masks from that paste, and it kept our complexions really clean. I *never* got pimples.

M: Would you talk more about using plants as cosmetics?

Ana: I've used Caribbean vervain *(la verbena)* on my daughter's hair to help it grow. I boil it, let it cool, wash her hair, and then I pour the vervain "tea" over her hair and leave it there. You can add any conditioner you like, but don't rinse out the vervain. She had hardly any hair growing out of the back of her head, and now she has a mane!

I even recommended that my clients with the same problem go out to the plaza and buy some vervain. After using it a while, they all thank me. The results have been very good!

M: I've heard about using Caribbean vervain as a fever remedy, but I never heard anyone talk about it as a cure for scant hair. I'm sure lots of people who read this will be trying it out!

Josefina: We also use rosemary *(el romero)* boiled up as a final rinse. It adds body and gives your hair a nice, dark color.

Ana: I use aloe to give hair body too, and it's great for getting rid of dandruff. I just peel a large stalk, cut it up into tiny pieces, put them in three or four cups of water and leave it all in the refrigerator. The next day, I blend up the mixture, strain it, and apply it to the hair after shampooing. I never rinse it out. You don't have to boil it, and if you make a decent quantity of it, you can store it in the refrigerator for future rinses. It doesn't go bad right away.

M: That aloe is an amazing plant!

María: So is the spineless *tuna* cactus. Believe it or not, they charge $3 for just one leaf of it in New York! You simply peel it, cut it up, and put it in water in a jar in the refrigerator. Then,

94

instead of drinking water from the faucet, you drink the cactus water. It's a tisane that cools the kidneys and increases urination. And it's also good if you're constipated!

M: By tisane, you mean an herbal preparation that hasn't been boiled?

Ana: Yes. When we say tisane, we mean a raw plant in water, "brewed" in the fridge. Sometimes, we chop it up first. The juice of the plant dissolves little by little into the water. Some people also put their boiled teas in the refrigerator to drink cold, but that's different. A tisane is made without heat.

María: I also prepare tisanes from a little plant called *la prenetaria*. It grows wild all over the place, wherever there's humidity, even through the cracks in the sidewalk! I just pick it, wash it, put it in a jar of water in the fridge, and drink it to clean out my kidneys.

There are medicinal plants for everything, even the heart! The leaves of the custard apple tree *(el corazón)* can be boiled up for a tea that's said to strengthen the heart as it lowers blood pressure.

I don't know. It seems that living in the city, you really tend to forget these good old remedies of the past!

Ana: But even scientists are still using plants as a source of medicine.

M: Scientists use the part or parts of a plant that they've determined to be most useful. But I believe that all parts of a plant are useful. Besides their strong, medicinal effects, they have so much to offer: minerals, vitamins, fiber, and a number of compounds that work together in a natural and perfect way . . .

Ana: They may be perfect, but some plants not only cure; they can also kill!

María: I know a plant that can kill. It has an exquisite flower, but you can die from drinking a tea of it. It's called the moon plant (*la campana*).

Ana: Another plant that both heals and kills is black nightshade (*la yerba mora*). The seeds are considered to be poisonous, but the leaf boiled in milk cures ulcers!

Josefina: Actually the seed is a purgative. Which reminds me of castor oil, another great purgative that was also used for intestinal worms. Nowadays it doesn't have much of a smell, but back then it was real "natural," if you know what I mean! *(laughter)*

And the leaves of the castor bean plant (*la higuereta*) were boiled up to make sitz baths for women suffering from congestion or inflammation of the womb area. After boiling a big handful of leaves in a large pot for 15 minutes or so, you strain the liquid and pour it into the warm bath water. Then you sit there for ten or 15 minutes or until you feel better.

Ana: After giving birth, we women used to drink a mixture of bittersweet chocolate boiled with *la yerba buena*. You simply boil half a bar of that chocolate with eight to ten leaves of *la yerba buena* in two cups of water, and drink it to help strengthen the womb after birth.

M: I bet lots of women enjoyed taking that medicine!

Josefina: Right! Not all home remedies are like castor oil! *(laughter)*

M: Besides *tuna* cactus, castor oil and other strong purgatives, what are some other remedies for constipation?

Josefina: A tea made from the young leaves of *el tártago*. But you have to make the tea out of the new leaf buds, because the mature parts of the plant contain poisons. It's one of the plants that can both cure and kill. The seed is poison, but the young bud cures constipation. I've given it to my daughter Maura and it really works!

Doña María had come for a beauty parlor appointment, and her husband has now arrived to pick her up, calling with long, steady beeps of his car horn. After she leaves, amidst many goodbyes and blessings, Ana and Josefina take me into the back yard, where broadleaf coriander (el recao), la prenetaria, life plant (la bruja), pigeon peas (gandules) and aloe plants grow alongside trees bearing abundant oranges, lemons, guanábanas and custard apples.

Ana: Do you know about the life plant? It's the best thing in the world for an earache. You warm up the leaf on the heat of the stove, and squeeze out the warm juice into your ear. You can cover it up with some cotton afterwards, but it's not always necessary. And life plant is special for another reason. If you hang one of the leaves up from a tack on a wall, it will sprout roots without ever touching the earth!

Oh, and when there's no toothpaste, pigeon pea leaves clean the teeth and strengthen the gums. You just place a leaf against the gums and rub as if it were a little brush.

M: I love hearing about plants that offer both medicine and food.

Ana: Well then you should know that the spineless *tuna* cactus we mentioned earlier makes a delicious stewed vegetable. It's something like okra. First you peel it, then you cook it up with garlic, onion, vegetables and cod fish or meat. I had some for the first time over at doña Julia's house and I didn't even realize it was *tuna* cactus. It's delicious, and it's got a nice, thick texture.

Speaking of food, lemon in warm salt water makes a great gargle. Because the salt cleanses your throat, and the lemon has lots of vitamin C to help fight off a cold or infection.

Josefina: Did you know that the root of coffee senna *(la hidionda chiquita)* is used by women to maintain a normal menstrual cycle? And the seeds are a good coffee substitute.

M: I look forward to tasting some "coffee" made from ground and toasted coffee senna seeds while I'm in Puerto Rico. They say it's delicious.

Josefina: Since you like those natural flavors so much, next time you get a cold, drink the juice of a green lemon boiled up with a little water and take an aspirin with it. Within a minute or two, your cold will simply disappear. And if you can get some sun while you're waiting, so much the better!

Ana: I use a similar remedy, but I add witch hazel solution to the lemon juice. I think the witch hazel works even better than aspirin!

And did you know that the same orange rind that's good for giving flavor to cakes and drinks can also be used as medicine for animals? My father used to put orange rind in the chicken's water when they had "fowl's pip," a sort of cold they get. And it cured them!

M: I hear plenty of roosters around here, and they all sound pretty healthy!

Ana: Those are doña Julia's. Let's go over to her place. She knows a lot about medicinal plants.

Josefina leaves to cook for her daughter; Ana and I visit doña Julia and her friend doña Monín, who has stopped by for a brief visit.

Julia: I was born on January 30 in 1919 and I've lived in Puerto Rico all my life. I learned about medicinal plants from my mother, who taught me that basil *(la albahaca)* is good for headaches and as an eyewash, that aloe whipped up with egg is very good for children when they had a cold . . . She had a remedy for everything. She even used head wraps made of tobacco leaves *(el tabaco)* to treat migraines.

M: What home remedies do you use yourself these days?

Julia: My son in law and I have really high blood pressure. So a Cuban friend of ours recommended that we boil up five leaves of broadleaf coriander with the papery outer peel and ends of three heads of garlic *(el ajo),* plus five leaves of common plantain herb *(el llantén)* and five orange leaves for 15 minutes or until the flavor is strong. Then, instead of drinking tap water or soda, we drink that herb water, cold from the ice box. When my blood pressure is sky high, I prepare it, drink it every day and, according to my doctor, the blood pressure does go down. And I can feel a difference, because when my blood pressure is really high, almost any little thing upsets me. But when I'm drinking the herb water daily, I'm calmer, and my blood pressure normalizes. So I'm talking from my experience.

M: What other conditions have you treated with home remedies?

Julia: For pain in my kidneys, I've prepared mallow *(la malva)* sitz baths. You just boil up some mallow leaves, and after the water has cooled off a bit, you add some Epsom salts. Then you sit in the water up to your waist for as long as you can, and it soothes the inflammation.

I've also used sitz baths of common plantain herb for vaginal and uterine complaints. You boil a good deal of it — one part leaves to three parts water — for about 20 minutes, and then you strain it and add it to your bath. It cools, cleans, and alleviates inflammation.

Another remedy for the same condition is a bath of wild eggplant leaves *(la berenjena cimarrona)*. You prepare it the same way as the plantain bath, and then you just sit for a while in that water while it's fairly warm. It helps a lot.

Ana: Doña Julia, what's the herb you use for wounds and sores?

Julia: *Yerba cangá,* dried. After you've washed the wound well, you sprinkle the pulverized leaf dust on it.

Ana: And when children get constipated?

Julia: When my kids had that problem, I always started out by giving them a teaspoon of cooking oil. Then I rubbed the hairs off of a few stems of el *cohitre blanco,* pressed the stems into a little ball, and covered it with oil before using it as a suppository. That's a good children's remedy.

Monín: For constipation, you can also mix the gelatin of a leaf of aloe with a washed and chopped-up leaf of spineless *tuna* cactus in the blender with two cups of water. Add honey and drink it throughout the day. Plus, eat fresh, natural food with lots of fiber. Nothing canned!

If a child gets indigestion, you can give him a remedy of

wood ashes. My mother used to take wood ashes from the hearth and put a pinch of those ashes in a cup of water. She let them settle for a while, and then the child would drink that water with half a teaspoon of cooking oil.

M: Now they sell modern charcoal pills at the drug store for gas and indigestion. It's even effective for food poisoning! It must be one of our most ancient medicines.

Monín: Charcoal is also good for absorbing odors in the refrigerator. So many of the old country ways are still valuable.

M: What did you all do when your children got high fevers?

Monín: We gave them special baths with plants.

Julia: For an unboiled bath, we would squeeze the juice of fresh aloe, *el poleo*, Caribbean mugwort *(la altamisa)*, garlic weed *(el anamú)* and everything else we could find into a bucket of water. Then we'd add some alcohol to the water and put it outside under the blazing sun. Within half an hour or so it was ready for a bath. We have a camphor tree *(al alcanfor)* here, but if there are no camphor leaves around, you can add half a camphor pastille to the water and that makes it even more refreshing. After straining the bath, we poured it over the child's head. Then the child would get all wrapped up so that he could sweat as much as possible.

M: Are there food products that you also use as remedies?

Julia: If you use a poultice of grated, raw potato directly after burning yourself, you'll see that the burn doesn't blister, and you might not even lose any hair from the burned spot!

Potato is also good for really bad headaches. Just grate it and mix it up with some witch hazel solution to make a cooling paste. Place that paste on your forehead, temples and neck, and lie down for a little while. What a delicious feeling! Pure relief! You're revived. And I'm speaking from experience!

Ana: You have a remedy for diabetes, don't you?

Julia: Yes, leaves from the mulberry tree *(la morera)*. Boil up five leaves for 15 minutes in about three cups of water, and drink it every day. I have diabetes, and it's really helped me. And when I worked as a nurse, I had a diabetic patient who was really sick. I told her: "Don't worry. Tomorrow I'm going to bring you a little mulberry tea, and that will take care of your condition." So I came home and boiled up some mulberry leaves and took her a big jar of it the next day. She hid the jar in her suitcase and every once in a while she took a swig. Well, when they checked her blood sugar, they found that it was quite low. And when she went home, her doctor told her to keep taking that "secret remedy" she'd been hiding, because it was extremely effective!

Monín: Doctors are aware. They realize that people have their own resources . . .

M: If someone is always tired, sleepy, and very low on energy, what would you recommend?

Julia: I'd suggest that she take a hemoglobin or red blood count. If it comes out low, I would suggest that she make lots of punches from all the most nourishing and strengthening things: grape juice, orange juice, malt. If the problem is a simple matter of fatigue from doing too much physical work, I would recommend a heavier diet, and I'd suggest drinking lots of broth. Of course, the best thing is always dove or pigeon broth. After drinking that, you feel a tremendous surge of energy almost immediately, and you say: "Yes I can!" Keep drinking it for two or three weeks, and you get "tough as a coconut," as they say in the country. Strong and resistant!

M: Those roosters are really something. How do you treat them when they get sick?

Julia: When they or the chickens get "the pip," which is contagious and leaves them with that heavy mucus, I just add lemon juice to their water. That takes care of it.

Ana: Look at her life plants!

M: Are they ever big and beautiful!

Julia: You know, when you pass by a plant you really should greet it. You should say: "Good morning, beautiful." If it's a life plant, maybe you say: "Love, give me a little leaf to help me out with this ear that's hurting." You should talk to it as if it were a person, as if it had a soul. Because if you have a plant and you tend it every day, giving it water, watching it grow, and wishing it well, that plant will become your friend.

M: Your *salvia* plant certainly looks happy!

Julia: I've always made teas out of *la salvia*. A tea of the leaves is very good for menstrual pains. Because those pains come from a cold condition, and *la salvia* is warming.

Ana: Tell her about the butter poultice!

Julia: When you've bruised yourself and the bruise starts swelling, use a poultice of butter, salt and sugar to bring the swelling right down. You just mix equal amounts of butter and sugar with about half the amount of salt. Put it all on top of the wound, and there will be no swelling.

M: I love to hear about remedies like this, because even if someone doesn't have a garden, everyone has a little butter, salt and sugar in the house.

Julia: Not to mention faith, which doesn't cost a thing! You know, before they operated on my eyes, everything I saw was in a blur. I couldn't thread a needle, so I couldn't do any mending. I couldn't even tend to the plants because, practically speaking, I was blind. Then one of my neighbors held a service at her house. Alicia and Ana here prayed for me, and I felt a marked difference afterwards. I can't say I could see perfectly the next day, but I came back here and worked with the plants and took care of my clothes. What could be greater or more beautiful than that?

M: You have a lot of faith in your home remedies too, don't you?

Julia: Yes, I take my medicinal teas and other home remedies. I drink everything folks offer me, and I do it with the faith that it will help me. Some people say: "I'll try this remedy and see if it does something for me." I say: "They're offering me this medicinal tea and it's second only to God!" I've always believed in home remedies, and I've come to trust them more and more because they've really worked for me.

Planting with the Moon in Caguas

Francisco (Panky) Negrón Maldonado

native bean   *habichuelas del país*

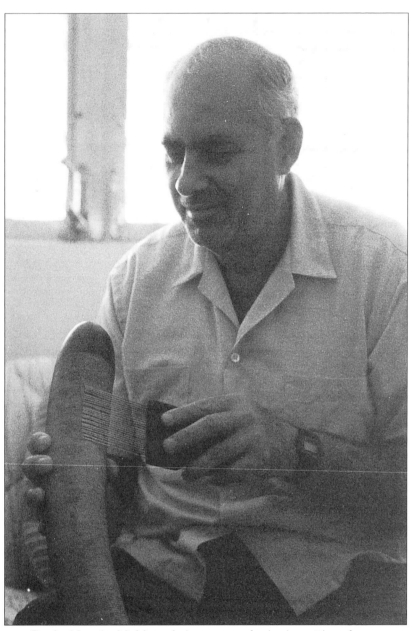

Panky Negrón Maldonado is an award-winning güiro player.

Planting with the Moon
in Caguas

Francisco (Panky) Negrón Maldonado

Not so very long ago, when the Puerto Rican people lived on food produced almost exclusively by their own labor on island soil, Francisco (Panky) Negrón Maldonado learned about working the land in the fields of Vega Alta. Trailing after his father and a pair of oxen, he learned to prepare the soil, to plant each seed and seedling at the proper depth, and to sow and harvest different vegetables at the most propitious times. According to his father, there is a time of year and even a time of month for planting almost everything that grows in Puerto Rico. Leonardo Negrón Santiago worked in harmony with the moon and the tides; he taught his son to do the same.

Since he left the farm when he was 17, Panky has made a living in urban settings, working mostly as a police officer. But he has always maintained small plots of land, suitable for growing fruits and vegetables for his table, and abundant crops of tender, native beans (las habichuelas del país).

The once-ubiquitous, cream colored native bean is almost impossible to find today because of a recent shift in agricultural and consumer practices. Thus, they are the envy of Panky's neighbors and the delight of co-workers and friends who eagerly buy the surplus.

Panky is a well-traveled individual, but his love for the earth and his understanding about planting are part of an island-based tradition of building and tending healthy, fertile soil in balance with nature.

Panky: The most valuable thing my father taught me in terms of agriculture is that nothing should be planted when the moon is new or waxing. If you break this basic rule, your plants will be tenderest just when the insects are hungriest, so you'll lose a good portion of your crops. The solution is to plant during the waning moon. That way, when the insects are ready to eat, the plants are no longer vulnerable. I've always planted during the waning moon, and I've had tremendous results.

I sow native beans on a tiny piece of land measuring only about 300 square meters, and from that piece of land I easily harvest 70 or 80 pounds of beans every time I plant. The last time I planted was in February, and I had my best crop, harvesting more than 80 pounds in April. I was able to give away and sell 40 pounds of the beans! Then, from the money I earned by selling them, I bought fertilizer. The other half of my crop is packed away in the freezer. They'll last me until the next crop is ready, in July.

M: What kind of fertilizer do you use?

Panky: I use natural fertilizers. There's a company here in Puerto Rico that packages the rich alluvial soil that's deposited along the river beds. That alluvium is then mixed with other soils, and it's great for the plants. Manure is also very good fertilizer. Chicken manure is one of the richest, but its nitrogen content is so high that if it's used before it sits for a year or two, it actually burns the plants. And what a stink! I brought some home once, and Margarita almost kicked me out! *(laughter)* So it's got to be "cured."

M: Do you follow the same rule of planting with the moon for everything you plant, or are there exceptions?

Panky: Actually, cassava *(la yuca)* and sugar cane *(la caña)* can be planted any time of month. They're both virtually immune to insect infestation, no matter when they're planted. But they're the only plants that have this quality as far as I know.

On the other hand, when planting plantain *(el plátano)* and banana *(el guineo)* plants, you want to observe not only the phases of the moon; you also want to work with the tide. Each tree produces six or seven seeds, which must be taken during low tide. Otherwise the seed is full of liquid and loses its sap. You want to take the seed with it's driest. That way it maintains its essence, and has the capacity to absorb the most from the earth.

Old-time farmers used to determine whether it was high or low tide simply by looking at the veins on their hands. If the veins were swollen, it was high tide. If they were flat, it was low tide. I never used my hands in that way, but from my own experience, I can tell you that it's very important to collect plantain and banana seed when the tide is low if you want an optimum yield from your plants. And then, of course, you plant the seeds during the waning moon.

M: Have you actually experimented by planting seeds at different times of month and taking banana plant seeds, let's say, during high tide?

Panky: Of course! Everything I'm telling you I've proven for myself. Nothing comes from books or lectures. I've experimented with taking seeds at high tide, and I've tried planting seeds during the waxing moon. Basically, I've seen that plants sown when the moon is waxing may sprout beautifully, but they won't yield a thing, because when they're about to produce their fruit, they're devoured by insects. It's a disaster!

M: What insects are these?

Panky: There are several. The worst threat is *la esperanza* (a type of grasshopper) at the larval stage, but there are several moths and flying insects that lay their eggs on the plants or in the earth near them. The eggs hatch, and you never see them while they're in the larval stage because they burrow into the earth. They do a great deal of damage unless you plant at the proper time.

People think that these old ways of farming are unnecessary. They say: "On the big farms in the United States, they don't plant by the moon." But they forget that on those big farms, airplanes spray insecticide all over the crops!

M: The bad thing is that the insecticide contaminates the earth and poisons the people!

Panky: And we don't know the effects of these poisons for the future. Plus, in many cases, insects actually develop immunity to the chemicals designed to kill them. Who knows? Maybe eventually there won't be anything that kills them . . . without killing us first! *(laughter)*

M: Do you ever use insecticide?

Panky: I have used it, but I've gotten the best results when I haven't. This year, for instance, I didn't use anything, and I didn't see any insects. None! So I saved money, and the soil is better off.

M: How would you describe the soil here in Caguas, near Cidra?

Panky: The land here, like on so much of the central part of the island, is excellent for growing vegetables, from yautía and cabbage and squash to celery root, plantains and sugar cane. Puerto Rican soil is tremendous. It's mostly red clay here, what we call "sweet clay." Just about the only things we don't grow in this part of the island are avocado and mango. Those crops grow better in the warmer areas of the island.

M: I was told recently that at the Mayagüez campus of the University of Puerto Rico, there's been a resurgence of interest in certain aspects of agriculture. Some classes are completely closed out for the first time! So I'm surprised I haven't seen more back yard gardens like yours.

Panky: During the mid-70s, before the era of food stamps, there was a great campaign supporting the development of back yard gardens. Everyone got enthused. Every household put a great deal of work into its garden, and there were prizes for the best ones. People were quite creative in making the most of the available space. There were even hundreds of rooftop gardens! And they were all a source of great pride.

But people lost interest all of a sudden when food stamps became available, because they figured: "Why should I sweat and get all dirty bending over to work the land if I can go to the supermarket and get what I need for free?"

It's such an easy system that only people who really love the land have chosen to maintain small family gardens during the past nine years or so. That's why the home garden program ended, and that's why the native beans are so scarce. Hardly anybody grows them anymore!

It's a shame, really. Because when people get things for free, they lose the pride that comes from working for what they have. It's a beautiful thing to sweat and work for the food you are going to eat. It's a beautiful thing to be able to say: "I'm eating from what I cultivated myself, and my children have shoes because I sold something that I produced."

Living on the Land

Cheo and Bárbara Rodríguez
of Orocovis

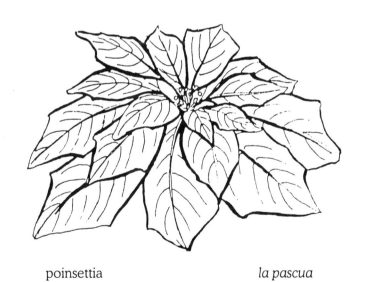

poinsettia   *la pascua*

Living on the Land

Cheo and Bárbara Rodríguez
of Orocovis

Cheo and Bárbara Rodríguez live in the central, mountainous zone of the island, tucked away nearly an hour's hike from the nearest paved road, with no phone and no TV. Since 1973, they have lived as close to the land as posible, working the soil in return for food and a vast array of medicinal plants. They avoid most animal products and adhere to a traditional diet, which means lots of viandas (starchy vegetables, mostly tubers such as celery root (el apio), cassava (la yuca), yautía, breadfruit and malanga.), plenty of whole grains, home-grown greens, fruits, seeds and pure, spring water that has been routed to flow through their kitchen.

Cheo and Bárbara are deeply concerned about Puerto Rico's cultural integrity. Here they share thoughts about how this integrity is related to — and reflected in — the diet, health, attitudes and agricultural practices of her people. As parents, farmers and lovers of nature, they study, cultivate and use medicinal plants, activities that were once part of Puerto Rico's daily cultural expression.

M: Living here in the country, so far away from the mainstream of society, what has been your motivation or inspiration, and what are your goals?

Cheo: When we moved here, my goal was to strengthen my own health and to test my belief that my physical problems were greatly due to the environment in which I lived. And coming to a healthy environment *has* helped me to become healthy again.

Bárbara: All of my family comes from the mountains, so when I was a child, I got lots of exposure to country life and small town life. Then my parents moved to the city, where I remained till I was 18. When I returned to the country as an adult, I felt as though I'd come home. It was a matter of falling in love with something that I'd already known. That's been my inspiration. My goal now is to raise my family in a healthy environment.

M: Would you talk about your relationship with the earth, and with the plants, especially?

Cheo: We keep in mind the fact that each one of us is part of everything, and we're involved in discovering relationships between ourselves and everything else. Even though we're distant from our human neighbors, we're surrounded by all the living creatures in the mountains, including the plants. And they offer us friendship, food, joy, health, life!

Bárbara: Without green plants in our lives, we couldn't survive! We'd die and become earth ourselves, so they're all important. Plants are very special beings. They live in a dimension parallel to our own, and they are here to help us.

Cheo: People used to live in such close quarters with nature, with the plants. And you can see that closeness in the beauty and strength of our grandparents and great grandparents. We're trying to rediscover that which worked so well in the past.

Bárbara: One thing we've discovered is that the plants used for health, be they food or medicine, aren't exotic or strange. They grow wild right outside our front door. They're from the environment we live in, and are sharing energy with us. When we live in cities, we forget that we're sharing the world with them.

My great grandmother always had all kinds of medicinal plants growing in her garden. She never ran to the doctor for pills or injections. In those days, everyone used the medicinal plants growing in their gardens. They knew how to prepare them because their parents and grandparents and their great grandparents had done it. The knowledge was passed on from one person to another, from one generation to another.

Every *jíbaro* household had its botanical garden, and every garden had Caribbean spearmint *(la yerba buena)*, marjoram *(la mejorana)*, rosemary *(el romero)*, peppermint *(la menta)*, lemon grass *(el limoncillo)*, rue *(la ruda)*, fragrant geranium *(el geranio oloroso)*, *la paletaria*, and much more. They were an important part of the household. In what looked like an ornamental flower garden, you could find medicine for just about anything! If you felt ill, you didn't go anywhere. Someone prepared you a little *guarapo* or they fixed you a hot bath and wrapped you up in warm blankets so that you could sweat. Women generally guarded the information about medicinal plants, while the men were more involved with cultivating the plants used for food.

But all of that knowledge, which for so long had been passed down from generation to generation, was cut off at the root because another wave of ideas took over completely. The new wave said: "How could you think that a bunch of weeds is really medicine? That's ignorance!" And since no one wants to be ignorant, the old ways were hidden, ignored, forgotten . . . and the new ways became the authority, dominating the entire scene.

We're losing a tremendous amount of important knowledge with the death of our elders, our grandparents, our midwives, the bonesetters and spiritual healers. But there are still old people in

117

the countryside and villages who will tell you that such and such a plant is good for certain conditions, and that if you mix it with this other plant and make a *guarapo,* you can treat such and such a problem. This information can still be recovered, especially from the oldest people on the island.

M: Do you have any favorite plants? Are there plants that you especially enjoy working with?

Cheo: The plant that has surprised us most in terms of its instantaneous effect is comfrey *(la consuelda mayor).*

Bárbara: We use it for all kinds of skin irritations. When the youngest was an infant, she was so plump that her little legs were always rubbing against one another. They got pretty badly irritated and soon she had a full-blown rash. I was worried because it simply wouldn't go away no matter what we tried.

    Then I got some comfrey, squeezed out some of the slippery juice from the long, thick stems with a rolling pin, and used that green juice as an ointment. Well, within ten or fifteen minutes, the irritation had disappeared, and the baby was fine! Nothing bothered her at all after that. That was the most dramatic and immediate reaction I've ever seen. Now we use comfrey all the time for skin irritations, and it always soothes.

    Then there's garlic *(el ajo)*! My grandfather had cancer for about 20 years, it seems, without anyone knowing about it. Instinctively, he ate raw garlic every day. My grandmother hated the smell, so in order not to bother her, he would mash it up, put it in a piece of soft bread, and swallow it like a pill every day. He never missed a day of taking his garlic, and it maintained his strength, his health. When the doctors operated on him, they couldn't figure out how he had lived so long! Because the cancer had spread throughout his entire body and even to his brain.

Meanwhile, he was still completely clear minded and coherent. He could carry on a conversation without your noticing that anything was amiss. The garlic seems to have been responsible for oxygenating his blood and keeping him alive.

M: Garlic is also used to control high blood pressure . . .

Cheo: And raw garlic counteracts the poisonous effects of alcohol.

Bárbara: Garlic doesn't even have to be eaten to be effective. You can wear it, and its antiseptic and other medicinal qualities are absorbed by the skin. And if someone has parasites, lukewarm enemas of garlic tea will help to control them.

Of course, it smells, whether you eat it or wear it!

Cheo: Once, cloves of garlic were tied around the ankles of small children. It was supposed to keep the poisonous snakes from biting them. They would avoid the smell. Now it's *people* who avoid the smell! *(laughter)*

Seriously, so many people today are looking for natural ways of balancing out the negative aspects of modern life.

Even people who take harmful drugs can use simple home remedies to make sure the drugs don't do too much damage! I know someone who, while recovering from cocaine addiction, used lecithin and orange tree leaves *(las hojas de naranjo)* to calm himself down and strengthen his nervous system. It eased what would otherwise have been an unbearably painful process.

Bárbara: Calcium also helps the nerves. You can get it from sesame *(el ajonjolí)*, from seaweed, from nettle leaves *(la ortiga)* from many sources besides milk, and it alleviates anxiety.

Cheo: Of course, lemon *(el limón)* is loaded with vitamin C, which can be used to fight the effects even of drugs as strong as heroin. In fact, our neighbor, doña Pancha's son, quit alcohol using lemon. Just lemon! So not only did he stop drinking, but the vitamin C strengthened him, physically.

Bárbara: It also strengthened his will power, his self esteem, his character. Every time he had the urge to drink alcohol, he drank lemon juice, straight. And since it was as bracing as rum, that sour juice allowed him to give up alcohol altogether.

M: I recently read about an experimental study being done in California in which alcoholics are injected with high dosages of vitamin C. It seems that the vitamin C enables them to stop drinking without the withdrawal symptoms.

Cheo: There is a tremendous amount of wisdom in the popular herbal tradition. One day science will catch up! *(laughter)*

Once, when I was living in rather primitive conditions, I had an infestation of cockroaches. Then one day a beautiful old lady came over and said to me: "Son, cockroaches hate *el poleo*. Put branches of it throughout your little home here, and they'll just disappear." I did that, and with only two or three branches in each corner, I got rid of every single cockroach!

M: An extract of *el poleo* would sell like crazy in New York if people knew about it!

Bárbara: *(laughter)* Plants offer so many possibilities to people: possibilities of maintaining one's health, of healing, of knowing a beautiful part of reality . . .

M: Tell me about another good home remedy!

Bárbara: There are so many! Did you know that the milky juice of the poinsettia *(la pascua)* plant eliminates warts? Just pick a few leaves and apply the milky inner juice to the warts four or five times a day. They'll disappear after just a few days.

Cheo: And the latex-like milk from the green papaya kills intestinal parasites! Cut some long slits into a just-harvested, green papaya. Then, with a teaspoon, collect the white latex that seeps out of the cuts. Since the latex is caustic, you should mix it with juice before taking it so as not to burn your lips. Take a teaspoonful or two a day, always on an empty stomach. Within three days you will have eliminated the parasites. And the same remedy can be used for poor digestion! Just take the latex-y milk mixed with juice after meals.

Bárbara: Tropical stinging nettle *(la ortiga)* is good for many types of fungus that grow on the hands, feet and between the legs. It's even used to cure *la culebrilla* (a painful, herpes-related neuritis that affects the skin). You pick the nettle leaves with gloves so as not to get stung, then you use a mortar and pestle or a rolling pin to crush them. Leave the crushed leaves and juice in water for three or four hours. (Or put the leaves in the blender with a little water.) Later, strain the water and keep it in the refrigerator. Every hour — at least six or seven times a day — wash the ailing area with the nettle water and let it dry in the air, without rubbing. Recuperation time depends on the gravity of the condition, but we've seen some amazing results.

The same nettle water has been used traditionally as a hair rinse to combat dandruff. You simply pour it over the scalp after shampooing, and leave it there without rinsing it off.

Cheo: There are also psychological levels of working with plants, with the symbols involved. For instance, they say that peppermint *(la menta)* affects *la mente,* the mind. And now it's proven that peppermint does stimulate the thinking process.

Bárbara: There are truths buried in so much of our folklore!

M: You use baths and sweats and teas and other herbal preparations to work on the psychological level of healing. Tell me how you prepare a healing bath.

Cheo: You can prepare a bath with an instruction manual, or you can do it in an improvised way, as if you were a singer inventing verses appropriate to a situation.

There are a great many factors. For instance, we have one tree that only blooms every two, three or five years. Conditions have to be just right or it simply won't flower. So if you go out to collect plants for a bath, and you notice that it's flowering, you say: "This will be a special addition to my bath!" And: "Over there *el cariaquillo* seems to be beckoning . . . and the *santa María!*" So you prepare your bath according to what's happening in the moment. It's an intuitive process, but it's based upon your knowledge about the properties of each plant.

When you're in charge of helping someone through a bath, you see the thread of ideas and feelings that are welling up in the person. If you know that the person is having love problems, you have some indication of how to go about soothing and easing, and you keep that in your mind when you go out looking for plants for his or her bath.

Then boil, for 15 or 20 minutes, the leaves, stems, flowers, seeds and roots you've chosen, and add them to the person's bath water. Sprinkle fresh flowers on top. Have the person listen to soothing music while bathing. Help him or her to feel safe and completely taken care of. Then see what happens. Using plants in therapeutic baths can have long-term effects on many levels.

M: During the three days I've been with you, I've noticed that you're always harvesting fresh vegetables for salad. You even eat salad for breakfast!

Cheo: It's important to eat greens and flowers while they're still vibrating with life. The best way to take in the goodness of the plants is to eat them as fresh as possible, so that their vital essence is maintained. But for our friends who live in the city, we also liquefy fresh plants and then freeze the liquid in little ice cubes. It's a good way of preserving their essence and the plants' special properties without having to dry, heat or use alcohol to preserve them. It's an instant lift full of the pure energy of the plants . . . as if you'd just cut and crushed a bunch of fresh plants and put them in your mouth. Delicious, cooling and nutritious!

M: A modern way to connect with plants! But tell me more about the tradition of home-based healing in Puerto Rico.

Bárbara: Besides the presence of back yard medicinal gardens in every home, besides the fact that everyone knew something about using plants for medicine, there was also always someone special in the community who dealt with the most difficult cases. That person would deal on the physical, emotional and spiritual levels all at once. She or he knew — and knows — that you can't separate a headache from an emotional trouble or frustration, for example. So you went to that person for a rub, for a blessing. You went to that person with the assurance that she or he would help you through good will, clear energy and good faith.

M: Money was never an object . . .

Bárbara: No. People would bring eggs or a chicken, some *viandas* or other necessities. But the people involved in healing usually had no monetary interest. They would give their lives to help people, and their own human qualities — their commitment, their energy — were part of the medicine. They had a genuine instinct for healing, and most were devoted to their calling. Their motivation was always simply to help, to alleviate pain, to heal.

All this has been made fun of. People laugh and say: "It's witchcraft," or "It's all in the mind; just psychological!" But the psychological aspects of health are very important, and have their place in medicine. The physical has always been related to the psychological and spiritual: to one's intentions, dedication and thoughts. They've always been one.

M: The relationship between the physical and psychological worlds is being studied seriously today by both scientists and medical professionals on the cutting edge of medical science. I'm thinking about the new medical field of psychoneuroimmunology.

Bárbara: But the typical doctor of today, who has invested so much money and spent so many years studying, without even having a life apart from his studies for so many years, wants to live it up a little, and feels like a total failure if he gets assigned to a hospital for poor people.

Meanwhile, the people who healed traditionally offered their services for free, from the heart: hot baths, rubs and adjustments, teas. Mostly, they were women.

In fact, the healer was also related to the birth giving process in some way. She had to do with everything that was life and health. She was probably a midwife, a *comadrona*. A man doing that work might have been called a *comadrón*. These people were very well respected until the destructive deculturization process started in with its: "You old people don't know anything. Let the professionals from the north teach you about real medicine."

That's how the baby formulas found their way to the shelves of new mothers. The people were told it was better than mother's milk. That mother's milk was for poor people who didn't know any better. They began to look down on our traditional midwives and healers, who were intimidated by being called "ignorant, uneducated, superstitious, country bumpkins. Hilbillies! *Jíbaros!*"

That brainwashing went on steadily during my mother's and my grandmother's generations. It all happened so fast! Our parents grew up in the new wave. Everyone my mother's age was born at home with a midwife. My mother suckled at my grandmother's breast until she was three years old! During that time, she slept in her parents' bed and went to the neighborhood healers for blessings and therapies, for herbal remedies and spiritual healings. These are still tremendous memories for her.

Meanwhile, everyone in my generation was born in the hospital. The bottle was better than the breast. We started out eating commercial baby foods. Modern psychology said that children should be separated from their parents as soon as possible. Everything was turned upside down in such a short time! It was like a guillotine that cut off people's relationship with tradition, with the land, at the roots. And it cut off a tremendous amount of knowledge as well.

People would actually deny they knew anything about plants so that they wouldn't be considered ignorant!

Cheo: Medicine is related to everything. We know that when one group of people sets out to destroy another, they prohibit the spiritual practices of the people. And medicine, people's work with plants, is closely related to these practices.

Destroying popular medicine is a way of weakening a nation. Because popular medicine, green medicine, keeps people close to one another, conscious of their natural environment, and physically strong. Besides, popular medicine is proof that a group of people can be self sufficient.

Bárbara: The *jíbaros* are a strong race. But strength and endurance have ben chipped away at both physical and ideological levels.

Cheo: I've seen it perpetrated through the educational system. As a child, I studied from books that pushed the idea that the old *jíbara* culture should be destroyed and replaced by the modern, industrial culture. The idea that the only "real" medicine comes in the form of pills and injections is an extension of that idea.

M: In general, I think that people are so used to equating price with quality that they find it hard to believe that something that's free, something that comes right out of the ground as a kind of gift, could possibly have as much value as something expensive, especially something expensive that comes from a far away, romanticized place.

Bárbara: Yes, but today, Puerto Rican people are going to these very expensive and exclusive health food stores to see what they can learn about their health, and they're finding — in classy little jars for ridiculously high prices — the very same herbs that their grandmothers used to give them. That's helping to open people's eyes a bit. They realize: "Hey, this is my grandmother's own medicine they're selling to us as if it were something new. We had this medicine first!"

Cheo: The people of Puerto Rico aren't blind. We see the alcoholism, the abuse of drugs like cocaine and heroin. Not to mention the fact that so many people have had bad experiences with prescription drugs and unnecessary surgery. We recognize that we have lost something important, something that can still be recovered.

We all have to realize that popular medicine isn't just a matter of prescribing remedies. It's part of an entire culture, and it involves a respect for the land. It also involves helping to maintain people's health by advising them about diet and nutrition.

The *jíbaros* ground corn in a mill made of native stone, and they knew how to increase the calcium content of the corn by adding lime to the soil. The corn was then mixed with beans to complement the protein, and food like that gives people tremendous strength. I've seen 70 and 80 year-old men and women working harder — and for a lot more hours — than most of the young people I know. Because no matter how muscular and athletic young people today may be, they don't have the endurance of our old timers, the people of two, three and four generations back. That has a lot to do with the way they lived, working every day close to the soil, and with their diet: locally grown whole grains, *viandas,* green vegetables, many of them wild, and a wide variety of fresh, native fruits.

Bárbara: On the large farms, they planted corn, rice, onions, garlic, *viandas* and beans for the entire year. Every afternoon or evening, they would grind the corn to be used for the next day's *sorullos* (hearth baked corn fritters stuffed with cheese or meat), which would be delivered to the men in the fields as they worked. Manure was used as fertilizer, to strengthen the plants . . . and the soil. No chemical products were used.

Of course, there was a time of great injustice, a time of great poverty, when most people didn't have land or anything to plant on it. And as a result, there was a great deal of illness. But if traditional knowledge and practices had been supported up to now, the world today would have a tremendous respect for the resources of Puerto Rico and for the strength and ingenuity of our people.

M: In closing, do you have a message for the people of Puerto Rico?

Bárbara: Yes. Let's recapture the wisdom of our grandparents. If we don't have grandparents, let's find people who can talk to us, who can tell us about the old ways, about the home remedies that were so convenient, wholesome and effective.

The plants are still with us. With a bit of effort and investigation, we can rediscover many things that have been forgotten because of the deculturization process, because of social pressures to forget. Some of our old people are still alive.

Cheo: Let's learn all we can now because when we leave our health to the chemical companies, our sickness ends up benefitting them as we jeopardize our well-being with the side effects of dangerous drugs. We should become more conscious, try to recuperate the lost wisdom of our healing traditions. This will strengthen us as individuals and as a people.

Bárbara: I think there's a type of awakening going on. People are beginning to take more interest in their health and in medicinal plants especially, because they know that their grandparents used them and they worked. And they still remember. Our tradition is very much alive in our folklore. It's under the rug right now, but it's very much alive.

Healing with Plants
for Sixty Years

María Otero Collazo
and
Eugenio Santiago Marrero

sweet scent · · · · · · · · · · · *la salvia*

María Otero Collazo   Eugenio Santiago Marrero

Healing with Plants
for Sixty Years

María Otero Collazo
and
Eugenio Santiago Marrero

*Doña María Otero Collazo de Santiago and her husband don
Eugenio Santiago Marrero were once the herbal physicians of their
barrio in the countryside of Mayagüez. Now 75 and 84 years old,
they continue to share a tremendous love for the natural world, and a
wealth of experience using plants as medicine during their lifetime.
Their knowledge comes from personal experience, both through
traditional family practices and through a willingness to experiment
with the plants growing around them. Plants, along with spiritual
practices such as prayer, are seen as optimum forms of medicine.*

*The following interview was held one May afternoon and
evening in Morovis after a wonderful dinner prepared by doña María.
Conversation ranged from the anecdotal to the encyclopedic as they
told of their experiences and shared their knowledge. Included here
are remedies for health problems ranging from unrelenting fever to
diabetes, women's infections, indigestion, headaches and asthma, as
well as preventive medicine like purslane* (la verdolaga) *for avoiding
bouts with intestinal worms and sheep tallow for toughening the
hands before doing rough manual labor. Noteworthy too, are the
uses of witch hazel solution* (Agua Maravilla) *for internal pain and
removing blood stains from clothing. Clearly, they did not specialize.*

*In the world of doña María and don Eugenio, there are few
rules, except those of good digestion. Don "Geño" — who was
around to see Halley's comet the first time — enjoys his cigarettes and
his daily shot of rum before dinner. He is proud to say that he has
never had a headache, and according to the local hospital, his heart
is "healthy as a child's."*

*Doña María makes it clear that everyone's system is different,
that we all have different needs. Indeed, although their knowledge
about plants is vast and they are aware of several properties of each
plant they name, doña María's message seems to be that each episode
of healing is an entirely unique experience. She doesn't follow recipes
for her medicinal formulas (or for her cooking), but she knows what
to do. The information she needs lives in her memory, and it is
accessed through her dreams, through prayer, and through the
intuitive act of preparing "green medicine." She has even performed
surgery when the occasion called for such a drastic measure.*

*Don Geño and doña María are living examples of Puerto Rico's
rich medical tradition, a tradition not only of information and
practice, but also of attitude. For this couple, health is not just an
absence of physical malaise; it takes root in a spirit of interdependence
with nature, and faith in a God who is always found in nature.
Healing is an every day experience, a sacred experience, widely
accessible, and not without humor.*

M: Doña María, you've spent a good part of your life working
with plants as a means of healing. How did you learn about this?

María: In the old days, every mother brought up her kids, always
telling them what was good for just about every condition. My
mother explained to me that teas of *la salvia* worked when a
women's period was late, when there was some irregularity in her
cycle. And she'd also say: "Listen, after drinking that tea, you

can't drink anything cold because it will give you cramps." So we learned as we grew, as the years went by.

I'm always picking and "bottling" plants, preparing them as medicine. That's because the way to cure yourself is to start trying things and see how you feel afterwards. If you use the plants, you'll learn which ones are good for you.

My daughter, in this world, plants are of the utmost importance.

Geño: Without them, what would we do? They supply us with food, with shelter, even oxygen!

M: Don Geño, what kind of experiences have you had using plants?

Geño: Well I know them pretty well. I was born in 1903, almost yesterday *(laughter),* and I've always been a farmer. I like medicinal plants. In fact, I used to dedicate a great deal of my time to working with them. I even used to prescribe for people. I would tell them how certain plants could be used as their medicine. And every time I get sick, I cure myself with plants. For instance, I take a strong tea of poleo when I get the flu or a bad cold. Sometimes, *los guarapos* work better than what a doctor might give you!

So I still go along planting herbs, although I do it less now that I'm old. It's a lot of work to condition the soil and keep all the different kinds of plants in their place. You have to fertilize them too, with cured cow and horse manures.

María: I also give the plants leftovers like potato peelings and coffee grinds. The bitterness and acid of the coffee kills harmful microbes in the soil.

Geño: But animal fertilizer and food leftovers should be put in one place until it all cures and becomes a nourishing soil in itself.

M: Now they call it compost! Plants love it! And getting back to the plants, please tell me about some of the medicinal plants you've both used over the years.

Geño: In Mayagüez, in Villa Angélica, there was a famous *anacagüita* tree, which looked like a *ceiba*. The *anacagüita* gives a lot of flowers good for making *guarapos* for cold and flu. Plenty of people would go there to look for them. Yes, plants have always been people's medicine!

María: Sweet verbena *(la yerba dulce)* has helped me a lot. You just boil it up, let it cool, put it in the refrigerator and drink it. Sweet verbena root is good for the stomach and for diabetes too, because although it tastes very sweet, it has no sugar.

Geño: You can also just chew the leaf whenever you pass by the plant! There's no mistaking the taste of sweet verbena!

María: Two years ago, I tested positive five different times for diabetes. They put me on a special diet, but I still tested positive. So I started drinking sweet verbena boiled up with a pinch of yellow allamanda *(el canario amarillo)* every day. Now, thank God, I've had more tests, and they can't find diabetes anywhere!

El cundeamor, which is very bitter, is also really good for diabetes. I boil the leaves up with the leaves of sweet verbena and it comes out like a *maví*. Actually, it's not so great tasting, but it's not too bad, cold. Just take a cup a day, right from the fridge.

I also had high blood pressure, and honey, they prescribed a mountain of pills! But the pills made me itch all over, so I threw them out. Now I use passion fruit *(la parcha)*. I just cut off the top and suck out the pulp of the fruit. Well, blessed cure that it is, I've had a bunch of tests done and I'm just fine!

So if they tell you you're about to die, well . . . *(laughter)*

Geño: If you live with *la doña,* you might be able to live at least 60 more years! *(laughter)* Lord have mercy! Since I married her, we've spent years running up and down seeing and prescribing and curing without charging a penny. Sometimes we'd be called at nightfall, and we wouldn't get home 'till ten or eleven in the morning of the next day. We traveled all over the countryside on foot, and everywhere we went, the plants that we needed were growing right where we happened to be.

M: Would you tell me some success stories?

Geño: I'd like to tell you about something that happened to a young girl in Mayagüez. Her name was Panchita. She worked in the factory with *la doña.* Like everybody else, the youngster had to have her chest examined for tuberculosis. She had a flu at the time, so she was in no condition to be examined, but she had to go. And when they checked her, they found a spot on her lungs. So they laid her off and told her to go to the sanatorium, that she couldn't work any more. When she heard that, she started to cry, and María saw her and asked her what was wrong. Panchita told her what had happened, and María said: "Don't worry. That little spot is nothing. I'm going to make you some medicine. I need a one gallon bottle and the following plants, and I promise that by the time you've drunk half of what I prepare, you'll pass any lung test they might give you.

Panchita took the medicine every day, and when she was almost finished, she went for another exam, and they didn't find a thing. She was in good health, and she never suffered from a lung problem again.

135

M: Do you remember the recipe?

María: Of course. I've used it so many times! Starting with the pharmacy: a four ounce bottle of each of the "seven syrups" *(los siete jarabes)* including *ipecacuana* syrup, chicory syrup *(la achicoria)*, cocillana syrup *(el jarabe pectoral)*, balsam syrup *(el tolú)*, star anise *(el anís de estrella)*, anise seed *(el anís de grano)* and witch hazel solution *(Agua Maravillosa)*. Then you peel three fat aloe leaves *(la sábila)* leaves and add all of the inside gelatin. Then juice large quantities of both watercress *(el berro)* and *el poleo* and add some almond or cooking oil and a little honey. Finally, you have to add a little rum or anisette in order to preserve it. When you're done, you should have a gallon of liquid. You don't have to cook it, but you do have to let it sit in the refrigerator for five or six days so that it really becomes one big syrup. Then drink it over a week's time. I'm telling you, my friend, many people have been cured with this formula!

M: Do you think that the ability to work with plants is a gift which only certain people have?

Geño: I think certain people have the blessing of being born to do that sort of work. They somehow know what to do.

M: I notice that you don't use any kind of recipe book as a source of remedies.

María: No, I invent everything. That's how it is when you're born to do something. I do everything from my head. And it's the same in the kitchen. You'll never find a cookbook around, although I can prepare all kinds of food. Once I try something and like it, I don't forget how I made it. I don't have to be tasting all the time. My mind is still crystal clear, thanks be to God.

And there's medicine in the kitchen, you know. Take cooking oil, for instance. It's a simple thing, but it's tremendous! Almost no-one believes in it anymore, but if you have a bad chest problem, take a tablespoon of cooking oil every morning, and the problem is eliminated little by little. The oil simply cleans out your chest. Nowadays everyone believes in fans and air conditioners, but they just weaken you.

Geño: There are lots of things the people of today don't know about. For example, hardly anyone uses sheep tallow sticks *(sebo Flandes)* these days.

María: When somebody has a fever, you take two pieces of tissue paper (the wrapping kind) just big enough to cover the soles of the person's feet. Actually, they should be a little big so that when you put socks on, the paper can fold around the feet. Rub the *sebo Flandes* into the paper. Then take a little salt, a little sugar, and roll a bottle over them until they're ground up fine. Then you put that powder on top of the paper covered with the sheep tallow and sprinkle some cooking oil on top of all that.

Next you prepare a bandage for the person's forehead that very same way. Exactly the same. Then you light a candle and use it to warm the bandage (don't put it too close, of course), and put the bandage on the person's head. Do the same with the paper soles, and put them on the soles of the person's feet. Finally, you put on some warm socks, and the person goes to sleep.

The person should sleep as much as she wants and you don't take off those little paper soles until the next day. That's the remedy for stubborn fevers that simply won't go down. It always works!

Geño: Working people use sheep tallow sticks too. Someone who does manual labor will use it to toughen up his hands. It heals and protects the skin. After work, you take a bath, and rub in some sheep tallow. The next day, your hands are as hard as iron. It's the best there is!

When I started doing manual labor, they put me to work with metal shafts, and they literally ripped up my skin. By the end of the first day, my hands were dripping with blood. But I'm the type to never say: "I can't go on," so I kept working. Then an older gentleman told me to rub some *sebo Flandes* into my hands for protection. As soon as I left work, I bought five little tallow sticks for a penny a piece. That night, I took one and rubbed it all into my hands. The next day, my hands were dry and strong, and I kept working with no problem. Every day after work, I put some more on my hands, and after that, nothing hurt them.

María: And he's talking from experience. He's tried it, just as I've tried all the things I've told you about.

Geño: You can also use it when someone has a flu or chest cold. Just rub it into a porous piece of cloth and apply the cloth to the person's chest, or put the sheep tallow directly onto the skin and then cover it up with cloth. I've seen it done both ways.

María: Another way of dealing with the same problem is by first rubbing the chest with a cloth soaked in *alcoholado* (herbs infused in alcoholic solution). Then you put plenty of Numoticina (a rubefacient used in chest plasters) on top of that cloth with some camphorated oil *(aceite alcanforado)*. That's your poultice, which must be worn, covered with cotton. Then you cover the poultice and cotton with a shirt and wait until the person begins to sweat and sweat. All the while, the person is breathing hard to get that medicated air. I've cured many a chest cold that way!

Of course, *la curía* is also very good for colds, and so is *la clavellina*, but only the yellow kind. White *clavellina* is just for show.

M: Doña María, your son-in-law told me that Alma once had a bronchial infection, and that her lungs were badly congested. From what I understand, you gave her a remarkable remedy.

María: When I took that girl in she was seven months old, and she weight seven pounds, fourteen ounces. My friend, her stomach was swollen, and if you gave her some milk, it would come out through her nose instead of going down into her stomach. Her little legs were bent backwards, completely immobile. And she was so weak, she could hardly cry. Geño said: "*Ay bendito,* we'll have to bury her in a few days." And I said: "Don't worry. She'll get better if God wills it so, and God is so very great!"

The next day I sent for a little bottle of castor oil, a dollar's worth of lime phosphate, and Elixir as a solvent. The medicine arrived that night. I gave her a little spoonful of the castor oil right away, and she slept through the night, quietly. The next day, she didn't even stir, and I thought she might be dying.

At six o'clock in the evening, I was totally absorbed, praying to the Virgin Mary when suddenly I was moved to pick the baby up and hold her. At that moment, her little intestines started working. "Geño," I called. "The girl is alive and she's moving her bowels!" My lord, she emptied herself out completely. She had been fed rice water without salt, and that caused her whole stomach to seize up with a terrible indigestion and blockage.

I stayed up all night with her, giving her herb teas with milk, feeding her. And the next day she woke up happy. Those remedies had done their work.

Afterwards, I asked permission from an aunt of mine to fish in the stream that ran by her house. "Sure," she said. "Come by whenever you like." So I went fishing at seven in the morning, when most of the creatures were still asleep. I caught a little fresh water crab *(la buruquena),* and I rubbed parts of its insides on the soles of the baby's feet in the sign of the cross. Then I took a special plant called traveler's joy *(el alfilerillo).* I boiled it, added a little rum as a preservative, and rubbed it into her knees and legs. And look at how strong she walks now!

Then, when she was older, she got that terrible chest condition, and I began to prepare the same remedy I had made for Panchita: the seven syrups, plant juices, oil, honey and rum. I gave that to her morning and night. By the time she was scheduled for her operation, there was nothing wrong with her. The doctor said it was a miracle, that her lungs were completely clean. He wanted to know what had cured her.

Geño: He even took a jar of the remedy with him. Said he was going to study it! *(laughter)*

M: You mentioned using rum to preserve your remedies. Up north, we prepare many remedies in alcohol because, since we have such a long cold season, we often need a plant when it's not available. Plus, it's much easier for people working outside of the home to take a few drops of tincture than it is to boil up a fresh or dried plant. Would you talk more about the importance of using alcohol in medicinal preparations here in Puerto Rico?

Geño: Yes, we preserve medicines with alcohol, and I'll tell you something. We all need a little alcohol. Not to get drunk on, but to use. Our bodies need a little bit of everything, and a little rum can be used by the body like medicine. It also helps to sustain you sometimes while you work. But only up to two shots! Any more will do more harm than good.

María: Sometimes we add witch hazel solution to a remedy, and that has alcohol in it. Witch hazel solution is the greatest thing for cleaning mucus out of the lungs. It's also great for blood-stained clothing. Throw your clothes in to wash with a bottle of witch hazel, and the blood comes right out!

Geño: Witch hazel is excellent for any internal pain you might have. But there are other things for pain, too. For instance, there are therapeutic baths that treat pain and illness. Several plants — such as eucalyptus *(el eucalipto)* and bitter orange leaves *(hojas de naranjo)* — serve for both internal and external use, for *guarapos* and for baths. *La santa María* is one of them. It's only used externally, as far as I know.

M: How do you prepare a bath?

Geño: We fill a big vat with water, and throw in all the plants once the water boils. Now it's not taking a bath, exactly; it's more like having a bath being poured over you. Because you can't use soap. You have to be clean already before receiving it. And you can't just splash the water every which place, either. You have to start at the top, at the head, and cover the entire body. That's how you receive the bath. Afterwards, you don't wash with soap, ever.

María: I'll tell you a little something about baths. For a good bath, you pick roses *(las rosas)* and all the other flowers that are around, along with the leaves of avocado *(el aguacate)*, mango *(el mangó)*, coffee *(el café)*, and more. You boil them all up in a pot as if you were making a big soup. Then you leave it for at least a few hours, because it shouldn't be too hot. (It could cause a shock upon walking out into the cool air afterward.) When you're prepared for the bath, just, get into the tub and receive

141

the stream of water as it's poured down over you from your head to your feet. *El higuillo oloroso* is *very* good for baths.

Geño: *La doña* has cured me a number of times using baths and just about everything else.

María: I've had plenty of challenges, plenty of tests. About 60 years ago, he was in bed for five months straight. And the whole time, he was delirious! If you could have seen him! He couldn't stop moving around in the bed, he didn't recognize anyone, and no one could understand what he was saying. I was with him all the time. The doctor came too, two or three times a day, but finally he gave up and said: "Bring this dead man to the sanatorium." The only medicines he gave after that were pain killers, by injection, so that Geño might die peacefully.

One night, Geño began screaming in a frightening way. I did my best to feed him. I boiled a chicken and some beef along with some baby doves. I added broadleaf coriander *(el recao)*, common plantain leaves *(el llantén)*, and pureed green banana cakes. Then I strained the whole thing so he could drink it as if it were a simple broth. The poor thing, he was all curled up like a little baby, and he tried to drink, but he couldn't stop screaming. It went on all night long.

The next night, he held on to his bladder, and how he screamed! Everyone in the house was just waiting for him to die. They'd even bought the funeral candles. But at six in the evening, I decided to do something. I went to a neighbor's house and asked: "Moncho, you have kids; do you have one of those syringes for the ears?" He did. So I went into the garden and gathered a bunch of *paletaria*, which I washed, boiled up and strained. Next I got rid of everyone who was in the room with him. I said: "Let me be alone with him for a while," and they all went into the living room.

I wrapped his penis in cloth, and I filled the syringe with *la paletaria* I'd prepared. Then I held him as I emptied the syringe into the urinary opening. The liquid stayed inside, and he was calm.

I emptied three syringes, and when I put a little basin out for him, there was a noise, "pum", and all that liquid came out. And then the blood came. Lots of it! He seemed to be emptying himself! And that was the blessed cure. He has never suffered again with any kind of bladder or kidney problem.

M: How did you get the idea to do that?

María: I knew that *la paletaria* is a good treatment for the bladder, and since it was originally a urinary problem, it seemed natural to work with it directly that way. I never had to give him any other treatment.

M: I've never heard of anyone using that method for men, but up north, women use similar "direct" methods. For vaginal infections, for instance, we use suppositories of garlic or other natural antiseptic medicines. Or we might do herbal douches or simply use tampons soaked in herbal formulas.

María: *La campana* is very good for women's inflammations and infections. It makes a very good douche solution, but it's hardly planted any more because it's been abused as a drug.

And there are ways to deal with bladder problems orally. For instance, the leaves of mallow *(la malva)* and black nightshade *(la mata gallina)* can be boiled up together, and you can add some *paletaria* and spineless *(tuna)* cactus too. You should take the remedy at least every day, and always at night. It usually cures completely, but you have to continue with the remedy for a while before it really takes effect.

Geño: She cured me of another problem during that same illness. I have an entire "map" of scars on my back to prove it.

María: He was just a pile of bones, lying in that bed! I spent lots of time bathing him. The problem was that he was always lying face up, and there was a great deal of friction with the sheets against his back, not only from his own restless movements in the bed, but from my pushing him this way and that when I tried to bathe him on one side, then the other, and then dry him. Of course, as he rubbed against the sheets, his skin got all scratched up.

One morning I woke up and saw a bunch of little maggots moving around in his bed. And since everything was so clean, I couldn't figure out where they were coming from. So I started looking, and I saw that it was his back, which was all burned from the friction. The little creatures were coming out of his bedsores!

At nightfall, when things were quiet, I calmly boiled some scissors. My mother-in-law asked me: "María, what are you doing?" And I said: "Oh, I'm just making some tea."

Then I took some cotton and began to cut the maggot-ridden area of his back. There was a sort of hollow spot where everything was rotten, so I had to cut through that flesh, and I left it sunken in. The only disinfectant we had in the house at the time was boric acid, so I washed it well with a boric acid solution and kept quiet about what I'd done.

Geño: Just in case she'd killed me! *(laughter)*

María: The next day, I washed it again with boric acid and I applied a special pomade. Then I told my mother-in-law what I had done. "You're going to kill that poor man," she said. And I said: "But if he's going to die anyway, he's going to die!"

Geño: And look at how well it turned out! *(Don Geño shows off his scars.)*

M: That's one kind of surgery they don't teach in medical school, and I'm sure you didn't learn it from your mother, either. Right, doña María? *(laughter)*

In the tradition of healing that I've studied, it's said that there are no rules, that each situation is completely unique, and that our intuition is a rich source of information. In the case you've just described, you received information, perhaps through prayer, and responded to a unique situation in a non-conventional but perfect way.

María: Yes, I've received a great deal of information through prayer, and also through my dreams.

Back in Mayagüez, we knew a man who was always sick with something or other. He suffered from terrible fevers and nerve-wracking headaches. He was a widower, and I felt sorry for him because he didn't have anyone else to talk with. So he came over to our house a lot.

One night, I dreamed I'd added salt to some of the ashes left over from the firewood we'd used to cook with, and put that mixture in hot water. Then I put a bandage soaked in that mixture on the man's forehead, and put his legs, from his knees down, into the bucket with the water, ashes and salt. The important thing was that both the water on his legs and the bandage on his forehead were really hot. Hot salt water with ashes.

That's what I dreamed, and I tried it the next day. He had a fever and a headache that was driving him crazy. It was as if all the blood in his body had gone to his head. Well, blessed be! The remedy I'd dreamed about brought that blood right down. He felt just fine afterwards, and calm.

145

Geño: You can talk about dreams, and you can talk about faith. After the Virgin appeared at the well in Sabana Grande thirty years back, sick people started going, and they still fill up the chapel. People go in wheelchairs and walk out without any help at all!

We had a neighbor who was paralyzed. The doctors had told her that she was incurable! She'd been ill for nine years but one day she decided to visit the well at Sabana Grande. And when she arrived in her little cart, she was healed. She simply stood up and told the woman who cared for her: "I want to walk back," and she did!

So at times, it's faith that does the healing, and not the medicine itself. It's the faith you have in the food or in the water or in the plant. You should see that shrine with all the writings of people who have been cured, and all the crutches that have been left there. There have been hundreds of miracles!

M: Nowadays, so many people live in cities, where it's easy to forget about the every-day miracle of life-giving plants. I'd like to hear more about your own relationship to the earth.

Geño: Very simply, plants are the best medicine, better than anything a doctor can prescribe. It's hard to understand, but most doctors today don't know a thing about plants.

I believe in plants. If I take some leaves for a *guarapo,* I look for certain properties. For instance, I'll look for a plant that's heating, or one that's cooling, which is good for when you've got a flu caused by heat. If your illness is caused by cold, you'd never administer a cooling plant, except perhaps in combination with heating plants.

María: *El cundeamor* is a heating plant.

146

Geño: It can even burn you!

María: The other day, one of our neighbors got sick, poor thing. They took her to the hospital and her legs were a real mess. they itched so much that she had to take injections. She just couldn't stop scratching her legs, and liquid was oozing out of the sores.

I went to see her and asked: "Can I prepare you a wash for your legs?" And she said: "Of course, my love. But you should know that I'm on my way out."

I came home and boiled up two gallons of *el cundeamor*, which she applied and also drank. Blessed cure! The itching disappeared and she was healed. Because *el cundeamor* is bitter, and it's warming.

So the doctor came and asked: "What in the world did you put on that?" She said: "A neighbor did me the favor with *el cundeamor*. And he said: "Don't tell me that *el cundeamor* is medicine!" But it certainly is!

And listen, the palma Christi or castor bean plant *(la higuereta)* is heating.

Geño: It's a very hot plant, and it's laxative, too.

María: It's good when a woman gives birth and part of the placenta remains inside. A sitz bath of palma Christi leaves boiled up will help to clean her out. Palma Christi is also good for animals who give birth and can't discharge the placenta.

Another form of using the palma Christi is to make a little necklace of its cut, hollow leaf stems. You just break the leaf stems up, string them together and hang them like a rosary on the person's body. It's good for any type of inflammation.

Geño: If you use the castor bean plant on the cows when milk balls form in their udders, they'll give more milk. You simply take the plant and boil it in a big tub. Then, after it has boiled long enough so that the water has taken on the color of the leaves, you skim off the foam. When you go to the cows the next morning, you take the liquid, and with the very same leaves you boiled, you wash the udder completely, and with lots of strength. Do this two or three times a day, and you'll see how those milk balls disappear! She'll get better soon, and I guarantee, she'll start giving more milk.

M: I'm really interested in learning more about which plants are hot, which are cooling, and the difference between the two kinds of plants.

Geño: *El poleo* is hot. It's great for chest colds. Aloe is hot. It's also very good for the chest, and so is *la malá,* which works in a similar way, almost as if it were aloe.

The root of *la yerba guinea* is hot. On the other hand, mallow is cooling; *guanábana* leaves are cooling; black nightshade is cooling.

Snake plant *(el chucho)* is hot.

María: Snake plant is really good for a bad cough, even a desperate case of the whooping cough. You just boil the grated root up with water or with coconut water and take it as needed.

Geño: Bitter orange leaves are cooling.

María: They're the best thing for your nerves.

Geño: And just about everybody knows that *la paletaria, el cohitre blanco* and purslane *(la verdolaga)* are all cooling, refreshing plants.

María: Purslane can be given to children to avoid their getting worms.

Geño: You boil it up and give it to them in tea, like wormseed *(el pazote)*. Wormseed is best, but it stinks so badly that you have to hold your nose in order to drink it. That's the bad part. But if you have worms, it will make them leave your body in droves!

María: What a stink! *(laughter)*

Geño: Sometimes the herbs that are the worst to take get the best results. Wormseed is the best thing in the world for parasites because it actually breaks them up into pieces before it expels them.

M: That reminds me of valerian *(la valeriana)*, which also has a terrible smell. But it's great for helping you sleep or even just relax when you're very anxious or under a lot of stress.

María: They sell valerian tincture in drops now at the drug store. You put some drops in water for your nerves.

Geño: Listen, the leaves and flowers of coffee senna *(la hidionda chiquita)* are good for gas. They make a great remedy mixed in a *guarapo* with anise seeds.

And you can use coffee senna seeds to make a type of coffee. Just toast them, but keep the flame low so they don't burn. Then grind them and boil them up. Delicious! I'd say that in general, coffee senna is hot.

María: Caribbean vervain *(la verbena)* is warming. The root boiled up in tea is very good for treating indigestion. When one has eaten too much, or when one has eaten something disagreeable, vervain gets rid of the discomfort. It makes a good gargle too, and it's effective in treating fevers.

Geño: Caribbean vervain is a warming plant, but you have to be able to recognize the medicinal vervain, which has a stalk that grows straight up above the main plant, and bears a little purple flower. The other vervain looks something like the real thing, but it's not too effective as medicine.

Japana *(la yapaná)* is also hot, and we use it in guarapo for colds, to get rid of any coldness in the body, and related conditions.

María: Common plantain is good for hemorrhage, and boiled up with black nightshade, it's a good, cooling treatment for stomach ulcers.

Geño: Plantain can have a warming effect too, and lemon grass *(el limoncillo)* is a hot plant.

María: Lemon grass tea is great for fevers.

Geño: All ginger *(el jengibre)* is hot. Sweet, native ginger *(el jengibre dulce)* is good for teas, and bitter ginger *(el jengibre amargo)*, grated and boiled in oil, is good for massages.

María: Bitter ginger in oil is great rubbed into arthritic joints. Sweet ginger with milk will help you to get rid of a bad cold in your chest. And sweet ginger with coconut milk tastes wonderful!

Geño: Ginger is good for so many things. If you're making coconut candy and you put in a little sweet ginger, those treats will have a phenomenal taste, while without the ginger, they won't taste like anything. You can add a bit of ground ginger to almost anything, even to your regular cooking and baking flour. It gives everything a good flavor.

New *tuatúa* leaves are cooling for the stomach.

María: Pull the *tuatúa* leaf down off the stem if you want your body to rid of waste from the bottom *(laughter)*. Pull it up off the stem if you want to throw up.

Geño: *El tártago* is like that. Take three leaves and pull them upward. Drink a tea of those leaves, and you'll throw up because you pulled them upward. A tea of tártago leaves pulled downward will get rid of your nausea. I've never done it, but all the old people of my day said it worked. I think it has to do with the sap of the plant being released more when you pull it one way or the other. I'd say *el tártago* is a warming plant.

María: One time, this guy here ate something that gave him bad indigestion and diarrhea. He was sick for days, and he was starting to look like a skeleton. He didn't want any medicine, but I finally told him: "Look, either you drink this tea I've made you or I'll pour it over your head." Well, I boiled up three leaves of *el tártago*, and then with some cooking oil I gave him a *santiguo*, rubbing his stomach gently in the form of a cross, pushing down and pushing cross-wise, too. Then I added a bit of salt and sugar to the tea I'd made, and he drank it. Miracle cure! He vomited what was in his stomach almost immediately, and the next day his stomach was so strong that he could have eaten a plate full of rocks!

We make our way into the loveliest part of the garden. I carry my book of pressed herbs, to which they contribute with the enthusiasm of newlyweds.

Geño: That tree over there is eucalyptus *(el eucalipto)*. It's really warming, and it's a good treatment for colds, something like *el anacagüita*.

María: For colds, there's also the warming flowes of *el cariaquillo*.

M: I've heard that the leaves and stems of pigeon peas *(los gandules)* are effective for diabetes.

María: Yes. They're quite bitter.

Geño: An area planted with pigeon peas is cooling, but I'd say that the leaves in tea are hot.
And Caribbean mugwort *(la altamisa)* is hot.

María: Caribbean mugwort is good for baths.
And yellow trumpet *(el saúco amarillo)* is hot. It's especially good for a cold in the chest.

Geño: There are two kinds of elder, you know. The yellow elder (yellow trumpet) is even more effective than white elder *(el saúco)* for a bad cold or flu.

María: Spineless *(tuna)* cactus is cool, and it's good for the kidneys.

Geño: Basil *(la albahaca)* is cooling, and it gives a good aroma to your food. It's also good for baths and for alcohol rubs. You add it to an alcohol solution *(el alcoholado)*, and when you have body pains, you give yourself a rub with it.

María: Besides that, basil makes a lovely tea, and its tiny seeds can be put into the inside corners of the eyes, very gently, so that they don't irritate. Left a little while there, they'll clear your vision. The seeds attract anything that shouldn't be in the eyes.

Geño: *La yerba buena* is good and cooling for the stomach. On the other hand, bay rum leaves *(la malagueta)* and *la salvia* are heating. And *la ipecacuana* is one of the most effective of the hot herbs. It's tremendous.

María: We used to take three little pieces of *la ipecacuana* and put them in a glass of water. That was boiled up, and it helped you to vomit up all the phlegm you might have in your chest. *La gran señora* is a hot herb that can be harvested in Mayagüez, but it's nowhere to be found around here. A *guarapo* of *la gran señora* is great for fever. In fact, I'd say it's the very best treatment for a flu with high fever, alternating hot and cold.

And rosemary *(el romero)* is a hot herb. They used to say that it was good for the memory, you know. But I've always had a good memory, so I've never used it for that.

M: What do you do to treat boils and other small growths?

María: Do you know about "the weed that even the goats won't chew?" Garlic weed *(el anamú)* has a strong smell, but the leaves used to be really popular as a hot compress for growths that wouldn't burst open. And the roots were used in the form of a tea when a woman didn't want to have children. It's abortive.

Geño: Almost any leaf heated up can be used to break open a boil or tumorous growth, because it's the heat, actually, that does the work. You can use hot leaves or hot cloths or even a hot, cooked egg! And as the growth opens up with the heat, you feel a tremendous relief.

153

M: What's that plant over there?

Geño: That's *la escobilla*. Before it flowers, it makes a lather, and you can actually wash with it. They used to use it to bathe horses, and even to wash dishes.

María: It's good for skin rashes, and it's great for washing little children when their sensitive skin gets irritated. You can bathe the tiniest baby with it.

And annato *(el achiote)* is good when someone has a painful inflammation. You put the leaf on top of the inflammation, and it's soothed. It's especially good for toothache.

Geño: Not to mention for headaches! You can rub the leaf with cooking oil and stick it on to your forehead. If it's doing the job, the leaf will dry out and break up until it's powder. It just draws the heat right out of you. If it stays wet and slides around, it's simply not the remedy you need.

María: Marjoram *(la mejorana)* is good for the inner ear. When you have an earache, you warm up some leaves and mash them up until the juice seeps out. Pick up that warm juice with a bit of cotton and squeeze it into the ear. Then cover it with the cotton.

Geño: In my opinion, arrowroot *(la maranta)* is the greatest, the starchy part, I mean. Down by our old farm, there was loads of arrowroot. It's a little like *la yautía*. Actually, the tuber part of the plant looks like a little *ñame*, and when you harvest it, you take the little egg-like tubers and, *¡Ave María!,* are they good in stew. I could win a contest eating *la maranta!*

Then for medicine, you just had to grate them and take the starch. The starch can also be used as baby powder to alleviate heat rash beneath kid's diapers.

María: Women also used arrowroot powder after bathing for other kinds of irritations. And that reminds me, rue *(la ruda)* is useful for uterine problems. So is broadleaf coriander, which is also great for lowering high blood pressure.

Geño: And you can add broadleaf coriander to almost any medicinal tea . . . or almost any plate of food!

María: Burnt *bálsamo* is tremendous. The ashes of that tree will cure any wound. Monche's son's cured himself with it. The trees have lots of leaves.

The oyster plant *(la sanguinaria)* is good for hemorrhages and also for irregular heartbeat. You boil it and drink it up, or you just mash it up a bit and place it in water, to drink as a tisane, but you shouldn't drink too much of it. Oyster plant is also good if you've bumped yourself. You mash it up with some salt and place it on the bruise as a poultice. It helps to heal it quickly.

Geño: Speaking of the heart, there's the custard apple *(el corazón)*, which is very good after someone has had a heart attack. The leaf is warmed up and placed over the heart. Taken in medicinal teas it also prevents further attacks.

María: There are so many herbs that can be boiled and served as medicinal tea, or cold from the refrigerator as if they were ice water or lemonade: lemon grass, bitter orange leaves, *la curía* and so many more!

Geño: You know, though I'm 84 years old, I have never once had a headache. Never in my life! And I don't think I'll have one in the next few years before I die either. In fact, I don't have any pains at all! Being old isn't painful for me. But people are always bothering me about my cigarettes, saying that they'll kill me, that they'll give me cancer. I tell them: "I've been smoking for almost 75 years, since I was ten years old. Smoking and drinking rum too, sometimes at the same time, losing nights of sleep, working day after day, and I'm alive! I'm just fine!

Five years ago, I was out milking the cows at six in the morning, and all of a sudden, I tripped over one of their ropes and I fell onto a big rock. I lay there unconscious for almost an hour. When I came to, I was all bruised and covered in blood. In fact, I was swallowing my own blood, but I did manage to drag myself home. My daughter wanted me to go to the doctor's office, but I didn't want to go. I told her there was nothing wrong. But a few days later when I went to the bathroom, it could have been that my eyes played a trick on me, but it seemed that I was bleeding a little. So I went to San Pablo Hospital, and I stayed there for seven days.

They did every kind of test on me, with all their fancy new equipment. I half expected them to put a periscope up my elbow so they could see what was up there. But they couldn't find any problem at all. Finally they let me go home and told me to come back in a week for another check up.

So I went back to see the doctor, and he gave me a check up. Afterwards, he asked me: "So, you smoke?" I said: "Of course I smoke." He said: "And your chest, is there anything wrong with your chest?" So I said: "Well once in a while I cough, but only what's normal." And he checked me out all over again and couldn't find anything wrong with me. He told me that my heart was like a child's. He said: "You're perfectly alright. You don't have any illness at all." That's when I told him I'd never even had a headache. He just looked at me, and you know what he said? He said I might just last another thirty years!

María: It's important to realize that everyone isn't the same. One person can smoke or drink something, and it does no harm at all, while if I do the very same thing, I'll be ready to die from it in no time at all.

For instance, I can't get away with drinking even a little bit of coffee. Not too long ago, I tried it again. I was cold all over because I hadn't eaten well during the day. I'd simply had no appetite. Then at about 9:30 at night, I drank some coffee and felt fine. But in the morning, I was so sick, so very sick, that I had to take a purgative.

Other people can drink coffee at any hour of the day or night and it does no harm at all. But even just the smell of coffee can make me sick.

Geño: Everyone is different, but I think that the way one eats is the most important thing. Not that you should only eat a little; you can eat all you want. But you should wait until it's time to eat. Because if you have a big lunch at twelve and you eat again at 1:30, you're interfering with the process of digestion. And if you keep on doing it, you're going to have trouble. Big trouble.

María: Eating too fast can give you gas. But if you're uncomfortable — or worse — after eating, there's anise, which is a warming remedy.

There's always a remedy for everything, you know. In this world, my daughter, plants are truly a wonder.

Don Geño passed away in November of 1987, six months after having participated in this interview. He wasn't sick, nor was he in pain. He died of heart failure just minutes after having tended the animals, when he settled down to watch TV.

Passing It On

epilogue

In April of 1987, I went to Puerto Rico for the first time, but I was going home. Home to *arroz con gandules* and *bacalao con pana,* to *arroz con coco,* the rich flavor of bright yellow *apio* and tall glasses of *refresco de guanábana.* Home to *la bendición* and holy week processions and plaster of Paris saints on bedroom altars. Home to the sound of roosters at all hours of the day and night, and *bomba, plena* and *salsa* in the city streets and local buses. I went home to outdoor concerts of *le lo lai,* African rhythms and indigenous flute sounds all in one. To where hospitality said "family" everywhere I went. Home to where country-raised elders and some very special young people know and work with the healing power of plants, and to where the pint-sized *pitirre* attacks and wins battles with the bandit *guaraguao.* Home to where the wind, sun, tides and red earth are guardians of the past and sacraments of all possibility.

But I also went home to a country struggling under an economy based not upon her strengths (abundant fresh water, fertile soil, small size, accessibility to diverse waterways and neighboring countries, capacity for solar, wind, sea and other types of safe, renewable energy generation) but upon her "insufficiency" of resources. Home to where industrial and military pollution of soil and water represents a serious risk for large segments of the population. And I went home to a people challenged by the devaluation of their own rich culture of planting and healing ways.

Earth and Spirit: Medicinal Plants and Healing Lore from Puerto Rico is based upon the knowledge and generosity of people in Mayagüez, Las Marías, Morovis, Carolina, Orocovis, Loíza, Río Piedras, Caguas, Luquillo and Fajardo. My investigation was limited to a six-week period, and even in such a short time I was able to glimpse a tremendous tradition of herbal medicine, spiritual healing and connection with the land. But along with the exciting stories of healing successes, I was also told stories of disappeared species, the poisoning of earth and precious water tables, and the disparagement and even ridicule of elders' knowledge and experience by those convinced that only modern pharmaceutical preparations can heal.

In Puerto Rico, traditional practices are rapidly disappearing, along with our elders. The unfortunate tendency to associate Puerto Rico's traditional medicine with ignorance, plus economic structures which have led to growing dependence upon non-indigenous products and practices, contribute to the rejection of a tremendously useful system of human exchange and mutual aid.

This system represents far more than the healing of people and animals. One of the most important aspects of folk medicine is its basic dependence upon healthy natural surroundings. Traditional healing practices help to maintain the integrity of the natural world, and folk healers educate others about the environment through harvesting, planting and related lore. In this way, traditional healers are also ecologists, supporting the web of life shared by all species.

As we are confronted with the deterioration of the Earth's ozone layer — as well as the foreseeable end of petroleum supplies and crises such as the proliferation of deadly nuclear waste — more than ever, we need safe, locally-based, renewable natural resources. For instance, we need biomass for alcohol to replace gasoline, natural rubber and fibers to replace those based on petrochemicals, green medicine to supplement and broaden the substances and possibilities of healing. For our own physical survival and the survival of generations to come, economic and social systems all over the world must prioritize the development of technologies and industries that are ecologically sound.

Yet, considering just one front of the problem, in the developing world, foreign debt forces countries to make way for capital-intensive but ecologically disastrous industries like petroleum exploration, lumbering and large-scale cattle grazing. As a result, our precious tropical rain forests are being destroyed at a rate of 50-100 acres per minute![1]

Tropical rain forests, though accounting for only 7% of the Earth's surface, provide habitat for 50%-80% of the world's plant and animal species. Utilizing carbon dioxide and producing a great deal of the world's oxygen, they give life in abundance and influence weather conditions throughout the world. Indeed, recent weather pattern changes are partly blamed on accelerated deforestation since the 1950s. At our present rate of destruction, 2/3 of Latin America's rain forests will have disappeared by the year 2000.

Dr. Oswaldo Guerrero, pharmacognosist at the University of Puerto Rico's College of Pharmacy, comments: "We're losing one species of life each day and we really don't know what we're destroying." Of course, this is true not only in terms of plant life, but also in terms of traditional knowledge and practices that are so closely related to the health and integrity of the area's ecology.

Dr. Guerrero is focusing his own study on Puerto Rico's endemic or native plants in danger of extinction. He explains that these plants promise to serve in diverse ways: from medicine and natural "diet" sweeteners to natural fibers, non-polluting insecticides, fertilizers, and other commercially valuable products.

---

[1] Rainforest Alliance, 65 Bleecker Street, New York, New York 10012. Tel: (212) 677-1900; fax: (212) 677-2187.

Magnolia splendens, for instance, is one of Puerto Rico's threatened species proven to have anti-bacterial action. And our own (Madagascar) periwinkle, *la playera (Catharanthus roseus),* contains more than thirty alkaloids, substances that cause marked physiological changes. Two of these alkaloids are being used effectively against Hodgkin's disease, a lymphatic cancer.[2]

As the twentieth century draws to a close, over 25% of all prescribed drugs in the U.S. still consist of (as in the case of psyllium seed) or contain plant material as the principal active ingredients. And almost all other drugs are based on molecular models found in land and sea plants including fungi and microbes. Throughout the western world, plants are — directly and indirectly — the source of almost all medical substances.

Three hundred of the more than 3,000 species of plants growing in Puerto Rico are already recognized by science as having positive medicinal action. And as evidenced throughout this book, many others hold the promise of medicinal, and perhaps commercial, value as well.

Although threatened by over-development and pollution, Puerto Rico's hills, plains, wetlands and forests still offer a plethora of useful botanicals and related information. And since a large part of the medicine used in the western world is derived from tropical environs, the archipelago [3] of Puerto Rico could take

---

[2] From *Plantas medicinales de Puerto Rico* by Dr. Esteban Núñez Meléndez (Editorial de la Universidad de Puerto Rico, 1982), p. 77.

[3] Although we may think of Puerto Rico as an island, it is certainly an archipelago, including the inhabited islands of Puerto Rico, Vieques and Culebra, the large uninhabited islands of La Mona and Desecheo, and hundreds of smaller islands and cays.

on a greater role in leading the search for natural medicines.

With an eye toward full-scale commercial development, research and funding for exploratory projects (involving the cultivation of medicinal plants and the manufacture of related products) is certainly called for.

Such valuable (and marketable!) plants include *la parcha (Passiflora edulis)*, which lowers blood pressure. (At present, since Puerto Rico lacks protective legislation that would ensure a market for native fruits, most of the *parcha* consumed here is imported from the Dominican Republic, where agricultural wages — and thus the fruit's market price — are lower.)

Aloe also holds tremendous promise as a money-making crop. It is currently used around the world as a tonic for the bronchial and digestive systems, a conditioner and cosmetic for hair and skin, a laxative, a first-rate ointment for burns, and as an adjunct to anti-viral therapies.

Sesame *(el ajonjolí)* might flourish as a source of high-quality cooking oil. The same, light-weight oil is ideal for cosmetic preparations (it even has sun-screen activity), and sesame seeds and its derivatives are a calcium-rich food.

Small-scale studies have already shown that Puerto Rico's well known *cundeamor (Momordica charantia)* and *anamú (Petiveria alliacea)* compare favorably with pharmaceutical preparations used as anti-fungal agents.

And several studies affirm popular knowledge that *la baquiña cerrada (Lepianthus peltata)* is effective in dissolving kidney stones.

According to Dr. Esteban Núñez Meléndez, professor emeritus at the College of Pharmacy at the University of Puerto Rico and author of *Plantas medicinales de Puerto Rico*: "The Caribbean region has contributed many essential oils, which are used in creams, unguents and liniments absorbed by the skin." The aromatic essential oils offered by citrus trees and other plants abundant in Puerto Rico are also highly valued throughout the hemisphere as flavoring agents for foods and medicines, as perfumes and in the field of aromatherapy, as antiseptics, fungicides, insect repellents, local anaesthetics, and as preservatives, especially for emulsions.

At the 1987 Congress of the North American Society of Phyto-chemistry held in Tampa, Florida, a study of 15 species selected from El Yunque, Puerto Rico's own tropical rain forest, found the plants to be precious enough so that: "germ plasm repositories should be created for future preservation of their chemical potential."

In fact, as we face new diseases as well as growing numbers of new and drug-resistant strains of viruses and bacteria, the value of environments such as El Yunque can only grow.

Although synthesized drugs (drugs not based on actual plant material, but almost always upon the molecular structure of plant-based compounds) mean the most extensive profits for pharmaceutical companies,[4] plants are now of greater importance in the development of medicine than ever before.

Dr. Mikhail Antoun, pharmacognosist at the University of Puerto Rico, emphasizes: "We're just beginning to learn about what nature has to offer. The only way to find the unimaginable, the truly new, is to work closely with nature, which is always full of surprises."

One of the greatest obstacles to the development and re-evaluation of natural medicine as a primary resource is the fact that Newtonian science tends to equate the whole of a substance

---

[4] According to the Herb Research Foundation's journal, titled *Herbalgram* (volume 15), a synthetic drug is patentable for 17 years, allowing pharmaceutical companies to recoup large profits on research and development investments and FDA-required tests for "new drug" status. (Approximately $120 million is spent on research and testing for each new drug!) Natural or "crude" drugs are not patentable, thus they offer less economic incentive.

with its molecular structure.[5] Thus, two substances: the natural vitamin C found in a ripe, juicy orange, for instance, and the synthesized vitamin found in a glass of artificially flavored Kool Aid are considered to be one and the same! The presence of a vital energy intrinsic in all beings warmed by the sun, cooled by night breezes, wet by the rain and rooted in fertile earth is not measurable by standard scientific equipment; thus it is ignored.

Some substances very obviously defy the Newtonian equation. For instance, in its natural state, crude camphor is a solid, crystalline resin. But its synthetic molecular "twin" is a liquid. Other natural compounds are either too unstable or just too difficult to synthesize. Thirty steps are involved in the process of synthesizing just one molecule of morphine. So poppies are still used as a source of morphine and other opium derivatives. And in spite of millions of U.S. dollars invested in efforts to synthesize or even cultivate ergot (a fungus found naturally in grains, used to stimulate and accelerate labor in childbirth), science has found no substitute for the real thing.

Our bodies too respond to many "immeasurable" differences. As our ancestors have always known, and as the new physics [6] is

---

[5] The term "Newtonian science" refers to the mechanistic science of pre-Einsteinian physics. Limited to a logical framework of cause and effect, Newtonian science simply can not explain or account for phenomena occurring in the atomic and subatomic realms.

Still working from a Newtonian base, "official" medical science depends for its validity, structure and progress upon repeatable phenomena as evidenced by replicated tests. Thus, synthesized products are favored, largely because their use eliminates variables that might interfere in processes of repetition and testing or measurement.

[6] The "new physics," derived from Einstein's and other scientists' ground-breaking discoveries, is based upon the observation of subatomic particles. As such, this discipline recognizes the virtual impossibility of repetition as well as the constantly changing context of every reality, a context dependent upon physical and non-physical factors.

teaching us, nature is far more complex than we could ever have imagined. In fact, the new physics recognizes what appears to be consciousness in even subatomic particles. In terms of healing, the implications validate the dignity of every energy-based healing approach, especially those involving spiritual cooperation with plants and the other beings in one's environment, and the shamanic skill of direct communication with disease itself on physical and non-physical levels.

Certainly, the use of whole plants, especially those harvested in the wild, may offer many benefits not yet recognized by laboratory science.

Andrew Weil, M.D., Harvard graduate and author of *Health and Healing*, explains that a plant taken in its whole state may work more slowly than the pharmaceutical drugs derived from it, but that the use of the plant itself may be distinctly advantageous. He shows how the currently outmoded use of foxglove leaf (digitalis) allowed heart patients and their doctors to monitor excessive dosages through clear warming signals: nausea meant that a dose should be cut back, far before any damage was done to the heart. Today's isolated, heart-stimulating compounds (digoxin and digitoxin) act quickly, and are invaluable in medical emergencies. But without the associate "non-active" compounds found in the crude plant form, there are no warning signs. Thus, patients who could benefit from the slow-acting and far safer "whole" cardiac tonic are unnecessarily exposed to the risk of iatrogenic (medicine caused) arrhythmia and even heart attack.

Coca (the source of cocaine), ephedra (source of ephedrine, the asthma medicine often consumed in spray form), and willow bark (a source of aspirin) are other examples of natural medicines whose isolated components are known to be addictive, carcinogenic or otherwise dangerous. Interestingly, however, these dangers are neutralized by other compounds found in the plants themselves.

166

As Dr. Weil asserts: "In general, isolated and refined drugs are far more toxic than their botanical sources. They also tend to produce effects of more rapid onset, greater intensity and shorter duration. Sometimes they fail to reproduce the desirable actions of the plants they come from, and sometimes they lack the natural safeguards present in those plants. They also lend themselves to methods of administration favoring abuse and toxicity.[7]

In the field of malaria treatment, the use of synthetic chloroquine has given rise to resistant strains of the offending mosquito *(Plasmodium falciparum)*. According to the World Health Organization, in malaria-plagued parts of the world, infections are once again being treated with a combination of drugs now including natural quinine, which had been abandoned for many years in favor of synthetics.

Meanwhile, some antimicrobial synthetics, especially antibiotics, have been found to cause cell wall irregularities, which may spawn new diseases. And it's becoming common knowledge that broad spectrum antibiotics — which (like pesticides) destroy useful, beneficial bacteria — are greatly responsible for the rise of the new (and largely non-diagnosed) overgrowth epidemic of the fungus *Candida albicans*. In the absence of beneficial bacteria that normally live in the digestive tract, this fungus overpopulates, feeding upon sugar. It compromises the immune system, leaving its victims prone to illness, fatigue, depression and/or anxiety.

Ironically, while "Say NO to Drugs" is practically the official billboard of Puerto Rico's metropolitan area, mile for mile, there is perhaps more pharmaceutical industry in Puerto Rico than

---

[7] Andrew Weil, M.D., *Health and Healing* (Boston: Houghton Mifflin Company, 1983) pp. 99-111.

anywhere else in the world. And while most of this industry produces for export, it's hard to ignore a relationship between the decline of the country's endemic medical culture and the rise of the petro-chemical-based pharmaceutical industry which, while offering obvious benefits including widespread employment, has also posed innumerable problems ranging from iatrogenic disease to local pollution, the exhaustion of irreplaceable underground water supplies, legalized addiction, and cultural alienation.

On the bright side, at the University of Puerto Rico, pharmacological research is at a point of transition, sparked by a resurgence of interest in natural products, including folk culture's highly valued medicinal plants. University faculty members have proposed the development of an Institute of Natural Products, designed for the purpose of studying the plants of Puerto Rico. It would work closely with the Department of Natural Resources and — in recognition of the value of ethnobotany — with the people of Puerto Rico who know, love and use the plants found in their surroundings.

The proposed Institute, and all such endeavors to link laboratory science and empirical knowledge are not just "good ideas." They are bridges that will help us to create and maintain healthy environments for ourselves while enabling us to face acute medical problems and emergencies with greater understanding and efficiency. Such facilities lead the way toward the making of medical professionals who will value and prescribe not only products of today's pharmaceutical industry but also plant extracts, infusions, decoctions, tinctures, homeopathic preparations, and other forms of natural medicine in the effort to live up to their Hippocratic oath to "do no harm." Closing the gap between science and popular culture, these practices, at a time of ecological crisis, may even prove necessary for human survival.

On a personal level, each of us can find ways of working to protect and preserve the natural environment. And we can preserve the body of traditional medicine that exists through the lore alive in our own memories and the memories and practices of family members, neighbors and friends.

Valuing the land and land-based traditions, recording botanical and healing lore, learning to recognize the plants that surround us, using and cultivating them ourselves, and encouraging others to do the same, we pass these irreplaceable traditions on.

In this way we will create and practice medicine which truly heals not only our own minds and bodies, but also our relationship with the Earth. And this is of the essence.

For the Earth is our past, and she is our only future.

Medicinal Plants and Healing Lore at a Glance

How to Prepare the Remedies

Contributors

A Practical Reference
of Botanical and Spiritual Folklore

It has been a privilege to compile this practical reference, which represents a good deal of the knowledge and experience shared by the people I interviewed during April and May of 1987 in ten *pueblos* of Puerto Rico. "Medicinal Plants and Healing Lore at a Glance" includes recipes and lore from all the interviews presented in this volume (including some remedies that were excluded from the published interviews). This chapter also offers recipes from several interviews that have otherwise not been included in this book.

How to Prepare the Remedies

Although variations do exist, below you will find the most common definitions for some of the traditional medical preparations used for generations in Puerto Rico. May these definitions facilitate your use of the remedies described on the following pages.

Before reading on, remember: **Each of us is unique** *as are our physical conditions. No remedy described will be right for everyone, and each should be tried with intuitive wisdom (taking into account one's own needs and personal experiences) and/or with the guidance of a person experienced in healing with plants.*

tea, decoction, "guarapo": *(This works best for stems, roots, bark, resins, leathery flowers and non-aromatic or tough leaves, including tough, yet fragrant sour orange leaves.)*

The traditional medicinal tea or *guarapo* of Puerto Rico is made (varying slightly from home to home) this way: To three or four cups of boiling water, add a handful of well-rinsed, fresh plant material. (If using dried plants, use 1/3 as much.*) Then lower the heat, cover and simmer for about 15 minutes, or until the water takes on a deep color, usually green. According to several contributors, *guarapos* should be drunk warm in the evening. During the day, they can be taken cool, in place of water or juice. Some are prepared with honey.

* *Water accounts for most of the weight and volume of fresh plants, so dried plants have a higher concentration of medicinal compounds. However, once plants are dried and processed, they tend to lose potency rather quickly. It is almost always best to use fresh, wildcrafted or organically-grown local plants.*

menorativa, menjunje, menjurio

Any tea or *guarapo* made with more than three, and up to a dozen or more ingredients.

infusion, unboiled tea *(This preparation is ideal for delicate, aromatic leaves and flowers.)*

Pour three or four cups of boiling water over a full handful of well-chopped fresh flowers or aromatic leaves and cover for a minimum of 20 minutes, and up to eight hours.

tisane ("tisana")

A medicinal drink made without heat. Plant material — which is sometimes chopped or crushed first — is steepcd in cool water for hours, over night, or days before consuming.

poultice

Most often, plant material mixed with cooking oil or pcnetrating cream (or a packet of cloth *(los paños)* soaked in a decoction) and placed directly upon an irritated or inflamed area of the body. Most poultices are used to soothe, increase circulation in an area, or draw out impurities and foreign matter.

bath

Most baths are prepared like giant *guarapos*. Plant material is added to a vat of water and boiled for 15-30 minutes before administering at room tempeature to a person who has already bathed with soap. The same water may also be used as a foot or sitz bath. See **Baths** on page 181 for more specific instructions.

alcoholado

A fragrant, analgesic, alcohol-based solution used for rubdowns and massages. Commercial brands are improved upon by the personalized addition of herbs for specific purposes.

Contributors

In "Botanical and Spiritual Folklore," the contributor of each remedy is identified by her or his initials, as follows:

AC: Ana Clausells de Costoso, Carolina
AG: Angel González, Mayagüez
BR: Bárbara Rodríguez, Orocovis
BS: Brígida Sotomayor Vargas, Mayagüez
BV: Brunilda Vargas Muñiz, Mayagüez
CC: Carmen Colón de Jorge, Luquillo
CM: Cruz María Santiago, Morovis
CMM: Carmen María Morales Serrano, Orocovis
CR: Cheo Rodríguez, Orocovis
CV: Carmen Vega, Mayagüez
CVS: Camila Vargas viuda de Sotomayor, Mayagüez
DB: Doña Bolina (Rafaela Parrilla), Loíza
DC: Doña Casimira (Casimira Osoris Fuentes), Loíza
FB: Félix Nicolás Beato, Fajardo
GS: Eugenio Santiago Marrero, Morovis
IL: Irenio López, Las Marías
IV: Inés Vargas Muñiz, Mayagüez
JP: Josefina Pizarro, Carolina
JS: Julia Santiago, Carolina
LF: Luisa Flores Rovira, Mayagüez
MC: María Cruz Avilés, Orocovis
ML: María Lagoa de González, Mayagüez
MO: María Otero Collazo de Santiago, Morovis
MOS: Ramona Ortiz Santana, Carolina
MS: María Salgado, Carolina
MSM: Mercedes Sotomayor de Martell, Mayagüez
PA: Petra Angleró, Mayagüez
PC: José (Pepe) Chávez, Botanical Gardens, Río Piedras
PN: Francisco (Panky) Negrón Maldonado, Caguas
PR: Providencia Rivera Rodríguez, Loíza
PS: Primi Socorro Vargas, Mayagüez
PV: Paula Valentín Mercado, Las Marías
TR: Tato Rodríguez Valentín, Las Marías

A Practical Reference of
Botanical and Spiritual Folklore

Alcohol and Drug Addiction

CR & BR: Every time you have the urge to drink an alcoholic beverage, drink a glass of lemon juice, straight. It's as bracing as alcohol, and the vitamin C fights the effects of that — or any other — drug in your system.
• Eat as much raw garlic as you can to counteract the poisonous effects of alcohol and other drugs.
• When withdrawing from an addiction to alcohol or other drugs, drink calming teas like those made from the leaves of the sour orange tree *(naranjo)*.
• Calcium-rich foods are calming, and they strengthen the nervous system. Try seaweed, cooked stinging nettle leaves *(la ortiga brava)*, sesame *(el ajonjolí)*!

MC: Catch a dozen *flinches*, those insects that scoot around on the top of the brook. Toast them over a low flame until they get reddish, and leave them for eight days in a bottle of rum. (The rum will turn pink.) Then strain the contents of that bottle into an empty one and make a gift of that "special" bottle to the person with the drinking problem. She'll get a tremendous case of diarrhea and nausea, but she may thank you for it because she'll never touch liquor again!

Allergies

DB: Drink lots of cooling teas, such as *la paletaria,* purslane *(la verdolaga),* white amaranth *(el blero),* black nightshade *(la yerba mora* or *la mata gallina),* and spineless *(tuna)* cactus.

Animal (including insect) Bites and Stings
Also, see *Cuts, Wounds and Sores*

BV: Apply crushed garlic *(el ajo)* so it won't swell up.

PS & M: When stung by wasps or jellyfish, apply fresh urine "straight" or mixed with clay-ish earth to make a poultice. Diluted commercial ammonia is also good.

M: Make a simple poultice of common plantain *(el llantén)* by chewing up a couple of leaves and placing them on bites, stings or cuts. If the problem is on a small area of the body, like a finger or toe, use a whole plantain leaf to tie the little poultice on.

Arthritis and Rheumatism

AG: Drink the unsweetened juice of a lemon mixed with water every day, twice a day.

PC: Massage the ailing joints with an *alcoholado* fortified with arnica flowers, camphor leaves or pastilles *(el alcanfor),* bay rum *(la malagueta)* and eucalyptus leaves *(el eucalipto).*

MSM: Boil the new leaves and woody stems of the pigeon pea bush *(el gandul)* and take as tea, two cups a day, for two weeks.

MO: Boil up some grated ginger *(el jengibre)* in cooking oil, strain and cool before rubbing into arthritic joints.

ML: Mash the flowers of the yellow trumpet *(el roble amarillo)* and massage them in, juice and all, or simply make a poultice of the mashed flowers to wrap directly over the afflicted area.
• Make a liniment! Fill a jar with rosemary *(el romero), el poleo* and marjoram *(la mejorana),* and then cover the herbs with *amoniaco* (an ammoniated solution used for rubdowns) plus a little *Aguarrás* (a petroleum distillate used for rubs). Let steep for two or three weeks, and use it to massage painful back muscles.

PA: Add bay rum leaves *(la malagueta)* and crushed camphor *(el alcanfor)* pastilles to *alcoholado* and let it sit a few weeks. Use as a massage liniment.

ML: Rub lemon juice or almond oil over the painful joints.

PV: Rub the grease of a guinea hen into the joints.

IL: For rheumatic pains, add the seeds, roots and leaves of *pata de perro,* a fibrous, bur-bearing plant, to a therapeutic bath.

GS: Add basil *(la albahaca)* to *alcoholado*, let sit a week or so, and give yourself cooling rubdowns.
• Take a therapeutic bath! (See **Baths** on page 181.)

Asthma, Coughs and Lung Congestion

PA: Mash up the stems of the elder bush *(el saúco)* to extract the juice. For every two tablespoons of juice, mix a teaspoon of olive oil and a pinch of salt. Take it several times a day.

• Peel two large, fleshy leaves of aloe *(la sábila),* cut the gel in cubes, and place in a quart-size glass or ceramic jar. (The aloe should fill 1/3 the jar.) Then add ½ cup of spices such as star anise, whole cloves and cinnamon sticks, and a full cup of honey. Top it off with rum. In three or four weeks it will be ready to take, liquid and solid, a tablespoon or two at a time. Besides treating asthma, coughs and colds, it's also good for indigestion!

IV: Boil up several *poleo* leaves, the chopped-up gel of one aloe leaf *(la sábila)* and a teaspoon of anise seeds *(el anís)* in two cups of water for 15 minutes. Drink with honey as needed.

MS: Boil up two thick leaves of *la malá* with a few anise stars *(el anís de estrella)* in a cup or two of water for 15 minutes, and then drink it. That will get rid of phlegm and bloody mucus as well.

MO: Take a tablespoon of cooking oil every morning, and the problem is eliminated little by little.
• For a bad cough, even whooping cough, boil up the grated root of the snake plant *(el chucho)* in coconut water. Drink as needed.
• Add a little witch hazel solution *(Agua Maravilla)* to any remedy to help eliminate phlegm from the lungs.
• Boil three small *ipecacuana* leaves in half a cup of water for ten minutes. Drink that tea to vomit up the phlegm in your chest.
• First rub the chest with a cloth soaked in *alcoholado.* Then put plenty of *numoticina* (a rubefacient used in chest plasters) on top of that cloth with some camphor ointment. Cover that poultice with cloth and cover the person with a heavy blanket. Let him sweat and sweat.
• For even the most serious bronchial complaint: Mix a four ounce bottle of each of the seven syrups *(los siete jarabes)* including *ipecacuana* syrup, chicory syrup *(la achicoria),* cocillana syrup *(jarabe pectoral),* balsam syrup *(tolú),* star anise *(el anís de*

estrella), anise seeds *(el anís en grano)* and witch hazel solution *(Agua Maravilla).* Add the gelatin of three fat aloe leaves *(la sábila)* plus a cup of the juice of both watercress *(el berro)* and *el poleo.* Add some almond or olive oil and plenty of honey. Finally, add a little rum or anisette to preserve it. When you're done, you should have a gallon of liquid. Let it set in the fridge for five or six days, then drink it all within a week's time.

PV & PR: Put the chopped-up gelatin of one aloe leaf *(la sábila)* into a small jug of water. Leave it outside covered with a little mesh during the night and drink that water during the next day. You may add lemon and honey to the drink.

IV: Boil the papery covering and ends of two whole heads of garlic *(el ajo)* with two shoots of *poleo* and a small handful of linden flowers *(el tilo).* Take with honey to taste.

GS: Rub sheep tallow *(sebo Flandes)* into the person's chest and then cover that area with a warm cloth.
• Try strong teas of *el poleo.*

BV: Add either aloe juice *(la sábila)* or lots of common plantain leaves *(el llantén)* to herbal teas to treat lung congestion.
• For a more serious complaint, take a small handful of *el cohitre blanco,* a chopped-up leaf of spineless *(tuna)* cactus, some Caribbean spearmint leaves *(la yerba buena)* and German chamomile or feverfew flowers *(la manzanilla),* some chopped up ginger *(el jengibre),* a small handful of *poleo* leaves, a small handful of *la paletaria,* two juicy aloe leaves and a small handful of basil *(la albahaca blanca).* Wash everything and boil it up all together, covered, for about 20 minutes in half a gallon of water. Add two tablespoons of witch hazel solution *(Agua Maravilla)* and take with honey as needed.

• Take teas of wild zinnia flowers *(el escopetón)*

CC: Make a steam bath by boiling eucalyptus *(el eucalipto)* and rosemary leaves *(el romero)* for 15 minutes on the stove. Turn off the flame and cover your head with a towel so that no steam escapes. Breathe in the steam as deeply as you can, for at least a good ten minutes or so, twice a day.

JP: Peel some thick aloe leaves *(la sábila)*. Cut the inside gelatin up in pieces, put it in a bowl with a little witch hazel solution *(Agua Maravilla)* and some honey, and let it sit a few days so that the plant's medicinal qualities are dissolved in the liquid. Take tablespoons of it as needed to loosen the phlegm from your chest.

PV: Boil the new leaves of *la ipecacuana* with Caribbean spearmint *(la yerba buena)* or lemon balm *(el toronjil)* or marjoram *(la mejorana)*. Take as tea. It really gets rid of phlegm.

IV: If a person has trouble breathing, warm three or four leaves of the life plant *(la bruja)* over some rising steam. Then squeeze the leaf juice into a small saucepan with two cups of water and boil for 15 minutes. Add a pinch of salt before serving.

AC: For a bad cough, drink papaya flower tea with honey.

PC: To alleviate asthma, boil several *flores de maga,* Puerto Rico's national flower, as a tea in two or three cups of water, and drink throughout the day.
• For a bad cough, boil up the flowers of the shell plant *(la pimienta Angola* or *dragón)* with some peppermint leaves *(la menta)* and drink as needed.

Baths
for body aches, fever, spiritual cleansing and renewal, relaxation, good luck, and more

GS: For a bath to treat body pain and illness, fill a big vat with water, and once it boils, put in the plants. You might include the leaves of eucalyptus *(el eucalipto)* and sour orange *(el naranjo), la santa María,* Caribbean mugwort *(la altamisa)* and many more. You have to be clean already before taking the bath, and you can't just pour the water any which way, either. You start at the top, at the head, and drench the entire body. That's how you receive the bath. Afterwards, you don't wash with soap, or even use a towel to dry off!

PV & TR: For a bath to treat fever, body pains and other physical and mental complaints, first you find the plants you want to use: avocado leaves *(el aguacate),* Caribbean vervain *(la verbena),* palma Christi *(la higuereta),* ginger root *(el jengibre), el higuillo oloroso, el sacabuche, la rompecota,* a little bit of everything. Use about three handfuls of fresh plant material for five gallons of water, and boil it covered, for a good half hour. Then, when that liquid has cooled, strain it, get into the shower, and have someone pour that bath over your entire body starting at the head, in a running stream. After the bath, don't rinse off, because you don't want to dilute the plant medicine.

MO: Pick roses and all the other flowers that are around, along with the leaves of avocado *(el aguacate),* mango *(el mangó),* coffee *(el café), el higuillo oloroso,* and more. Boil them all up as if you were making a big soup, then leave it for the next day, or at least until it's cooled down. After you've taken a bath for cleanliness, get into the tub and receive the stream of water as it is poured down over you from your head to your feet.

BV: For fever and muscle aches, boil up the leaves of Caribbean mugwort *(la altamisa)*, bay rum *(la malagueta)*, *el higuillo oloroso, la vara prieta, la campana,* and *el tártago.* After it cools a bit, have the person get all soaped up. (The strained bath water you prepared will be used to rinse the soap off.) Then pour that bath so that it runs over the person's entire body. Wrap her up in warm clothes and blankets to encourage heavy sweating. The very process of sweating helps to eliminate the illness.

PS & BV: Use *la vara prieta* along with *el cariaquillo* and mango leaves *(el mangó)* to make a bath that's effective at removing all negative energies. It's also good for muscle aches and arthritis.

DC: First you have to boil the plants you'll be using, and let that water cool. Then, after bathing with soap and water, you let the plant bath flow over you from your head to your toes, over every part of your body. Get out of the tub without drying yourself off. Don't sit in the water, because the water has taken with it all the negativity that you don't want or need any longer.
• For luck, prepare a bath with white basil *(la albahaca blanca)*, Caribbean spearmint *(la yerba buena)* and marjoram *(la mejorana)*.
• To counteract spiritual problems or manipulation by others, use *el poleo,* wormseed *(el pazote), la salvia,* Caribbean mugwort *(la altamisa),* aloe *(la sábila)* and Caribbean vervain *(la verbena)*.

ML: Use sour orange leaves *(las hojas del naranjo),* basil *(la albahaca), la salvia, la curía,* marjoram *(la mejorana),* Caribbean spearmint *(la yerba buena)* and rosemary *(el romero)* as a healing, aromatic bath.

DB: If you think you have something like bad energy following you around, take a bath of marjoram *(la mejorana),* Florida water

(Agua de Florida), Caribbean spearmint *(la yerba buena)* or Caribbean mugwort *(la altamisa)*.
• Bathe in the ocean to cleanse the body and soul of all negativity.
• For relaxation, bathe with tranquilizing, soothing herbs. The leaves and flowers of the sour orange tree *(el naranjo)* are especially effective.

JS: To make an unboiled bath for a child with fever, squeeze the juice of fresh aloe *(la sábila)*, *el poleo*, Caribbean mugwort *(la altamisa)*, garlic weed *(el anamú)* and other plants into a five-gallon bucket of water. Add some alcohol to the water and put it outside under a strong sun. Within half an hour or so it's ready for a bath. If there are no camphor leaves around *(el alcanfor)*, you can add half a camphor pastille to the water and that makes it even fresher. After bathing the child with the stream of fragrant water, wrap him up so he can sweat as much as possible.

CR: Choose plants according to knowledge and intuition. Go out of doors to collect plants for a bath, and notice: "The *santa María* is in flower; I should take some for my bath." Or, "over there, *el cariaquillo* seems to be beckoning." Prepare your bath according to what is happening in the moment. Boil the leaves, stems, flowers and roots you've chosen for 15 or 20 minutes, and add them to the person's bath water. The bath is very relaxing, but you might want to play some soothing music as well. The idea is to help the person feel completely safe and taken care of.

Blood Stains

MO: Pour a bottle of witch hazel solution *(Agua Maravilla)* in with your clothes as you wash them, and the blood comes right out.

Boils and External Cysts

CM: At bedtime, use a feather to paint the boil or tumor with the yolk of a raw egg. Put some towels underneath the area to absorb the liquid when the boil opens.

MO: Heat leaves of garlic weed *(el anamú)* with some steam, and use them as a hot compress for a growth that won't burst open.

GS: Almost any leaf heated up can be used to explode a boil because it's the heat that does the work. Use hot leaves, a hot cloth, even a hot, cooked egg. What a relief!

PS: Boil up some *tuatúa* leaves for about 15 minutes. While that water is cooling, warm and soften up a large, fresh leaf by passing it back and forth over a low flame. Wash the area with the warm "tea," then put the warm leaf on the cyst. You may want to cover it with a little oil in order to keep it stuck to the skin, and/or you may want to use a towel to hold the leaf on. The leaf will draw out to the surface whatever is causing the problem internally. After the boil explodes, wash the area with more warm *tuatúa* water and — if you like — apply an antiseptic cream.
• Follow the same procedure using mallow leaves *(la malva)*. You can also drink the refreshing mallow water.

ML: Make a poultice, binding the warm, mashed pulp of the root of the tuberose *(la azucena)* onto the area with a cloth.

Broken Bones and Sprains

PA: For sprains, heat up the leaves of Madeira vine *(la suelda consuelda)* with the steam from your teapot. Then chop them up and mix them in a little bowl with warm cooking oil. Apply that poultice all over the affected area, and cover it with gauze or other fabric. Leave it on for two days before changing it.

LF: In case of a broken bone, grate the tuberous roots of Madeira vine *(la suelda consuelda)*, and make a heavy, sticky paste, adding some milky liquid from the bread fruit *(la pana)* and some olive or almond oil. Once the bone has been set, use this paste as a poultice, and bind it on with cloth to keep it in place. It's the "cast" of the old days. It really helps the bones knit together.

Bruises, Bumps

PS: Wrap the bruised area with rags soaked in cold salt water.
• If the skin swells and blackens without going down after two or three days, use rags soaked in very hot salt water to bring down the swelling.

MO: Chop or mash up the leaves of the oyster plant *(la sanguinaria)* and mix that up with some salt. Apply that damp material to the bruise as a poultice.
• Apply the ashes of the *bálsamo* tree. (Also good for wounds!)

JS: Mix butter, sugar and salt in proportions of 2:2:1. Apply that mixture to the bruise, and there will be no swelling.

Burns

JS: Place a poultice of grated raw potato directly on the burned area. It's very cooling. If applied soon enough, the burn won't blister, and you may not even lose any hair from the burned spot.

BS: Rub aloe gel *(la sábila)* all over the burned skin, frequently.

Callouses and Corns

PS: Rub the sap of *el tártago* on corns or callouses with a little piece of cotton, daily.

ML: Make a poultice, wrapping the warm, mashed pulp of the root of the tuberose *(la azucena)* onto the area with a cloth.

Calming the Nerves

BR: Eat calcium-rich foods, such as seaweed, stinging nettle leaves *(la ortiga brava)*, sesame *(el ajonjolí)*. There are so many sources besides milk!

PV & DB: Drink soothing teas of chamomile *(la manzanilla)*, linden tree flowers *(el tilo)* or sour orange leaves *(las hojas del naranjo)*.

PS: Teas of valerian root *(la valeriana)* are very effective.

Cancer
(at the onset and/or for relief of pain)

DC: Drink the boiled seeds of *el cundeamor* with shoots of garlic weed *(el anamú)* and common plantain leaves *(el llantén)*.

CC: Extract the juice from a handful of garlic weed leaves *(el anamú)* and another handful of common plantain *(el llantén)* by adding them both to a blender along with a cup and a half of water. Strain and take twice daily.

Chewing Gum

BV: Cut through the bark of a breadfruit tree *(la pana)*. The next day, you'll have some sap that serves as a natural chewing gum!

Childbirth
during labor

BV: Drink nutmeg *(la nemoscá)* tea and apply cloths soaked in analgesic ointments like "belladona" for the pain.

MC: Take a strong tea of anise seeds *(el anís de grano)* with the flowers and leaves of coffee senna *(la hidionda chiquita)*. It will help to eliminate gas while relieving pain as well.

post partum tonics and care

PA: The calabash *(la higüera)* or white gourd medicine is actually a type of tisane. The traditional way of making it is as follows: First bore a hole in one end of a large, unripe, calabash and pour into that hole as many whole cloves *(los clavos de especia)*, anise seeds *(el anís de grano)* and anise stars *(el anís de estrella)* as fit into one's hand. Then, seal the gourd and bury it for a couple of days until a liquid forms inside. That's part of the medicine. The spices keep the gourd from going bad, but it does ferment a little.

If you want to be more modern, you can make it by scooping the pulp and seeds from the gourd into a glass bowl, adding the spices and leaving it in the refrigerator for a few days before offering it to the woman. But she shouldn't take it cold from the fridge! Any way it's prepared, the dose is about one cup a day — of both the spicy liquid and the pulp — for about nine days straight, and during that time she should rest! In fact, if she wants to preserve her womb, she shouldn't do any heavy work at all for a full 40 days!

AC: To strengthen the womb after childbirth, boil up half a bar of bittersweet chocolate with two cups of water and eight or ten leaves of Caribbean spearmint *(la yerba buena)* for about 15 minutes. Drink and enjoy!

MO: When a woman gives birth and part of the placenta remains inside her womb, a sitz bath of boiled palma Christi leaves *(la higuereta)* will help to clean her out.

IL: After childbirth, a vaginal wash of boiled mallow *(la malva)* leaves (strained through a cloth) with a few drops of almond oil gently soothes and cleanses.

BV: After giving birth, drink lots of chicken broth with burnt bread.

Circulation

PS: To improve the circulation, drink ginger tea *(el jengibre dulce)* every day.

M: Exercise daily!

BV: Boil up the leaves of annato *(el achiote)* and soak the legs and feet for poor circulation or muscle spasms.

Clear Mind

DB: Take teas made of the leaves and skin of the *jobo* fruit.
• Relax!

Coagulate Milk

BV: To coagulate milk quickly for making cheese, add the little fruits from *la maya* or simply add lemon juice to the milk.

Coffee Substitute

GS: Toast the seeds of coffee senna *(la hidionda chiquita)* over a low flame so they don't burn. Then grind them and boil them up. Delicious!

Colds

CM: Rub the chest with some warm Vicks and drink teas of eucalyptus *(el eucalipto)* or ginger *(el jengibre)* mixed with warming spices such as cloves *(clavos de especia)* and cinnamon *(la canela)*.

AC: At the onset of a cold, drink hot lemon juice with a half teaspoon of witch hazel solution *(Agua Maravilla)*.

MO: Take teas of yellow trumpet *(el saúco amarillo)* stems and flowers.
• Drink boiled teas of *anacagüita* flowers.
• Drink teas made from the boiled-up flowers of *el cariaquillo*.
• Boil some chopped ginger in a little water for ten minutes or so, and add to hot milk. Season with honey, and enjoy its warmth.

PV: Take teas of elder flowers *(el saúco)* with sour orange leaves *(las hojas del naranjo)* and ginger *(el jengibre)*. Add honey to taste, if you like.
• Drink strong teas of *el poleo*.

GS: The warming teas of *la yapaná* get rid of any coldness in the body, and all sorts of related conditions.

DB: Drink star anise tea *(anís de estrella)* with honey and lemon.
• To get rid of a condition of cold in the body, make a coffee poultice. Simply prepare a paste of dry coffee mixed with cooking oil, and apply it to the forehead. Secure it with a towel.

BV: Take teas of sour orange leaves *(las hojas del naranjo)*.

ML: For a "watery" cold with runny eyes and nose, mix lemon juice *(el limón)*, honey and rum in equal parts. Drink warm as often as needed.

Colic

DB: Warm up a leaf of the castor bean plant *(la higuereta)*, rub some olive oil (or castor oil) on it, and place it, oily side down, on the baby's belly, covered with a towel.

CVS: Give the child a weak tea of *tártago* leaf buds.

IV: Give the baby a warm tea made from kale leaves *(la col blanca)* and anise seeds. I boil up three medium-size leaves in two to three cups of water for 15 minutes) with ½ teaspoon of anise seeds *(el anís de grano)*.

PA: There's nothing like kale leaf tea *(la col)* with a pinch of salt.

Complexion

AC: Let raw rice sit in water until it softens, then mash it up until it forms a paste. Use that paste as a cleansing facial mask.

PS: Rub aloe gel *(la sábila)* on spots and blemishes.
• To moisturize a dry complexion, massage very ripe avocado pulp into the skin and leave that mask on for 20 minutes to half an hour before rinsing well.
• Rub half a lemon on oily skin to cut grease and eliminate dark spots.

Constipation

JP: Drink teas made from the young leaf buds of *el tártago*.

JS: A good treatment for children is to first give the child a teaspoon of olive oil. Then rub the little hairs off a few stems of *el cohitre blanco,* press the stems into a little ball, cover with cooking oil, and use as a suppository.

DB: Drink lots of coconut water with lemon *(el limón)*.

ML: Eat tamarind fruit *(el tamarindo)* raw, or drink the syrupy juice made by soaking the pulp in water and then blending it up (without the pits!) with water and brown sugar in the blender.
• Break up a pod of purging cassia *(la caña fístula)* and boil up a piece measuring a few inches long in a cup or so of water. Take throughout the day in small amounts.

IL: Make a *paño* or towel poultice of mallow leaves *(la malva)*. Simply boil the leaves, as if for a tea, then soak a towel in that warm solution, wring it out, and place it over the abdomen.

MOS: Mix the gelatin of one leaf of aloe *(la sábila)* with a washed and chopped-up leaf of spineless *(tuna)* cactus in the blender with two cups of water. Add honey and drink throughout the day.
• Eat fresh, fibrous foods, nothing canned . . . and exercise!
• Eat your last meal by 6 PM so that your food has a chance to fully digest and doesn't ferment as you sleep.

MS: Cut up a fat leaf of spineless *(tuna)* cactus and put the pieces in juice or water in a jar in the refrigerator. Instead of drinking water from the faucet, drink the thick "cactus juice."

M: Take a puff or two of a freshly cured cigar.

Cooling, Nourishing Drinks
(all will increase urination)

MS: Cut up a fat leaf of spineless *(tuna)* cactus and put the pieces in juice or water in a jar in the refrigerator. Instead of drinking water from the faucet, drink that "cactus juice."
• Pick and wash a handful of *la prenetaria*, put it in a jar of water in the fridge, and drink during the day instead of other beverages.

GS: Drink teas of *la paletaria, el cohitre blanco* and purslane *(la verdolaga)* separately or mixed, in any combination, hot or cool.

BV: For a condition of inner heat or inflammation, boil up a big leaf of the spineless *(tuna)* cactus with a handful of coarse, raw corn in a quart of water and drink it throughout the day.

CM: Rinse and crush a handful of mallow leaves *(la malva)* and put them in a pitcher. Cover with water, leave in the fridge and drink as desired throughout the day.

Cuts, Wounds and Sores

CM: Wash the cut or dog bite with warm salt water (with the saltiness of one or two teaspoonfuls of salt in ½ cup water).

TR: Bathe the open sore, cut or wound with a tea of *el guaco.* It's a good antibacterial wash.

PS: For bloody wounds, apply a dry poultice made of wood ashes and freshly ground coffee. Secure it with a towel.

JS: Sprinkle dried, powdered *yerba cangá* on the clean wound.

MO: Apply the ashes of the *bálsamo* tree directly on the wound.

BV: For a cut, chop up a leaf of *la suelda consuelda,* add some cooking oil and stick it to the wound as a poultice.
• Mash up *malá* leaves and tie them on to the cut to stop the bleeding. Then for quick healing, apply udder balm, belladonna ointment or kerosene that's been burned for a few hours in a lantern. Kerosene is especially good for animals because besides cleansing and healing, it keeps the flies out of their wounds.

LF: For suppurating sores on the legs, extract the juice of wild eggplant leaves in a blender with a bit of water, strain the liquid, soak a towel in that liquid, and use the towel as a poultice.

Diabetes
(to lower blood sugar)

JS: Boil up five mulberry leaves *(la morera)* for 15 minutes in about three cups of water, and drink that tea every day.

CC: Mix (in the blender) three handfuls of the following greens: *el cundeamor*, pigeon pea leaves *(el gandul)*, stinging nettle *(la ortiga brava)* and lemon grass *(el limoncillo)* with three cups of water. Strain and drink daily, one cup every five or six hours.

MO & GS: Drink pigeon pea *(el gandul)* leaf tea frequently.
• Make a tea of sweet verbena root *(la yerba dulce)* with *el cundeamor*, then put it in the refrigerator and drink it all day long.

BV: Drink teas of pigeon pea buds *(el gandul)* or the new leaves of the almond tree *(el almendro)* as if they were water, cool during the day and warm at night.

ML: Drink teas of broadleaf coriander *(el culantro del monte)*.
• Drink teas of the leaf buds of the almond *(el almendro)* and star apple *(el caimito)* trees.

Diarrhea

CM: Drink a strong, green tea of black nightshade *(la mata gallina)* with sal de Eno (a sodium bicarbonate-based digestive).

JP: Put raw rice in water and leave it there for an hour or more. Drink the rice water.

DC: Take teas of basil *(la albahaca blanca)* mixed with cashew husks *(el pajuil)* and *hicaco* fruit.

BV: Drink teas of Caribbean vervain *(la verbena)* with lemon.

LF: Sip teas of the small, new leaves of *el tártago* mixed with oregano *(el orégano chiquito)*.

Digestive Aids
(See also **Indigestion**)

GS: Eat all you want, but wait until it's time to eat. Because if you have a big lunch at noon and you eat again at 1:30, you're interfering with the process of digestion. And that could cause you lots of problems. Big problems!

MO: Eat slowly.

IV: Take the juice of a lemon in water twice daily if you have trouble digesting greasy foods.

PS: Eat lemon along with heavy, greasy foods like shellfish.

PA: Try my aloe-based remedy on page 178.

Dying

CMM: When a dying person is in pain, chop up a couple of handfuls of Caribbean spearmint *(la yerba buena)* and boil for 15 minutes in enough milk to cover the herbs. Soak a small towel in that milk while it's warm, and apply it to the person's stomach and abdomen. It smells good, comforts, strengthens and eases pain.

Earache

AC: Warm a leaf of the life plant *(la bruja)* and squeeze the warm juice into your ear. Cover it up with some cotton if desired.

BV: Warm up a leaf of the life plant *(la bruja)*, then crush it and

soak up the juice with a little cotton. Place the warm cotton in
your ear. The liquid seeping from the cotton heals the inner ear
and kills the pain.

MO & ML: Warm up some marjoram leaves *(la mejorana)* and
chop them up. Pick up their warm juice with a pad of cotton and
squeeze it into the ear. Cover it up with the cotton and lie down.

Edema

MOS: If you suffer from swollen legs and ankles, boil the stems
and leaves of the tamarind tree *(el tamarindo)*. Once that water
has cooled, soak your feet up to your knees in it.
• Or drink teas of boiled tamarind leaves and leaf stems.

CMM: Drink teas of new *guanábana* leaves.

M: Drink teas of *la paletaria, la verdolaga* and/or the *tuna* cactus.

Erysipelas

CM: Pick the leaves of stinging vine *(la pringamoza)* with gloves,
then heat them in oil over a low flame until the oil turns green.
Then use a clean feather to paint that oil all over the irritated skin.

Eyes

MO: For clouded vision, place a few of the tiny seeds of the basil
plant *(la albahaca)* in the inner corners of the eyes, very gently so
that they don't irritate. Leave them in a while so they can attract
mucus and foreign matter.

DB: For cloudy vision, put some well-rinsed leaves of common plantain *(el llantén)* alone or with rue *(la ruda)* in a clean glass of water, and leave outside (covered with a little mesh) or on your window ledge during the cool dampness of the night. When you get up in the morning, rinse your eyes with that water.

BV: For conjunctivitis, leave half a dozen fairy roses *(la rosa cienhojas)* in a small cup of water overnight, and rinse your eyes with that water throughout the entire next day.

PA: Cool purslane tea *(la verdolaga)* makes an excellent eye wash.

Fatigue and Weakness

IV: While chopping up a free-range, native chicken for soup, cut the bones up as well, so that the marrow can be cooked right into the broth. You can prepare the broth with the meat if you want, or cook the meat aside. The marrow is the most important part of the soup! Strain and drink!

JS: Drink dove or pigeon broth every day for two or three weeks!

DB: Every day, drink a punch made from two fresh, raw eggs, a cup of fresh milk, half an ounce of brandy, and some brown sugar to taste.

Fertilizer

PN: Use alluvial soil and cured manure. Chicken manure must be cured for over a year before it can be used.

MO: For good fertilizer, add coffee grounds and potato peelings to manure as it's curing.

Fever
(also see **Baths**)

MO: Drink teas of the leaves and stems of *la gran señora*.
• Lemon grass tea *(el limoncillo)* — made from the whitish leaf bases of the plant — is very effective.
• Drink Caribbean vervain *(la verbena)* tea.
• Take two pieces of tissue paper (the wrapping kind) just a little bigger than the soles of the feverish person's feet. Rub beef or sheep tallow *(el sebo Flandes)* into the paper. Then take a little salt, a little sugar, and roll a bottle over the grains until they're ground up fine. Put the powdered salt and sugar on top of the paper covered with tallow, and sprinkle some cooking oil on top of all that. Next, you prepare a bandage to be tied onto the person's forehead exactly the same way. Then you light a candle and use it to warm the bandage. (Don't put it too close, of course), and put the bandage on the person's head. Do the same with the papers, and put them on the soles of her feet. Finally, put on some warm socks, and she goes to sleep. She should sleep as much as she wants, and don't take off those little paper soles until the next day. That's the remedy for stubborn fevers that simply won't go down. It always works!

PV: Take teas of Caribbean vervain *(la verbena)* and common plantain *(el llantén)*.
• Peel and mash up the roots, or at least the lowest part of the stems of lemon grass *(el limoncillo)* and then boil them up with anise *(el anís de grano)*. Drink as needed.
• Drink teas of the leaves of the sour orange tree *(las hojas del naranjo)* with *poleo* and yellow trumpet leaves *(el saúco amarillo)*.

• Stick *salvia* leaves on to the soles of your feet, with camphor cream *(el alcanfor)* and stick another leaf on your forehead. Lie down covered with a blanket. This also works for headaches.
• Drink teas of black nightshade *(la mata gallina)* mixed with Caribbean vervain *(la verbena)*.

BV: Common plantain *(el llantén)* and *la curía* cut fever and pain. The leaves of both plants can be added to any tea.
• Boil up the leaves of German chamomile or feverfew *(la manzanilla)*, Caribbean spearmint *(la yerba buena)*, black nightshade *(la mata gallina)* and *tuna* cactus. Drink that tea throughout the day.

CVS: Run a little "bath" of a young child's fresh urine over the forehead of the feverish person, and then rub his forehead with sheep tallow *(el sebo Flandes)*.

DC: Administer teas or — even more effective — the juice, of the wild lettuce plant *(achicoria)* by the tablespoonful.

PC: Take teas of *el quinino del pobre.*

PS: Take teas of *la gran señora* and *el botón de cadete,* alone or mixed together.

Flu

MC: Drink fragrant geranium *(el geranio oloroso)* leaf tea.

GS: Drink strong teas of the leaves of *el poleo.*

BV: Take teas of *la gran señora* or *el botón de cadete* mixed with lemon grass *(el limoncillo)*.

• For a flu with a cough, rinse and boil the following ingredients in a half gallon of water in a covered pot: a handful of *el cohitre blanco*, a chopped-up leaf of spineless *(tuna)* cactus, some Caribbean spearmint leaves *(la yerba buena)* and German chamomile or feverfew leaves and flowers *(la manzanilla)* plus a small handful of *la paletaria,* the juice of two aloe leaves *(la sábila)*, and a handful of basil *(la albahaca blanca)*. After boiling for 20 minutes, it will be ready to drink with honey as needed.

PA: Drink teas of the root and/or the whitish bases of the leaves of lemon grass *(el limoncillo)*.
• Mulberry leaf tea *(la morera)* is very effective.

ML: Chop up a peeled, sour orange *(la naranja),* including the white, inner rind, and add it to any "flu formula" green tea.
• Grate a green papaya and boil it for five to ten minutes, covered over a low flame. Drink the juice.
• Drink teas of eucalyptus leaves *(el eucalipto)*.
• For a flu with a cough, take teas of *la curía*.
• Prepare a large *menorativa* for the whole family, boiling up a piece of the royal palm root *(la palma real)*, the coconut palm root *(la palma de coco)*, a carrot *(la zanahoria)*, a small, green papaya, a small piece of purging cassia *(la caña fístula)* and — from the pharmacy — *maná canelón* (a cinnamon-based sweetener used as flavoring). Everyone takes a cup. That cleans out the system and helps to prevent and/or get rid of the flu.

Fowl's Pip

AC & JS: Add orange rind or lemon juice to the birds' water supply.

Full Harvest

PN: Always plant during the waning moon. Only sugar cane and tubers like cassava *(la yuca)* can be planted at any time of month.
• Take "babies" from banana plants for replanting during the waning moon at low tide.

Hair Care

AC: To help hair grow, boil up some Caribbean vervain *(la verbena)*, let it cool off, and use this "tea" as a final hair rinse after shampooing. Leave it in 'till next shampoo and repeat.

JP & PA: Rosemary *(el romero)* boiled up and applied after a shampoo as a final rinse adds body and gives your hair a nice, dark color. It also prevents hair from falling out.

AC: To give hair body and get rid of dandruff, peel a large aloe leaf *(la sábila)* and mix in the blender with ½ cup of water. After washing your hair, apply the aloe mixture, and don't rinse it out. You can make a lot and store in the refrigerator for future rinses.

BR: For dandruff, collect several stinging nettle leaves *(la ortiga brava),* using gloves, of course. Then crush the leaves in a mortar and pestle or using a rolling pin. Place crushed leaves and juice in water and let sit for a few hours. Then strain the water, pour it over the scalp after shampooing, and leave it there without rinsing it out. If you make a lot, it will keep in the fridge. (Or use the blender method, adding, ½ cup of water to six or seven large leaves, and straining the blended liquid before applying.)
• For baldness, massage daily with a rosemary oil *(el romero)* made this way: First fill a jar with fresh, organic rosemary. Then

201

cover it with olive oil and let it sit for a month or so before straining. Regular, brisk massages with that oil will stimulate hair growth. (The massages should last a good five to seven minutes!)

BV: For dandruff, use the raw, blended-up gelatin of aloe *(la sábila)* as if it were shampoo.

PS: When someone starts losing their hair, I recommend regular scalp massages with fresh, home-made coconut oil.
• For head lice, boil up some vines of *el cundeamor* until the water turns dark green. Then use it as if it were a shampoo, but leave it on the person's head for a good 15 -20 minutes. That kills the lice, and it's good for the scalp. Repeat in a week.

Headaches

JS: Grate some raw potato up fine and mix it up with some witch hazel solution *(Agua Maravilla)* to make a cooling paste. Apply it to your forehead, temples and neck, and lie down for a while. What a relief!

GS: For a headache caused by heat that needs to be drawn out, rub a leaf of annato *(el achiote)* with cooking oil and stick it on to your forehead. If it's working, the leaf will dry out and break up until it's powder. If it stay's wet and slides around, it's not the remedy you need.

PS: For a migraine, heat up some *salvia* leaves, enough to cover your entire forehead and temples. Then add a paste of roasted coffee and cooking oil on top of the leaves, and tie it on to your forehead with a towel. Lie down for a few hours!

MO: To treat a migraine headache, place a mixture of native wood ashes and salt in a bucket of hot water. Wrap the person's forehead in a bandage soaked in that mixture, and put his legs, from the knees down, into the bucket.

PV: Simply place your feet in a big bucket of hot water. You might want to place some fragrant alcoholado in the water and/or a bag of ice on your head and around the neck area.

IL: Place *salvia* leaves on the forehead, neck and temples. You can use cooking oil, camphorated oil or Vicks to make them stick and increase their effect. Tie them on, and go lie down.

Heart

GS: After a heart attack, place a warmed-up leaf from the custard apple tree *(el corazón)* over the heart. The same leaf, taken in the form of medicinal teas, will also prevent further attacks.

Hemorrhage

MO: Take teas of common plantain *(el llantén)*.

BV: Drink teas of *la malá* or chew the leaves.

High Blood Pressure

JS: Every day, in a quart of water, boil up five leaves of broad leaf coriander *(el recao)* with the outer peel and ends of three heads of garlic *(el ajo)*, plus five common plantain leaves *(el* *llantén*) and five sour orange leaves *(las hojas del naranjo)* for 15 minutes or until the flavor is strong. Then, instead of drinking water or juice, drink that herb water, cold if you like, all day long.

MO: Drink broadleaf coriander tea *(el culantro del monte)* daily.

PS: Cut a *jagua* fruit in quarters, put it in a pitcher of water in the refrigerator and, after a day or so, start drinking that water and prepare a new batch every two days. No sugar is needed!

BR & CR: Eat raw garlic daily.

PV: Eat lots of passion fruit *(la parcha)* and drink the juice.

CVS: Drink teas of the new leaves of the guava bush *(el guayabo)*.

Indigestion

MS: Take teas of young *guanábana* leaves with *poleo*.

AC: Drink a tea of new mango leaves with *guanábana* leaves.

PV: Try a tea of chamomile or feverfew flowers *(la manzanilla)*.
• Teas of lemon balm *(la melisa)* with Caribbean spearmint *(la yerba buena)* are great for treating nausea.
• Teas of sour orange leaves *(las hojas del naranjo)* are soothing.

MOS: Put a pinch of wood ash in a cup of water. When the ashes have settled, drink the water with ½ teaspoon of olive oil.

CM: Drink strong, green teas of black nightshade *(la yerba mora)* with new *tuatúa* leaves.

DC: Drink mint tea *(la menta).*
• *El poleo* and new *guanábana* leaves are excellent for an upset stomach. Each can be brewed up as a simple tea, or they can be combined.

GS: Take teas of Caribbean spearmint *(la yerba buena).* They're good and cooling for the stomach.
• If you want to throw up and start fresh, drink a tea made from three *tártago* leaves, which have been picked by pulling upward from the stems. To settle your stomach, make the same tea, but take the leaves by pulling them downward from the stalk.

MO: For gas and indigestion, try anise seed tea *(anís de grano).*
• Teas of Caribbean vervain root *(la verbena)* are good.
• Drink lemon balm tea *(la melisa)* daily for better digestion.

BV: Caribbean spearmint tea *(la yerba buena),* chamomile *(la manzanilla)* and *la paletaria* are all great, alone or combined.
• Caribbean vervain tea *(la verbena)* with lemon is good.

ML: If you feel as though food is rotting in your stomach, drink cooling coconut water.

CMM: For gas, nausea and indigestion, take teas of custard apple leaves *(el corazón),* alone or with the young leaves of the guava bush *(el guayabo)* or the sour orange tree *(el naranjo).*

Infertility (women)

BV: For a condition of "congested tubes," boil up grated arrowroot tubers *(la maranta)* and eat by the tablespoonful, as if it were cereal.

Inflammation

MO: Cut the hollow leaf stems of the castor bean plant *(la higuereta)* into ½ inch pieces. Then string them so you have a necklace, bracelet or belt of the appropriate size, and place them on the person's body. This is great for all kinds of inflammation.

PV: Heat and chop up the leaf of the castor bean plant *(la higuereta)* and make a poultice by mixing the chopped leaf with belladonna ointment, and wrapping it around the swollen, inflamed area. This is good for any kind of inflammation, including for animals, when they are swollen after giving birth.

Insects (see *Pests* and *Animal Bites and Stings)*

Insomnia

DB: Put a camphor pastille *(el alcanfor)* in a glass of water, and place that glass under your bed before retiring.

ML: If a child can't sleep, give her a tea of sour orange leaves *(las hojas del naranjo)*.

Internal Pain

IV: Take a big handful of garlic weed *(el anamú)*, and mash it up or put it in a blender with a cup and a half of water and strain. Drink as needed.

Intestinal Gas

PA: Take a strong tea of anise seeds *(anís de grano)* with the root and flowers of coffee senna *(la hidionda chiquita)*.

• I recommend teas of basil (*la albahaca blanca*) alone or with anise seed (*el anís de grano*) or star anise (*anís de estrella*).

LF: Take a tea of coffee senna root (*la hidionda chiquita*) boiled up with slices of ginger (*el jengibre*).

CMS: Take chamomile flower infusions (*la manzanilla*).

Intestinal Parasites

BR & CR: Cut some long slits into a just-harvested green papaya. Then, with a teaspoon, collect the caustic white latex that seeps out of the cuts. Take a teaspoonful or two a day, diluted in juice, on an empty stomach. In a few days you'll be rid of the parasites.
• Administer enemas of lukewarm garlic tea (*el ajo*) or simply place a whole clove of raw garlic in the rectum.

CVS: Drink the juice of the wormseed plant (*el pazote*) on an empty stomach, a tablespoon at a time.

MO: Purslane tea (*la verdolaga*) prevents infestations of worms.

GS: Wormseed tea (*el pazote*) is the best, but it stinks. Make it strong, and hold your nose when you drink it. The worms will leave your body in droves.

Kidney Pain and Inflammation

JS: Boil up lots of common plantain (*el llantén*) — one part leaves to three parts water — for 20 minutes. Strain and use that water for a sitz bath. What a relief!

PV & BV: Cut a leaf of the spineless *(tuna)* cactus into two fat slices. Then heat them in the oven and, once cooled, place them, gel-side down, on the person's back over the kidneys. Cover that poultice with a towel.

PA: For kidney pain, warm up some leaves of *la baquiña cerrada* with the steam of your teapot, then rub cooking oil or camphor ointment on top of them, and place over the kidneys. Cover with a towel and allow the oil or ointment to seep into the skin.

GS & MO: For kidney stones, take teas of *Juana la blanca* or *la baquiña cerrada.* Drink freely of *la baquiña,* but don't take *Juana la blanca* for more than three days in a row.

DC: For kidney stones, boil common plantain *(el llantén)* with *la baquiña cerrada* and *Juana la blanca.* Strain and serve each morning with the water of an entire, green coconut.

PS: Drink cooling teas of mallow leaves and flowers *(la malva).*
• Drink lots of coconut water.

BV: Drink teas of amaranth *(el blero)* and/or *el cohitre blanco.*
• Boil up a leaf of spineless *(tuna)* cactus, a scant handful of *la paletaria* and a scant handful of black nightshade *(la mata gallina)* in three cups of water for 20 minutes. Drink throughout the day.

Medicated Ointment or Oil for Rubs and Poultices

PA: Melt a five-ounce jar of Vaseline in a little saucepan over a low flame. Then mash two camphor pastilles *(el alcanfor)* until they're just powder, and add that powder to the Vaseline on the stove. When it's dissolved, pour it back into the same jar.

• If you prefer, add the powdered camphor to cooking oil as it is heated upon the stove. For a solid consistency, add grated wax (bees wax is best) to the oil as it cooks.

Menstrual Irregularities

JP: Boil up some coffee senna root *(la hidionda chiquita)* and take as a tea to bring on and normalize menstruation.

MO: Teas of garlic weed* leaves and roots *(el anamú)* bring on a late period.

MO & PS & PV: Teas of rue* *(la ruda),* fennel *(el hinojo)* and broadleaf coriander *(el recao)* regulate the cycle and alleviate menstrual pain.

CV: Lemon verbena (la *yerba Luisa)* and *salvia* teas bring on a late period.

PA: For menstrual pain, boil up the paper-like peel and ends of a couple of heads of garlic *(el ajo)*, and drink as tea.

JS & MO: *Salvia* leaf tea warms the womb and brings down the bloods.
> * *Use these herbs with caution. May cause abortion.*

Muscle Cramps

PV: For leg cramps and other body pains, add a few handfuls of roasted — softened — bitter ginger *(el jengibre amargo)* to one quart of *alcoholado.* Use for rubs. (It gets stronger as it sets.)

BV: For muscle spasms, boil up some annato leaves *(el achiote)* and soak legs and feet in the warm liquid.
• Rub fresh, warm urine into the cramped leg or foot.

BS: Rub corn silk into the cramped area.

Peace of Mind

DC: Pray for guidance and live in a grateful way, always carrying with you a symbol of thanks in your thoughts.

FB: Tend a home garden of vegetables, fruits and herbs. Enjoy the fruit of your labor, and share with the neighbors.

Pests

AC: To get rid of ticks, fill a bucket with *poleo* leaves, and cover the leaves with water. Then simply leave the *poleo* there to steep from one day to the next, under glass in the sun. Pour that water in and around the doghouse, or wherever the ticks are. The water has a strong smell, and the ticks will move on quickly.

BV: To get rid of fleas, lice, ticks and other pests, mix *Aguarrás* (a petroleum distillate used for rubdowns, available in pharmacies) with undiluted ammonia solution and mop the house with it.

ML: To keep moths and cockroaches away, put mashed up pieces of vetiver root *(el pacholí)* in drawers and closets.

CR: Cockroaches hate *el poleo*. Every few days, put branches of fresh *poleo* in every corner of your home, and they'll disappear.

Skin Care

irritation

PV: For itching, bathe in a boiled solution of *el cundeamor* or palma Christi *(la higuereta)*.

MO: To make a skin powder for heat and diaper rash, grate arrowroot tubers *(la maranta)* and dust with the silky starch.
• When there's irritation, bathe in a solution of *la escobilla*. It soothes the most sensitive skin, and is an ideal wash for baby.

BR & CR: Crush the juice from the long, thick stems of the comfrey plant *(la consuelda mayor)* and use the juice as a lotion.

PV: To treat heat rash internally, drink teas of *la paletaria*. It's cooling, and very effective for children's skin irritations.

to toughen skin

GS: For manual laborers: At night, work an entire stick of sheep tallow *(el sebo Flandes)* into your hands. The next day, the skin on your hands will be hard and strong.

BV: To fit into tight shoes without getting corns and blisters, rub feet with sheep tallow *(el sebo Flandes)* the night before wearing the shoes, and then again, just before and after wearing them.

sunburn

PV: Pass aloe gel *(la sábila)* over the skin as if it were a lotion.

skin fungus

PA: Fill a bottle with fresh *cundeamor* and cover it all with three parts cooking oil and one part rubbing alcohol. Leave it for a few days so that the medicinal qualities and color of the plant seep into the liquid. Apply to the affected area as often as needed.

MO: Boil up some *cundeamor*, and when the water is a deep green color, let it cool and apply that "tea" frequently.

BR & CR: Use gloves to pick several stinging nettle leaves *(la ortiga brava)*. Crush the leaves in a mortar and pestle or using a rolling pin. Place the crushed leaves and their juice in water and let sit for a few hours. Then strain the water, and wash the ailing area with the nettle water every two hours. Let it air-dry, without rubbing. (Or use the blender method, adding ½ cup of water to six or seven large leaves, and straining the blended liquid before applying.) This lotion keeps well in the fridge.

ringworm

CM: Cut a 7" piece of the trunk of dumb cane *(el rábano cimarrón)* lengthwise and put some salt into the cut. Leave the sliced cane outside overnight to absorb the cool, damp night air. During that time, the salt dissolves into the liquid from the cane, and in the morning you paint the ringworm with that liquid using a feather. It burns a bit, but that's how ringworm is cured.

BV: Mix squash resin in equal proportion with the crushed leaves of the ringworm tree *(el talantalán)* and apply as a poultice.

IL: Mash up the leaves of the ringworm tree *(el talantro)* and apply the juice all over the affected area, as needed.

Stomach Ulcers

PS: Toss a couple of handfuls of common plantain *(el llantén)* in the blender with two cups of water. Add some black nightshade *(la mata gallina),* blend, strain, divide in two, and drink morning and night on an empty stomach.

MO: Boil up a couple of handfuls of common plantain *(el llantén)* with a couple of handfuls of black nightshade *(la mata gallina)* in a quart of water and drink throughout the day.

DB: Boil up some black nightshade *(la yerba mora)* in milk, either alone or combined with common plantain leaves *(el llantén).* Drink on a regular basis.

ML: Take teas of *tuatúa* leaf buds with black nightshade leaves *(la mata gallina)* ½ hour before meals.

IV: Every day, wash two handfuls of *el cohitre blanco,* and place in a large mortar. Mash it 'till the juice comes out, then boil both fiber and juice in a quart of water over a low flame for 20 minutes or so. Strain and drink three times daily without sugar. A bit of honey may be added.

MOS: Boil a peeled, white onion for 20 minutes and drink the water. Take this remedy twice a day for ten days.

Swollen Glands and Mumps

CM: Rub swollen glands with sheep tallow *(el sebo Flandes).*

Teeth and Gums
(people and animals)

ML: For toothache, rinse the mouth with *amoniaco* (a dilute ammonia solution sold in pharmacies).
• For gum problems, chop up a peeled aloe leaf *(la sábila)* and leave in water over night. Strain and use as a mouthwash.
• If your gums hurt and you have false teeth, place a piece of *salvia* leaf between gums and teeth and change daily. The juice then has a chance to enter the system throughout the day.
• A little tea of tuatúa leaf buds will relieve a teething child's pain.

AC: If you don't have a toothbrush handy, place the leaf of the pigeon pea bush *(el gandul)* against your gums and rub as if it were a little brush.

PV: Make a little packet of lemon grass root *(el limoncillo)* and rub it over your gums as if it were a toothbrush. It freshens up the breath and makes your mouth feel great!

CM: To combat an infection in the mouth, rinse with warm salt water for long periods of time, every chance you get.

TR: For a tooth or gum infection, swish a tea of the boiled root of *el morivivi* in your mouth as often as needed. If the tooth is loose, this will help it to drop out.

PC: For toothache, rinse your mouth with a tea made from the leaves of *el guayacán.*

BV: After losing a tooth, place salt in the hollow where the tooth was. That will cleanse the wound and cut the bleeding fast.
• If there is hemorrhage, wash a bud of *salvia,* chew it up and

hold it in place on the gum itself. *La salvia* will coagulate the blood and ease the pain.
• Or hold a piece of *la malá* over the gum area. It stops bleeding.

CM: When your cows have loose teeth, squeeze everything out of a bunch of lemons (some people roast their lemons first) and add some salt and sugar. Then rub that lemon juice along the cows' gums, and don't give them water right away. In a pinch, you can use iodine solution. That also tightens their teeth right up.

Throat Problems

AC: Gargle with lemon juice in warm salt water. Both the salt and the lemon cleanse the throat, and the lemon has lots of vitamin C.

CM: Drink *salvia* tea or chew the young leaf buds.
• For serious throat problems, squeeze some lemon juice into a cup with a little water and add some white vinegar and salt. Heat it up and start gargling with it, as hot as you can take it, every hour or two, all through the day and night.

Udder Congestion

GS: If your cow or goat is suffering from a congested udder, boil up about 15 castor bean leaves in a couple of gallons of water as if for a bath, and then leave it to cool overnight. Next morning, wash her udder completely, with lots of strength, using the very same leaves you boiled as if they were a washcloth. You do this two or three times a day and the milk will flow. Lots of milk! I guarantee it!

Urinary Tract Inflammation

CM: Boil up some *prenetaria* mixed with spineless *(tuna)* cactus and drink that tea throughout the day.
• Make a simple tisane of *la prenetaria*. Just wash the plant, crush it up a bit, add it to a jar of water, juice and all, and after it's been setting for some hours, drink all day long, as much as you want.

MO: Boil the leaves of mallow *(la malva)* and black nightshade *(la mata gallina)* in a quart of water. You can add some *paletaria* and spineless *(tuna)* cactus too. Take a cupful of this tea at least twice a day, and always again at night. This remedy usually cures completely, but you have to continue with it for a while.

PV: Take strong teas of rue *(la ruda)*.

Uterine Inflammation

JP: After boiling about seven castor bean leaves *(la higuereta)* in a two-gallon pot for 15 minutes, strain the liquid and pour it into warm bath water in a tub big enough to sit in. Sit there for 15 or 20 minutes, or until you feel better.

JS: Boil up some wild eggplant *(la berenjena cimarrona)* leaves. Then, just sit for a while in that water, while it's fairly warm.
• Boil up some mallow leaves *(la malva)*. After the water has cooled off a bit, add Epsom salts and sit in that water as long as you can.

MO: Boil up some *campana* leaves and use as a vaginal wash.

PS: Drink mallow leaf tea *(la malva)* strained through a cloth.

Warming "Pleasure" Drinks

PV: Try a tea of marjoram *(la mejorana)* with native ginger *(el jengibre dulce)*, some elder flowers *(el saúco)* and honey.
• Mash up some native ginger *(el jengibre dulce)* and boil it in a little water for 10 to 15 minutes. Then add a cup of hot milk and honey to taste. Enjoy its comforting warmth!

Warts

ML: Place a poultice of the mashed pulp of the tuberose root *(la azucena)* directly on the warts and secure with a cloth bandage.

BR & CR: Apply the milky juice that flows from the cut leaves and stems of the poinsettia plant *(la pascua)* to the warts four or five times a day. They'll disappear after just a few days.

Plants by Name and Family

The plants mentioned in this volume (specifically, those used in Puerto Rico) are herein presented in alphabetical order according to their names in Spanish.*

INDEX I

*Index II, on page 231, is organized in alphabetical order, by English.

PUERTO RICAN NAMES	SCIENTIFIC NAMES	ENGLISH NAMES	BOTANICAL FAMILIES
achicoria, chicoria	*Lactuca intybacea*	wild lettuce	Compositae
achiote, bija	*Bixa orellana*	annato	Bixaceae
aguacate	*Persea americana*	avocado	Lauraceae
ajo	*Allium sativum*	garlic	Liliaceae
ajonjolí	*Sesamum indicum*	sesame	Pedaliaceae
albahaca (blanca)	*Ocimum basilicum*	basil	Labiatae
alcanfor	*Cinnamomum camphora*	camphor	Myrtaceae
alfilerillo, tente en el aire	*Cassytha filiformis*	love vine	Lauraceae
almendro	*Terminalia catappa*	tropical almond	Combretaceae

PUERTO RICAN NAMES	SCIENTIFIC NAMES	ENGLISH NAMES	BOTANICAL FAMILIES
alumbre, prenetaria, paletaria, frescura	*Peperomia pellucida*	shine bush, ice'n glass, silver bush	Piperaceae
altamisa, artemisa	*Ambrosia peruviana*	Caribbean mug-wort, ragweed	Compositae
anacagüita	*Sterculia apetala*	Panama tree	Sterculiaceae
anamú	*Petiveria alliacea*	garlic weed, congo root	Phytolaccaceae
anís de grano	*Pimpinella anisum*	anise seed	Umbelliferae
anís de estrella	*Illicium anisatum*	star anise	Magnoliaceae
apio	*Apium graveolens*	celeriac	Umbelliferae
árnica	*Arnica montana*	arnica	Compositae
arroz	*Oryza sativa*	rice	Gramineae
artemisa, altamisa	*Ambrosia peruviana*	Caribbean mug-wort, ragweed	Compositae
azucena antillana	*Polianthes tuberosa*	tuberose	Amaryllidaceae
bálsamo, péndula	*Citharexylum fruticosum*	fiddlewood	Rubiaceae
baquiña cerrada	*Lepianthes peltatum*	monkey's hand	Piperaceae
berenjena cimarrona	*Solanum torvum*	wild eggplant	Solanaceae
berro	*Nasturtium officinale*	watercress	Cruciferae
bija, achiote	*Bixa orellana*	annato	Bixaceae
blero, bledo, espinaca criolla	*Amaranthus viridis*	calaloo, white amaranth	Amaranthaceae

Plants by Name and Family (Spanish)

PUERTO RICAN NAMES	SCIENTIFIC NAMES	ENGLISH NAMES	BOTANICAL FAMILIES
botón de cadete, molinillo	*Leonotis nepetifolia*	lion's ear, hollow stalk, shandilay	Labiatae
bruja, yerba bruja, siempreviva	*Kalanchoe pinnatum*	life plant	Crassulaceae
cadillo de fibra, pata de perro	*Urena lobata*	bur	Malvaceae
café	*Coffea arabica*	coffee	Rubiaceae
caimito	*Chrysophyllum cainito*	star apple	Sapotaceae
calabaza	*Cucurbita moschata*	pumpkin, squash	Cucurbitaceae
campana	*Datura suaveolens*	moon plant	Solanaceae
caña de azúcar	*Saccharum officinarum*	sugar cane	Gramineae
caña fístula	*Cassia fistula*	purging cassia	Caesalpiniaceae
canario amarillo	*Allamanda cathartica*	yellow allamanda	Apocynaceae
canela	*Cinnamomum zeylanicum*	cinnamon	Lauraceae
capá prieto, vara prieta	*Cordia alliodora*	Spanish elm	Boraginaceae
cariaquillo	*Lantana camara*	red sage, yellow sage	Verbenaceae
cebolla	*Allium cepa*	onion	Liliaceae
ceiba	*Ceiba pentandra*	silk-cotton tree, kapok	Bombacaceae
chicoria, achicoria	*Lactuca intybacea*	wild lettuce	Compositae

PUERTO RICAN NAMES	SCIENTIFIC NAMES	ENGLISH NAMES	BOTANICAL FAMILIES
china	*Citrus sinensis*	(sweet) orange	Rutaceae
chincha, cilantro, cilantrillo	*Coriandrum sativum*	coriander	Umbelliferae
chucho, cocuisa	*Sansevieria metallica*	snake plant, bowstring hemp	Liliaceae
cilantrillo, cilantro, chincha	*Coriandrum sativum*	coriander	Umbelliferae
clavellina	*Caesalpinia pulcherrima*	Barbados pride, dul-dul	Caesalpiniaceae
clavo de especia, clavo dulce	*Syzygium aromaticum*	clove	Myrtaceae
cocillana	*Guarea rusbyi*	cocillana	Meliaceae
coco(tero), palma de coco	*Cocos nucifera*	coconut palm	Palmaceae
cocuisa, chucho	*Sansevieria metallica*	snake plant	Liliaceae
cohitre	*Commelina spp.*	French weed	Commelinaceae
col blanca	*Brassica oleracea*	kale	Cruciferae
consuelda mayor	*Symphytum officinalis*	comfrey	Boraginaceae
corazón	*Annona reticulata*	custard apple, bullock's heart	Annonaceae
culantro del monte, recao	*Eryngium foetidum*	broadleaf coriander, fitweed	Umbelliferae
cundeamor	*Momordica charantia*	wild balsam apple, sorossie	Cucurbitaceae
curía, tilo (mata)	*Justicia pectorialis*	green balsam, carpenter's grass	Acanthaceae

Plants by Name and Family (Spanish)

PUERTO RICAN NAMES	SCIENTIFIC NAMES	ENGLISH NAMES	BOTANICAL FAMILIES
curía panacea, yapaná	*Eupatorium triplinerve*	japana	Compositae
dragón, pimienta Angola	*Alpinia zerumbet*	shell plant	Zingiberaceae
escobilla, escoba blanca	*Sida spp.*	soap bush, wire weed	Malvaceae
escopetón	*Zinnia peruviana*	wild zinnia	Compositae
espinaca criolla, blero, bledo	*Amaranthus viridis*	calaloo, white amaranth	Amaranthaceae
eucalipto	*Eucalyptus spp.*	eucalyptus	Myrtaceae
frescura, paletaria, alumbre, prenetaria	*Peperomia pellucida*	shine bush, ice'n glass, silver bush	Piperaceae
gandul	*Cajanus cajan*	pigeon pea	Fabaceae
geranio oloroso	*Pelargonium odoratissium*	fragrant geranium	Geraniaceae
gran señora		bitter mint	Labiatae
guaco	*Mikania spp.*	guaco	Compositae
guanábana	*Annona muricata*	soursop	Annonaceae
guayabo	*Psidium guajava*	guava	Myrtaceae
guayacán	*Guaiacum officinale*	lignum vitae, pockwood	Zygophyllaceae
guineo	*Musa spp.*	banana	Musaceae
güiro, güícharo	*Lagenaria siceraria*	gourd (musical)	Cucurbitaceae
hamamelis	*Hamamelis virginiana*	witch hazel	Hamamelidaceae
hicaco	*Chrysolbalanus icaco*	coco plum	Chripobalanceae

PUERTO RICAN NAMES	SCIENTIFIC NAMES	ENGLISH NAMES	BOTANICAL FAMILIES
hidionda chiquita	*Senna occidentalis*	coffee senna	Caesalpiniaceae
higüera	*Crescentia cujete*	calabash, gourd	Bignoniaceae
higuereta, ricino, palmacristi	*Ricinis comunis*	castor bean, palma Christi	Euphorbiaceae
higuillo oloroso	*Piper marginatum*	black wattle, soot soot, jointwood	Piperaceae
hinojo	*Foeniculum vulgare*	fennel	Umbelliferae
ipecacuana	*Pedilanthus tithymaloides*	slipper plant	Euphorbiaceae
jagua	*Genipa americana*	genipap	Rubiaceae
jengibre amargo	*Zingiber zerumbet*	bitter ginger	Zingiberaceae
jengibre dulce, jengibre del país	*Zingiber officinale*	ginger	Zingiberaceae
jobo	*Spondias dulcis*	yellow mombin	Anacardiaceae
Juana la blanca	*Borreria laevis*	iron grass	Rubiaceae
lechosa, papaya	*Carica papaya*	papaya	Caricaceae
limón	*Citrus limon*	lemon	Rutaceae
limoncillo	*Cymbopogon citratus*	lemon grass	Gramineae
llantén	*Plantago major*	common plantain	Plantaginaceae
maga	*Montezuma grandiflora*	maga wood	Malvaceae
maíz	*Zea mays*	corn	Gramineae
malá blanca	*Senecio aizoides*	stipti	Compositae
malagueta	*Pimenta racemosa*	bay rum	Myrtaceae

Plants by Name and Family (Spanish)

PUERTO RICAN NAMES	SCIENTIFIC NAMES	ENGLISH NAMES	BOTANICAL FAMILIES
malanga	*Colocasia esculenta*	dasheen, taro	Araceae
malva	*Malachra capitata*	mallow	Malvaceae
mangó	*Mangifera indica*	mango	Anacardiaceae
manzanilla	*Chrisanthemum parthenium*	feverfew	Compositae
	Tanacetum parthenium	feverfew	" "
	Matricaria recutita	German camomile	" "
	Anthemis nobilis	(Roman) camomile	" "
mapén, pana, panapén	*Arctocarpus altilis*	bread fruit	Moraceae
maracuyá, parcha	*Passiflora edulis*	passion fruit, bell apple, water lemon fruit	Passifloraceae
marañon, pajuil	*Anacardium occidentale*	cashew	Anacardiaceae
maranta, yuquilla	*Maranta arundinaceae*	arrowroot	Marantaceae
mata (de) gallina, yerba mora	*Solanum americanum*	black nightshade	Solanaceae
maya	*Bromelia pingüin*	wild pineapple	Bromeliaceae
mejorana	*Origanum marjorana*	marjoram	Labiatae
melisa, toronjil	*Melisa officinalis*	lemon balm	Labiatae
menta	*Menta piperata*	peppermint	Labiatae
molinillo, botón de cadete	*Leonotis nepetifolia*	lion's ear, hollow stalk, shandilay	Labiatae
morera	*Morus nigra*	(black) mulberry	Moraceae
moriviv
í	*Mimosa pudica*	sensitive plant	Mimosaceae

PUERTO RICAN NAMES	SCIENTIFIC NAMES	ENGLISH NAMES	BOTANICAL FAMILIES
ñame	*Dioscorea alata*	Mexican yam, tropical yam	Dioscoreaceae
naranjo (agrio)	*Citrus aurantium*	sour orange	Rutaceae
nuez moscada, nemoscá	*Myristica fragrans* *Ocotea moschata*	nutmeg, Puerto Rican nutmeg	Myristicaceae " "
orégano chiquito	*Lippia micromera*	Puerto Rican oregano	Verbenaceae
ortiga brava	*Urera baccifera*	(giant) stinging nettle	Urticaceae
pacholí, baúl de pobre	*Vetiveria zizanioides*	vetiver	Gramineae
pajuil, marañon	*Anacardium occidentale*	cashew	Anacardiaceae
paletaria, prenetaria, alumbre, frescura	*Peperomia pellucida*	shine bush, ice'n glass, silver bush	Piperaceae
palmacristi, higuereta, ricino	*Ricinis comunis*	castor bean, palma Christi	Euphorbiaceae
palma de coco, cocotero	*Cocos nucifera*	coconut palm	Palmaceae
palma real, palma de yaguas	*Roystonea borinquena*	Puerto Rican royal palm	Palmaceae
pana, panapén, mapén	*Arctocarpus altilis*	breadfruit	Moraceae
papa	*Solanum tuberosum*	potato	Solanaceae
papaya, lechosa	*Carica papaya*	papaya	Caricaceae

Plants by Name and Family (Spanish)

PUERTO RICAN NAMES	SCIENTIFIC NAMES	ENGLISH NAMES	BOTANICAL FAMILIES
parcha, maracuyá	*Passiflora edulis*	passion fruit, bell apple, water lemon fruit	Passifloraceae
pascua	*Euphorbia pulcherrima*	poinsettia	Euphorbiaceae
pata de perro, cadillo de fibra	*Urena lobata*	bur	Malvaceae
pazote	*Chenopodium ambrosioides*	wormseed	Chenopodiaceae
péndula, bálsamo	*Citharexylum fruticosum*	fiddlewood	Rubiaceae
pimienta Angola, dragón	*Alpinia zerumbet*	shell plant	Zingiberaceae
piñon, tártago	*Jatropha curcas*	physic nut	Euphorbiaceae
playera	*Catharanthus roseus*	Madagascar periwinkle	Apocynaceae
poleo	*Lippia stoechadifolia*		Verbenaceae
prenetaria, paletaria, alumbre, frescura	*Peperomia pellucida*	shine bush, ice'n glass, silver bush	Piperaceae
pringamoza	*Tragia volubilis*	stinging vine	Euphorbiaceae
quinino del pobre, viernes santo	*Phyllanthus niruri*	gale of the wind	Euphorbiaceae
rábano cimarrón	*Dieffenbachia seguine*	dumb cane	Araceae
recao, culantro del monte	*Eryngium foetidum*	broad leaf coriander, fitweed	Umbelliferae

PUERTO RICAN NAMES	SCIENTIFIC NAMES	ENGLISH NAMES	BOTANICAL FAMILIES
ricino, higuereta, palmacristi	*Ricinus comunis*	castor bean plant, palma Christi	Euphorbiaceae
roble amarillo, saúco amarillo	*Tecoma stans*	yellow trumpet, ginger Thomas	Bignoniaceae
romero	*Rosmarinus officinalis*	rosemary	Labiatae
rompecota	*Scleria spp.*	sawgrass	Cyperaceae
rompe zaragüey, santa María	*Eupatorium odoratum*	bitter bush	Compoitae
rosa cienhojas	*Rosa centifolia*	fairy rose	Rosaceae
ruda	*Ruta chalepensis*	rue, garden rue	Rutaceae
sábila, zábila	*Aloe spp.*	aloe, semper vivy	Liliaceae
sacabuche	*Physalis spp.*	ground cherry	Solanaceae
salvia (olorosa)	*Pluchea symphytifolia*	sweet scent, cattle tongue	Compositae
sanguinaria	*Rhoeo spathacea*	oyster plant	Commelinaceae
santa María, rompe zaragüey	*Eupatorium odoratum*	bitter bush	Compositae
saúco amarillo, roble amarillo	*Tecoma stans*	yellow trumpet, ginger Thomas	Bignoniaceae
saúco blanco	*Sambucus mexicana*	(Mexican) elder, sirrio	Caprifoliaceae
siempreviva, bruja, yerba bruja	*Kalanchoe pinnatum*	life plant	Crassulaceae
suelda consuelda	*Anredera leptostachys*	Madeira vine	Basellaceae
tabaco	*Nicotiana tabacum*	tobacco	Solanaceae

Plants by Name and Family (Spanish)

PUERTO RICAN NAMES	SCIENTIFIC NAMES	ENGLISH NAMES	BOTANICAL FAMILIES
talantro, talantalán, talantrillo	*Senna alata*	ringworm tree	Caesalpiniaceae
tamarindo	*Tamarindus indica*	tamarind	Caesalpiniaceae
tártago, piñón	*Jatropha curcas*	physic nut	Euphorbiaceae
tautúa, tuatúa	*Jatropha gossypifolia*	wild physic nut, belly ache bush, body cata	Euphorbiaceae
tente en el aire	*Cassytha filiformis*	love vine	Lauraceae
tilo (árbol)	*Tilia spp.*	linden	Tiliaceae
tilo (mata), curía	*Justicia pectoralis*	green balsam, carpenter's grass	Acanthaceae
tolú	*Myroxylon balsamum*	(tolu) balsam	Fabaceae
tomate	*Lycopersicon lycopersicum*	tomato	Solanaceae
toronjil, melisa	*Melisa officinalis*	lemon balm	Labiatae
tuatúa, tautúa	*Jatropha gossypifolia*	wild physic nut, belly ache bush, body cata	Euphorbiaceae
tuna	*Opuntia ficus-indica*	spineless tuna cactus	Cactaceae
valeriana	*Valeriana scandens*	valerian	Valerianaceae
vara prieta, capá prieto	*Cordia alliodora*	Spanish elm	Boraginaceae
verbena	*Stachytarpheta jamaicensis*	Caribbean vervain, worry vine	Verbenaceae

PUERTO RICAN NAMES	SCIENTIFIC NAMES	ENGLISH NAMES	BOTANICAL FAMILIES
verdolaga	*Portulaca oleracea*	purslane	Portulacaceae
viernes santo, quinino del pobre	*Phyllanthus niruri*	gale of the wind	Euphorbiaceae
yapaná, curía panacea	*Eupatorium triplinerve*	japana	Compositae
yautía	*Xanthosoma sagittifolium*	tanier, yautía	Araceae
yerba bruja, siempreviva, bruja	*Kalanchoe pinnatum*	life plant	Crassulaceae
yerba buena	*Mentha nemorosa*	Caribbean spearmint, red mint	Labiatae
yerba cangá	*Ludwigia octovalvis*	primrose willow	Onagraceae
yerba dulce	*Lippia dulcis*	sweet verbena	Verbenaceae
yerba de Guinea	*Panicum maximum*	guinea grass	Gramineae
yerba Luisa	*Aloysia triphylla*	lemon vervain	Verbenaceae
yerba mora, mata (de) gallina	*Solanum*	black nightshade *americanum*	Solanaceae
yuca	*Manihot esculenta*	cassava	Marantaceae
yuquilla, maranta	*Maranta arundinaceae*	arrowroot	Marantaceae
zábila, sábila	*Aloe spp.*	aloe, semper vivy	Liliaceae
zanahoria	*Daucus carota*	carrot	Umbelliferae

Plants by Name and Family

The plants mentioned in this volume (specifically, those used in Puerto Rico) are herein presented in alphabetical order according to their names in English.*

INDEX II

*Index I, on page 219, is organized in alphabetical order, by Spanish.

ENGLISH NAMES	SCIENTIFIC NAMES	PUERTO RICAN NAMES	BOTANICAL FAMILIES
almond (tropical)	*Terminalia catappa*	almendro	Combretaceae
aloe, semper vivy	*Aloe spp.*	sábila, zábila	Liliaceae
amaranth (white), calaloo,	*Amaranthus viridis*	blero, bledo, espinaca criolla	Amaranthaceae
anise (seed)	*Pimpinella anisum*	anís, anís de grano	Umbelliferae
annato	*Bixa orellana*	achiote, bija	Bixaceae
arnica	*Arnica montana*	árnica	Compositae
arrowroot	*Maranta arundinacea*	maranta, yuquilla pitsilén	Marantaceae
avocado	*Persea americana*	aguacate	Lauraceae

ENGLISH NAMES	SCIENTIFIC NAMES	PUERTO RICAN NAMES	BOTANICAL FAMILIES
balsam (tolu)	*Myroxylon balsamum*	tolú	Fabaceae
banana	*Musa spp.*	guineo	Musaceae
Barbados pride, dul dul	*Caesalpinia pulcherrima*	clavellina	Caesalpiniaceae
basil	*Ocimum basilicum*	albahaca blanca	Labiatae
bay rum	*Pimenta racemosa*	malagueta	Myrtaceae
bell apple, passion fruit, water lemon fruit	*Passiflora edulis*	parcha, maracuyá	Passifloraceae
belly ache bush, body cata, wild physic nut	*Jatropha gossypifolia*	tautúa, tuatúa	Euphorbiaceae
bitter bush	*Eupatorium odoratum*	santa María, rompe zaragüey	Compositae
bitter ginger	*Zingiber zerumbet*	jengibre amargo	Zingiberaceae
bitter mint		gran señora	Labiatae
black night-shade	*Solanum americanum*	yerba mora, mata (de) gallina	Solanaceae
black wattle, jointwood, soot	*Piper marginatum*	higuillo oloroso	Piperaceae
body cata, belly ache bush, wild physic nut	*Jatropha gossypifolia*	tautúa, tuatúa	Euphorbiaceae
bowstring hemp, snake plant	*Sansevieria metallica*	chucho, cocuisa	Liliaceae
breadfruit	*Arctocarpus altilis*	pana, panapén, mapén	Moraceae

Plants by Name and Family (English)

ENGLISH NAMES	SCIENTIFIC NAMES	PUERTO RICAN NAMES	BOTANICAL FAMILIES
broad leaf coriander, fitweed	*Eryngium foetidum*	recao, culantro del monte	Umbelliferae
broad leaf or common plantain	*Plantago major*	llantén	Plantaginaceae
bullock's heart, custard apple	*Annona reticulata*	corazón	Annonaceae
bur	*Urena lobata*	cadillo de fibra, pata de perro	Malvaceae
calabash, gourd	*Crescentia cujete*	higüera	Bignoniaceae
calaloo, white Amaranthaceae amaranth	*Amaranthus viridis*	blero, bledo, espinaca criolla	
camphor	*Cinnamomum camphora*	alcanfor	Myrtaceae
Caribbean mugwort, ragweed	*Ambrosia peruviana*	altamisa, artemisa	Compositae
Caribbean spearmint, red mint	*Mentha nemorosa*	yerba buena	Labiatae
Caribbean vervain, worry vine	*Stachytarpheta jamaicensis*	verbena	Verbenaceae
carpenter's grass, green balsam	*Justicia pectoralis*	curía	Acanthaceae
carrot	*Daucus carota*	zanahoria	Umbelliferae

ENGLISH NAMES	SCIENTIFIC NAMES	PUERTO RICAN NAMES	BOTANICAL FAMILIES
cashew	*Anacardium occidentale*	pajuil, marañon	Anacardaceae
cassava	*Manihot esculenta*	yuca	Marantaceae
castor bean plant, palma Christi	*Ricinus comunis*	higuereta, ricino, palmacristi	Euphorbiaceae
cattle tongue, sweet scent	*Pluchea symphytifolia*	salvia	Compositae
celeriac	*Apium graveolens*	apio	Umbelliferae
chamomile (Roman & German, resp.)	*Anthemis nobilis Matricaria recutita*	manzanilla	Compositae " "
cinnamon	*Cinnamomum zeylanicum*	canela	Lauraceae
clove	*Syzygium aromaticum*	clavo de especia, clavo dulce	Myrtaceae
cocillana	*Guarea rusbi*	cocillana	Meliaceae
coconut palm	*Cocos nucifera*	coconut palm	Palmaceae
coco plum Chripobalanceae	*Chrysolbalanus icaco*	hicaco	
coffee	*Coffea arabica*	café	Rubiaceae
coffee senna Caesalpiniaceae	*Senna occidentalis*	hidionda chiquita	
comfrey	*Symphytum officinalis*	consuelda mayor	Boraginaceae
common or broadleaf plantain	*Plantago major*	llantén	Plantaginaceae

Plants by Name and Family (English)

ENGLISH NAMES	SCIENTIFIC NAMES	PUERTO RICAN NAMES	BOTANICAL FAMILIES
congo root, garlic weed	*Petiveria alliaceae*	anamú	Phytolaccaceae
coriander	*Coriandrum sativum*	cilantrillo, chincha	Umbelliferae
corn	*Zea mays*	maíz	Gramineae
custard apple, bullock's heart	*Annona reticulata*	corazón	Annonaceae
dasheen, taro	*Colocasia esculenta*	malanga	Araceae
dul dul, Barbados pride	*Caesalpinia pulcherrima*	clavellina	Caesalpiniaceae
dumb cane	*Dieffenbachea seguine*	rábano cimarrón	Araceae
elder	*Sambucus mexicana*	saúco (blanco)	Caprifoliaceae
eucalyptus	*Eucalyptus spp.*	eucalipto	Myrtaceae
(fairy) rose	*Rosa centifolia*	rosa cienhojas	Rosaceae
fennel	*Foeniculum vulgare*	hinojo	Umbelliferae
feverfew	*Chrisanthemum parthenium* or *Tanacetum parthenium*	manzanilla	Compositae
fiddlewood	*Citharexylum fruticosum*	bálsamo, péndula	Rubiaceae
fitweed, broadleaf coriander	*Eryngium foetidum*	recao, culantro del monte	Umbelliferae
fragrant geranium	*Pelargonium odoratissium*	geranio oloroso	Geraniaceae
French weed	*Commelina spp.*	cohitre	Commelinaceae

ENGLISH NAMES	SCIENTIFIC NAMES	PUERTO RICAN NAMES	BOTANICAL FAMILIES
gale of the wind	*Phllyanthus niruri*	quinino de pobre, viernes santo	Euphorbiaceae
garlic	*Allium sativum*	ajo	Liliaceae
garlic weed, congo root	*Petiveria alliacea*	anamú	Phytolaccaceae
genipap	*Genipa americana*	jagua	Rubiaceae
geranium (fragrant)	*Pelargonium odoratissium*	geranio oloroso	Geraniaceae
ginger	*Zingiber officinale*	jengibre dulce, jengibre del país	Zingiberaceae
ginger (bitter)	*Zingiber zerumbet*	jengibre amargo	Zingiberaceae
ginger Thomas, yellow trumpet	*Tecoma stans*	saúco amarillo, roble amarillo	Bignoniaceae
gourd, calabash	*Crescentia cujete*	higüera	Bignoniaceae
gourd (musical)	*Lagenaria siceraria*	güiro, güícharo	Cucurbitaceae
green balsam, carpenter's grass	*Justicia pectoralis*	curía	Acanthaceae
ground cherry	*Physalis spp.*	sacabuche	Solanaceae
guaco	*Mikania spp.*	guaco	Compositae
guava	*Psidium guajava*	guayabo	Myrtaceae
guinea grass	*Panicum maxicum*	yerba guinea	Gramineae
hollow stalk, lion's ear, shandilay	*Leonotis nepetifolia*	botón de cadete, molinillo	Labiatae

Plants by Name and Family (English)

ENGLISH NAMES	SCIENTIFIC NAMES	PUERTO RICAN NAMES	BOTANICAL FAMILIES
ice'n glass, shine bush, silver bush	*Peperomia pellucida*	paletaria, alumbre, frescura, prenetaria	Piperaceae
iron grass	*Borreria laevis*	Juana la blanca	Rubiaceae
japana	*Eupatorium triplinerve*	yapaná, curía panacea	Compositae
jointwood, soot soot, black wattle	*Piper marginatum*	higuillo oloroso	Piperaceae
kale	*Brassica oleracea*	col blanca	Cruciferae
kapok, silk cotton tree	*Ceiba pentandra*	ceiba	Bombacaceae
lemon	*Citrus limon*	limón	Rutaceae
lemon balm	*Melisa officinalis*	melisa, toronjil	Labiatae
lemon grass	*Cymbopogon citratus*	limoncillo	Gramineae
lemon verbena	*Aloysia triphylla*	yerba Luisa	Verbenaceae
life plant	*Kalanchoe pinnatum*	bruja, siempreviva yerba bruja	Crassulaceae
lignum vitae, pockwood	*Guaiacum officinale*	guayacán	Zygophyllaceae
linden	*Tilia spp*	tilo	Tiliaceae
lion's ear, hollow stalk, shandilay	*Leonotis nepetifolia*	botón de cadete, molinillo	Labiatae
love vine	*Cassytha filiformis*	afilerillo, tente en el aire	Lauraceae

ENGLISH NAMES	SCIENTIFIC NAMES	PUERTO RICAN NAMES	BOTANICAL FAMILIES
Madagascar periwinkle	*Catharanthus roseus*	playera	Apocynaceae
Madeira vine	*Anredera leptostachys*	suelda consuelda	Basellaceae
maga wood	*Montezuma grandiflora*	maga	Malvaceae
mallow	*Malachra capitata*	malva	Malvaceae
mango	*Mangifera indica*	mangó	Anacardiaceae
marjoram	*Origanum marjorana*	mejorana	Labiatae
Mexican yam, tropical yam	*Dioscorea alata*	ñame	Dioscoreaceae
monkey's hand	*Lepianthes peltatum*	baquiña (cerrada)	Piperaceae
moon plant	*Datura suaveolens*	campano	Solanaceae
mulberry (black)	*Morus nigra*	morera	Moraceae
nettle (giant stinging)	*Urera baccifera*	ortiga brava	Urticaceae
nutmeg	*Myristica fragrans*	nuez moscada, nemoscá	Myristicaceae
onion	*Allium cepa*	cebolla	Liliaceae
orange (sour)	*Citrus aurantium*	naranjo (agrio)	Rutaceae
orange (sweet)	*Citrus sinensis*	china, naranjo dulce	Rutaceae
oregano (PR)	*Lippia micromera*	orégano	Verbenaceae
oyster plant	*Rhoeo spathacea*	sanguinaria	Commelinaceae

Plants by Name and Family (English)

ENGLISH NAMES	SCIENTIFIC NAMES	PUERTO RICAN NAMES	BOTANICAL FAMILIES
palma Christi, castor bean	*Ricinus comunis*	higuereta, ricino, palmacristi	Euphorbiaceae
Panama tree	*Sterculia apetala*	anacagüita	Sterculiaceae
papaya	*Carica papaya*	papaya, lechosa	Caricaceae
passion fruit, bell apple, water lemon fruit	*Passiflora edulis*	parcha, maracuyá	Passifloraceae
peppermint	*Mentha piperata*	menta	Labiatae
periwinkle (Madagascar)	*Catharanthus roseus*	playera	Apocynaceae
physic nut, piñon	*Jatropha curcas*	tártago	Euphorbiaceae
pigeon pea	*Cajanus cajan*	gandul	Fabaceae
plantain (common or broadleaf)	*Plantago major*	llantén	Plantaginaceae
pockwood, lignum vitae	*Guaiacum officinale*	guayacán	Zygophyllaceae
poinsettia	*Euphorbia pulcherrima*	pascua	Euphorbiaceae
potato	*Solanum tuberosum*	papa	Solanaceae
primrose willow	*Ludwigia octovalvis*	yerba cangá	Onagraceae
Puerto Rican nutmeg	*Ocotea moschata*	nemoscá	Myristicaceae
Puerto Rican oregano	*Lippia micromera*	orégano	Verbenaceae

ENGLISH NAMES	SCIENTIFIC NAMES	PUERTO RICAN NAMES	BOTANICAL FAMILIES
Puerto Rican royal palm	*Roystonea borinquena*	palma real, palma de yaguas	Palmaceae
pumpkin	*Cucurbita moschata*	calabaza	Cucurbitaceae
purging cassia	*Cassia fistula*	cañafístula	Caesalpiniaceae
purslane	*Portulaca oleracea*	verdolaga	Portulacaceae
ragweed, Caribbean mugwort	*Ambrosia peruviana*	artemisa, altamisa	Compositae
red mint, Caribbean spearmint	*Mentha nemorosa*	yerba buena	Labiatae
red sage, yellow sage	*Lantana camara*	cariaquillo	Verbenaceae
rice	*Oryza sativa*	arroz	Gramineae
ringworm tree	*Senna alata*	talantro, talantalán, talantrillo	Caesalpiniaceae
rose (fairy)	*Rosa centifolia*	rosa cienhojas	Rosaceae
rosemary	*Rosmarinus officinalis*	romero	Labiatae
royal palm (Puerto Rican)	*Roystonea borinquena*	palma real, palma de yaguas	Palmaceae
rue	*Ruta chalepensis*	ruda	Rutaceae
sawgrass	*Scleria spp.*	rompecota	Cyperaceae
semper vivy, aloe	*Aloe spp.*	sábila, zábila	Liliaceae
sensitive plant	*Mimosa pudica*	moriviví	Mimosaceae

Plants by Name and Family (English)

ENGLISH NAMES	SCIENTIFIC NAMES	PUERTO RICAN NAMES	BOTANICAL FAMILIES
sesame	*Sesamum indicum*	ajonjolí	Pedaliaceae
shandilay, lion's ear, hollow stalk	*Leonotis nepetifolia*	botón de cadete, molinillo	Labiatae
shell plant	*Alpinia zerumbet*	pimienta Angola, dragón	Zingiberaceae
shine bush, silver bush, ice'n glass	*Peperomia pellucida*	paletaria, alumbre, frescura, prenetaria	Piperaceae
silk cotton tree, kapok	*Ceiba pentandra*	ceiba	Bombacaceae
sirrio, elder	*Sambucus mexicana*	saúco blanco	Caprifoliaceae
slipper plant	*Pedilanthus tithymaloides*	ipecacuana	Euphorbiaceae
snake plant, bowstring hemp	*Sansevieria metallica*	chucho, cocuisa	Liliaceae
soap bush, wire weed	*Sida spp.*	escobilla, escoba blanca	Malvaceae
soot soot, black wattle, jointwood	*Piper marginatum*	higuillo oloroso	Piperaceae
sorossie, wild balsam apple	*Momordica charantia*	cundeamor	Cucurbitaceae
sour orange	*Citrus aurantium*	naranjo (agrio)	Rutaceae
soursop	*Annona muricata*	guanábana	Annonaceae
Spanish elm	*Cordia alliodora*	capá prieto, vara prieta	Boraginaceae

ENGLISH NAMES	SCIENTIFIC NAMES	PUERTO RICAN NAMES	BOTANICAL FAMILIES
spearmint (Caribbean), red mint	*Mentha nemorosa*	yerba buena	Labiatae
spineless (tuna) cactus	*Opuntia ficus-indica*	tuna	Cactaceae
star anise	*Illicium anisatum*	anís de estrella	Magnoliaceae
star apple	*Chrysophyllum cainito*	caimito	Sapotaceae
stinging nettle (giant)	*Urera baccifera*	ortiga brava	Urticaceae
stinging vine	*Tragia volubilis*	pringamoza	Euphorbiaceae
stipti	*Senecio aizoides*	malá (blanca)	Compositae
sugar cane	*Saccharum officinarum*	caña de azúcar	Gramineae
sweet scent, cattle tongue	*Pluchea symphytifolia*	salvia	Compositae
sweet orange	*Citrus sinensis*	china	Rutaceae
sweet verbena	*Lippia dulcis*	yerba dulce	Verbenaceae
tamarind	*Tamarindus indica*	tamarindo	Caesalpiniaceae
tanier	*Xanthosoma sagittifolium*	yautía	Araceae
taro, dasheen	*Colocasia esculenta*	malanga	Araceae
tobacco	*Nicotiana tabacum*	tabaco	Solanaceae
tomato	*Lycopersicon lycopersicum*	tomate	Solanaceae

Plants by Name and Family (English)

ENGLISH NAMES	SCIENTIFIC NAMES	PUERTO RICAN NAMES	BOTANICAL FAMILIES
tropical almond	*Terminalia catappa*	almendro	Combretaceae
tropical yam, Mexican yam	*Dioscorea alata*	ñame	Dioscoreaceae
tuberose	*Polianthes tuberosa*	azucena antillana	Amaryllidaceae
tuna cactus (spineless)	*Opuntia ficus-indica*	tuna	Cactaceae
valerian	*Valeriana scandens*	valeriana	Valerianaceae
vervain (Caribbean)	*Stachytarpheta jamaicensis*	verbena	Verbenaceae
vetiver	*Vetiveria zizanioides*	pacholí, baúl del pobre	Gramineae
watercress	*Nasturtium officinale*	berro	Cruciferae
water lemon fruit, bell apple, passion fruit	*Passiflora edulis*	parcha, maracuyá	Passifloraceae
white ama-ranth, calaloo	*Amaranthus viridis*	blero, bledo, espinaca criolla	Amaranthaceae
wild balsam apple	*Momordica charantia*	cundeamor	Cucurbitaceae
wild eggplant	*Solanum torvum*	berenjena cimarrona	Solanaceae
wild lettuce	*Lactuca intybacea*	(a)chicoria	Compositae
wild physic nut, body cata, belly ache bush	*Jatropha gossypifolia*	tautúa, tuatúa	Euphorbiaceae
wild pineapple	*Bromelia pingüin*	maya	Bromeliaceae

ENGLISH NAMES	SCIENTIFIC NAMES	PUERTO RICAN NAMES	BOTANICAL FAMILIES
wild zinnia	*Zinnia peruviana*	esopetón	Compositae
wire weed, soap bush	*Sida spp.*	escobilla, escoba blanca	Malvaceae
witch hazel	*Hamamelis virginiana*	hamamelis	Hamamelidaceae
wormseed	*Chenopodium ambrosioides*	pazote	Chenopodiaceae
worry vine, Caribbean vervain	*Stachytarpheta jamaicensis*	verbena	Verbenaceae
yam (Mexican, tropical)	*Dioscorea alata*	ñame	Dioscoreaceae
yellow allamanda	*Allamanda cathartica*	canario amarillo	Apocynaceae
yellow elder, yellow trumpet	*Tacoma stans* roble amarillo	saúco amarillo,	Bibnoniaceae
yellow mombin	*Spondias dulcis*	jobo	Anacardiaceae
yellow sage, red sage	*Lantana camara*	cariaquillo	Verbenaceae
yellow trumpet, yellow elder	*Tacoma stans*	saúco amarillo, roble amarillo	Bibnoniaceae
zinnia (wild)	*Zinnia peruviana*	esopetón	Compositae

A Glossary of
Spanish and Puerto Rican
Words and Expressions
used in this book

abuelita: an affectionate way of saying *abuela,* grandma.

aceituna: olive.

alcoholado: an cooling analgesic infusion of herbs in dilute rubbing alcohol, used for rubdowns and massages.

al sereno: placed out of doors from sunset to sunrise, in order to absorb the cool, moist energy of the night.

apio: celeriac root.

arroz con dulce: also known as *arroz con coco,* this is a sweet, sliceable, coconut-rice pudding, seasoned with cloves, cinnamon, ginger, vanilla, raisins and other delectables.

arroz con gandules: one of Puerto Rico's national dishes, this is a mixture of rice with pigeon peas spiced with local condiments.

ay bendito: an expression that appeals to the sympathy of the Puerto Rican heart. In its most common usage, it could roughly be translated as "pretty please," or "for the love of God . . . " But it could also mean, simply, "poor thing."

bacalao con pana: salted codfish served with velvety-smooth (incomparable!) breadfruit.

barrio: translated as "neighborhood" in urban North America, in Puerto Rico this word most often denotes a rural community.

bendición: literally, "blessing." It usually takes the form of a hello and goodby greeting such as "May God bless you and protect you always." Traditionally, children (at any age) ask for the *bendición* from their parents and other elders at every meeting and leave-taking.

bomba, plena and *salsa: Bomba* and *plena* are African-derived musical forms developed in the coastal towns of Puerto Rico. Both are characterized by call and response song patterns and popular themes ranging from historical events and social commentary to discussions of the musical event in progress. *Bomba* is typically played with three barrel-shaped drums, one of which responds to song lyrics and the movements of solo dancers. *Plena* is typically played at sports events, social protests and festivals with three or four hand drums or *panderetas* and a *güiro* (a scored gourd scraped in time). *Salsa* or *mambo* is a popular dance form based on a complex of Afro-cuban and jazz rhythms, played by a full band of instruments including percussion, brass, piano, reeds, etc.

campesina(o): often translated as "peasant," this word most accurately describes a rural subsistence farmer. See *jíbaro.*

como Dios manda: as God intended.

coquí: a small island tree frog which, during the night, sings a gentle, high-pitched version of his name. Native only to Puerto Rico — and reportedly unable to survive in any other environment — the *coquí* (*Eleutherodactylus spp.*) has become a symbol of the importance of maintaining Puerto Rico's ecological balance and cultural integrity.

don, doña: titles of respect used for older men and women.

dulce de coco: a soft candy made from grated coconut, brown sugar, ginger and other spices.

espiritista: a diviner and spiritual healer, usually a medium. Most often, a member of the popular religious *espiritista* sect that holds meetings in order to do divination, healings and exorcisms involving communication with the world beyond.

guaraguao (Buteo jamaicensis): a hawk common in the mountainous regions of Puerto Rico.

guarapo, té, tesito, tesesito: a traditional medicinal tea. See page 171 for details.

jíbaro: the proud, independent and capable agricultural people of the Puerto Rican countryside. Also, in popular usage, a "country bumpkin" who has yet to learn the street-wise ways of urban life.

le lo lai: folk music of the Puerto Rican mountains, with an emphasis on stringed instruments such as the guitar and the ten-stringed *cuatro*. Time is kept by scraping a scored gourd, known as the *güiro*. Lyrics are most often written in the form of *décimas*, (10-line poems, 8 syllables per line, typically with a rhyme scheme of ABBAACCDDC. Performance of *le lo lai* often involves a great deal of improvisation.

mauí: a traditional, fermented island "root beer" made from the bark and roots of the mabí tree *(Colubrina spp.)*. Besides being a popular beverage, it is also considered to have medicinal qualities.

menorativa, menjunje: a boiled tea or potion made with more than three, and up to a dozen or more ingredients.

pasteles: a popular island dish (similar to Central American corn *tamales*) but made of green plantain and other starchy vegetables, and stuffed with meat, olives, sometimes chickpeas and raisins. They are wrapped in softened banana leaves and boiled before serving. Variations include rice, cabbage-wrapped, and vegetarian *pasteles*.

pitirre (Tyrannus dominicensis): a small bird, native to Puerto Rico, and famous for its courage and ferocity. This flycatcher attacks and even wins territorial battles with the relatively enormous hawks. The *pitirre* is often used to symbolize Puerto Rico's nationalist struggle.

pollo guisado con papas: stewed chicken with potatoes and spices.

pueblo: a village or township. Also, the general population of a country or region.

refresco de guanábana: a thick, chilled drink made of the soursop or *guanábana* fruit, water or milk, perhaps a sweetener, and ice.

rellenos de papa: potato dough stuffed with meat, olives and sometimes raisins, then fried to a crisp, golden brown.

Sabana Grande: located in southwestern Puerto Rico, this town is the site of a 20th century appearance of the Blessed Virgin Mary.

San Germán and Maricao: two towns to the south and east of Mayagüez, respectively.

sancocho: a satisfying stew featuring several types of viandas, other vegetables and one or more types of meat.

santiguo: one of many types of spiritual massage, the *santiguo* is generally limited to the stomach and abdominal area, and is most often used to ease the passage of fermented and often hardened food material found to be congesting the digestive system.

sofrito: the source of authentic island flavor, *el sofrito* is the first and most important step in for cooking meats, beans or colored rice. A typical *sofrito* includes onion, garlic and other condiments, sauteed in olive oil. The main ingredients are then added to this base.

viandas: starchy vegetables such as cassava, tropical yam, tanier, taro, breadfruit, potatoes, green plantains and bananas.

A Bilingual Subject Guide*

*In order to avoid repetition, when a plant or other theme has been mentioned as part of an interview and also as part of the remedy reference (pages 175-217), only the latter entry is noted.

The last (italicized) page number noted for each plant corresponds to its listing by name and botanical family, pages 219-244.

achicoria (wild lettuce)   178, 199, *219*

achiote (annato)   154, 188, 202, 210, *219*

Africa(n)   57-58, 69, 70, 71, 75, 246

Agua Maravilla, hamamelis (witch hazel)   178, 179, 180, 183, 189, 202, *223*

aguacate (avocado)   181, 191, *219*

Aguarrás   177, 210

ajo (garlic)   xiii, 175, 176, 179, 203, 204, 207, 209, *219*

ajonjolí (sesame)   163, 175, 186, *219*

albahaca (basil)   177, 179, 182, 194, 196, 200, 207, *219*

alcanfor (camphor)   165, 176, 177, 178, 183, 199, 203, 206, 208, 209, *219*

alcohol addiction   175

alcohol for external use (*alcoholado*) 173, 176, 177, 178, 183, 209, 211

alfilerillo, tente en el aire (love vine)   140, *219*

alkaloids   xiii, xiv

Allamanda cathartica   (See *canario amarillo* or yellow allamanda.)

allergies   176

Allium cepa   (See *cebolla* or onion.)

Allium sativum   (See *ajo* or garlic.)

alluvial soil   197

almendro (tropical almond leaves)   194, *219*

almond leaves, tropical (*almendro*)   194, *231*

almond oil   177, 179, 185, 188

aloe *(sábila)*   xv, 163, 178, 179, 180, 182, 183, 186, 191, 192, 200, 201, 202, 211, 214, *231*

Aloe spp.   (See *sábila* or aloe.)

Aloysia triphylla   (See *yerba Luisa* or lemon verbena.)

Alpinia zerumbet   (See *dragón* or shell plant.)

altamisa (Caribbean mugwort)   181, 182, 183, *220*

Amaranthus viridis   (See *blero* or calaloo.)

Ambrosia peruviana   (See *altamisa* or Caribbean mugwort.)

ammonia *(amoníaco)*   176, 177, 210, 214

anacagüita   189, *220*

Anacardium occidentale   (See *pajuil* or cashew.)

anamú (garlic weed)   153, 163, 183, 184, 186, 206, 209, *220*

animal bites & insect stings   176, 193

anís de grano, anís de semilla   (anise)   178, 179, 187, 190, 198, 205, 206, 207, *220*

anise *(anís de grano)*   178, 179, 187, 190, 198, 205, 206, 207, *231*

anís de estrella (star anise)   178, 187, 190, 207, *220*

anisette   179

annato *(achiote)*   188, 202, 210, *231*

Annona muricata   (See *guanábana* or soursop.)

Annona reticulata   (See *corazón* or custard apple.)

Anredera leptostachys   (See *suelda consuelda* or Madeira vine.)

Anthemis nobilis   (See *manzanilla* or chamomile.)

Antoun, Mikhail, Ph.D.   164

Apium graveolens (See *apio* or celeriac root.)

Arctocarpus altilis   (See *pana* or breadfruit.)

apio (cereleriac root)   115, 159, *220*

arnica *(árnica)*   176, *231*

Arnica montana   (See *árnica* or arnica.)

arrowroot *(maranta)*   154, 205, 211, *231*

arroz (rice)   159, 191, 194, *220*

arthritis & rheumatism   176-177

ashes   193, 203, 204

asthma & lung congestion   177-180

avocado *(aguacate)*   181, 191, *231*

azucena antillana (tuberose)   184, 186, 217, *220*

balsam *(tolú)*   178, *232*

bálsamo (fiddlewood)   185, *220*

banana *(guineo)*   201, *232*

baquiña cerrada (monkey's hand)   163, 208, *220*

Barbados' pride *(clavellina)*   139, *232*

basil *(albahaca)*   177, 179, 182, 194, 196, 200, 207, *232*

baths for bodily aches, fever, spiritual cleansing and renewal, relaxation, good luck, etc.   *xv,* 173, 181-183

bay rum *(malagueta)*   28, 176, 177, 182, *232*

bees' wax   209

belladona ointment   187, 193, 206

belly ache bush *(túatúa)*   184, 204, 213, 214, *232*

bendición   159, *246*

berenjena cimarrona (wild eggplant)   193, 216, *220*

berro (watercress)   179, *220*

bitter bush *(santa María, rompe zaragüey)*   181, 183, *232*

bitter ginger *(jengibre amargo)*   209, *232*

<u>Bixa</u> <u>orellana</u> (See *achiote* or annato.)

black nightshade *(mata de gallina, yerba mora)*   176, 194, 199, 204, 208, 213, 216, *232*

bladder *&* urinary tract   216

bleeding   203

blero, espincaca criolla (calaloo)   176, 208, *220*

blood stains   183

blood pressure   203-204

boils *&* external cysts   184

bomba   159, *246*

<u>Borreria</u> <u>laevis</u> (See *Juana la blanca* or iron grass.)

botón de cadete, molinillo (lion's ear)   199, *221*

brandy   197

<u>Brassica</u> <u>oleracea</u> (See *col blanca* or kale.)

bread   188

breadfruit *(pana, panapén)*   115, 159, 185, 187, *232*

broad leaf coriander *(culantro del monte, recao)*   *xvi,* 194, 203, 203, 209, *233*

broken bones *&* sprains   184-185

<u>Bromelia</u> <u>pingüin</u> (See *maya* or wild pineapple.)

brown sugar   197

bruises, bumps   185

bruja, yerba bruja (life plant) 180, 195, *221*

bur *(cadillo de fibra)*   177, *233*

burns   185-186, 211

butter   185

cadillo de fibra, pata de perro (bur)   177, *221*

Caesalpinia pulcherrima (See *clavellina* or Barbados pride.)

café (coffee)   181, 190, 193, 198, 202, *221*

caimito (star apple)   194, *221*

Cajanus cajan   (See *gandul* or pigeon pea.)

calabash *(higüera)*   187-188, *233*

calabaza (pumpkin, squash)   212, *221*

calaloo, white amaranth *(blero, espinaca criolla)*   176, 208, *233*

callouses & corns   186

campana (moon plant)   182, 216, *221*

camphor *(alcanfor)*   165, 176, 177, 178, 183, 199, 203, 206, 208, 209, *233*

caña fístula (purging cassia)   191, 200, *221*

canario amarillo (yellow allamanda)   134, *221*

cancer   162, 186-187

Candida albicans   167

canela (cinnamon)   178, 189, *221*

cariaquillo (red sage)   182, 183, 189, *221*

Caribbean spearmint, red mint *(yerba buena)*   179, 180, 182, 183, 188, 195,199, 200, 204, 205, *233*

Caribbean vervain *(verbena)*   181, 182, 194, 198, 199, 201, 205, *233*

Carica papaya   (See *lechosa* or papaya.)

carpenter's grass *(curía)*   182, 199, 200, *233*

carrot *(zanahoria)*   200, *233*

cashew *(pajuil)*   194, *234*

cassava *(yuca)*   109, 115, 201, *234*

Cassia fistula   (See *caña fístula* or purging cassia.)

Cassytha filiformis   (See *afilerillo* or love vine.)

castor bean plant, palma Christi *(higuereta, ricino)*   181, 188, 190, 206, 211, 215, 216, *234*

castor oil   139

Catharanthus roseus   (See *playera* or Madagascar periwinkle)

Ceiba petandra   (See *ceiba* or kapok.)

celeriac root *(apio)*   115, 159, *234*

cebolla (onion)   213, *221*

ceiba (kapok)   134, *221*

chamomile *(manzanilla)*   186, 204, 205, 207, *234*

cheese   189

Chenopodium ambrosioides   (See *pazote* or wormseed.)

chewing gum   187

chicken   188, 197, 200

childbirth   187

china (orange)   200, *222*

chocolate   188

Chrisanthemum parthenium   (See *manazanilla* or feverfew.)

chromatography   xiv

Chrysolbalanus icaco   (See *hicaco* or coco plum.)

Chrysophyllum cainito   (See *caimito* or star apple.)

chucho (snake plant)   178, *222*

cilantrillo, chincha (coriander)   194, 203, 304, *222*

Cinnamomum camphora   (See *alcanfor* or camphor.)

Cinnamomum zeylanicum   (See *canela* or cinnamon.)

cinnamon *(canela)*   178, 189, *234*

circulation   188

Citharexylum fruticosum   (See *bálsamo* or fiddlewood.)

Citrus aurantium   (See *naranjo* or sour orange.)

Citrus limon   (See *limón* or lemon.)

Citrus sinensis   (See *china* or orange.)

clavellina (Barbados pride)   139, *222*

clavo dulce (clove)   178, 187, 189, *222*

clay   176

cloves *(clavos dulces)*   178, 187, 189, *234*

cocaine   166

cocillana   178, *222*

cockroaches   210

coco (coconut)   159, 178, 191, 200, 202, 205, 208, *222*

coconut *(coco)*   159, 178, 191, 200, 202, 205, 208, *234*

coco plum *(hicaco)*   194, *234*

Cocos nucifera   (See *coco* or coconut.)

Coffea arabica   (See *café* or coffee.)

coffee *(café)*   2, 4, 181, 190, 193, 198, 202, *234*

coffee senna *(hidionda chiquita)*   187, 189, 206, 207, 209, *234*

coffee substitute   189

cohitre (French weed)   179, 191, 192, 200, 208, 213, *222 col blanca* (kale)   190, *222*

colds   189-190

colic   190

Colocasia esculenta   (See *malanga* or taro.)

comfrey *(consuelda mayor)*   211, *234*

Commelina spp.   (See *cohitre* or French weed.)

common plantain *(llantén)*   176, 179, 186, 197, 198, 199, 203, 207, 208, 213, *234*

complexion   191

constipation   191-192

consuelda mayor (comfrey)   211, *222*

cooking oil (generally olive)   177, 178, 179, 185, 190, 191, 193, 196, 198, 202, 203, 204, 208, 209, 211

cooling, nourishing drinks   192

coquí   36, 246,

corazón (custard apple)   203, 205, *222*

Cordia alliodora   (See *vara prieta* or Spanish elm.)

coriander *(cilantrillo)*   194, 203, 204, *235*

Coriandrum sativum   (See *cilantrillo* or coriander.)

corn *(maíz)*   192, 210, *235*

corns & callouses   186

coughs   177-180

Crescentia cujete   (See *higüera* or calabash.)

Cucurbita moschata   (See *calabaza* or pumpkin.)

culantro del monte, recao (broadleaf coriander)   *xvi*, 194, 203, 203, 209, *222*

cundeamor (wild balsam apple)   xv, 163, 186, 194, 202, 211, 212, *222*

curía (carpenter's grass)   182, 199, 200, *222*

curía panacea, yapaná (japana)   190, *223*

custard apple *(corazón)*   203, 205, *235*

cuts, wounds & sores   193

Cymbopogon citratus   (See *limoncillo* or lemon grass.)

cysts & boils   184

dasheen, taro *(malanga)*   115, *235*

Datura suaveolens   (See *campana* or moon plant.)

Daucus carota   (See *zanahoria* or carrot.)

diabetes   193-194

Dieffenbachia seguine   (See *rábano cimarrón* or dumb cane.)

digestion   204-205
digitalis, digoxin, digitoxin, foxglove   166
Dioscorea alata   (See ñame or Mexican yam.)
diuretics   192
dove or pigeon broth   197
dragón, pimienta Angola (shell plant)   180, *223*
drug addiction   168, 175
drugs, research and development   xiii-xiv, 162, 164-168
dumb cane *(rábano cimarrón)*   212, *235*
dying   195

earache   195-196
ecology   x-xi, 160, 161
edema   196
eggs   184, 197
Einstein and the new physics   165-166
elder, Mexican *(saúco blanco)*   177, 190, 217, *235*
energy generation   159
ephedra   166
ergot (ergotina)   xiii, 165
Eryngium foetidum   (See *culantro del monte* or broadleaf coriander.)
escobilla (soap bush)   211, *223*
escopetón (zinnia)   180, *223*
espinaca criolla, blero (calaloo)   176, 208, *223*
espiritista   ix, 59-76, 247
essential oils   xiii, 163
eucalyptus *(eucalipto)*   176, 180, 181, 189, 200, *235*
Eucalyptus spp.   (See *eucalipto* or eucalyptus.)
Eupatorium odoratum   (See *santa María* or bitter bush.)
Eupatorium triplinerve   (See *yapaná, curía panacea* or japana.)
Euphorbia pulcherrima   (See *pascua* and poinsettia.)
exercise   188
eyes   196-197

fairy rose *(rosa cienhojas)*   197, *235*
fatigue & weakness   197
fennel *(hinojo)*   209, *235*
fertility   205
fertilizer   x-xi, 197-198

fever   198
feverfew *(manzanilla)*   179, 199, 200, 204, *235*
fiddlewood *(bálsamo)*   185, *235*
fleas   210
"flinches"   175
Florida water   183
Foeniculum vulgare   (See *hinojo* or fennel.)
folk medicine   ix, xi-xvi, 159-160, 166, 168-169
foxglove, digitalis   166
fragrant geranium *(geranio oloroso)*   199, *235*
flu   199-200
fowl's pip *(moquillo)*   200
foxglove, digitalis, digoxin, digitoxin   166
French weed *(cohitre)*   179, 191, 192, 200, 208, 213, *235*
fungus   211-212

gale of the wind *(quinino del pobre)*   199, *236*
gandul (pigeon pea)   159, 176, 194, 214, *223*
garlic *(ajo)*   xiii, 175, 176, 179, 203, 204, 207, 209, *236*
garlic weed *(anamú)*   163, 183, 184, 186, 206, 209, *236*
gas (intestinal)   206-207
genipa *(jagua)*   204, *236*
Genipa americana   (See *genipa* or jagua.)
geranio oloroso (geranium, fragrant)   199, *223*
geranium, fragrant *(geranio oloroso)*   199, *236*
ginger *(jengibre)*   177, 179, 181, 188, 189, 190, 207, 217, *236*
gran señora   198, 199, *223*
ground cherry *(sacabuche)*   181, *236*
guaco   193, *223*
Guaiacum officinale   (See *guayacán* or pockwood.)
guanábana (soursop)   159, 196, 204, 205, *223*
guaraguao   159, 247
guarapo (tea)   172
Guarea rusbyi   (See *cocillana*.)
guava *(guayabo)*   204, 205, *236*
guayabo (guava)   204, 205, *223*
guayacán (lignum vitae)   214, *223*
Guerrero, Oswaldo, Ph.D.   xiv, 161-162
Guinea grass *(yerba de guinea)*   148, *236*

guinea hen   177
guineo (banana)   201, *223*
güiro (gourd, musical)   105, 246, 247, *223*
gums & teeth   214-215

hair   201-202
hamamelis, Agua Maravilla (witch hazel solution) 178, 179, 180, 183, 189, 202, *223*
harvest   201
headaches   202-203
head lice   202, 210
hemorrhage   203
heart   203
hicaco (coco plum)   194, *223*
hidionda chiquita (coffee senna)   187, 189, 206, 207, 209, *224*
high blood pressure   203
higüera (calabash)   187-188, *224*
higuereta, ricino (castor bean plant, palma Christi)   181, 188, 190, 206, 211, 215, 216, *224*
higuillo oloroso (jointwood)   181, 182, *224*
hinojo (fennel)   209, *224*
Hodgkin's disease   162
honey *(miel de abejas)*   178, 179, 180, 189, 190, 192, 213, 217

ice'n glass *(prenetaria, paletaria)*   175, 179, 192, 200, 205, 208, 211, 216, *237*
<u>Illicium anisatum</u>   (See *anís de estrella* or star anise.)
indigestion   178, 204-205
infertility   205
inflammation   206
infusion   173
insect pests   210
insect stings   176
insomnia   206
Institute of Natural Products   168
internal pain   206
intestinal gas   206-207
intestinal parasites   207
ipecacuana (slipper plant)   178, 180, *224*

iron grass *(Juana la blanca)* 208, *237*

jagua (genipa) 204, *224*
japana *(yapaná, curía panacea)* 190, *237*
Jatropha curcas (See *tártago* or physic nut.)
Jatropha gossypifolia (See *tautúa* or wild physic nut.)
jengibre (ginger) 177, 179, 181, 188, 189, 190, 207, 217, *224*
jengibre amargo (bitter ginger) 209, *224*
jíbaro 117, 125, 126, 127, 246
jobo (yellow mombin) 189, *224*
jointwood *(higuillo oloroso)* 181, 182, *237*
Juana la blanca (iron grass) 208, *224*
Justicia pectoralis (See *curía* or carpenter's grass.)

Kalanchoe pinnatum (See *bruja* or life plant.)
kale *(col)* 190, *237*
kapok *(ceiba)* 134, *237*
kerosene 193
kidney pain & inflammation 207-208

labor (childbirth) 187-188
Lactuca intybacea (See *achicoria* or wild lettuce.)
Lagenaria siceraria (See *güiro* or gourd.)
Lantana camara (See *cariaquillo* or red sage.)
lechosa (papaya) 8, 180, 200, 207, *224*
le lo lai 159, 247
lemon *(limón)* 175, 176, 177, 179, 189, 190, 191, 194, 195, 200, 215, *237*
lemon balm *(melissa, toronjil)* 180, 204, 205, *237*
lemon grass *(limoncillo)* 194, 198, 200, 214, *237*
lemon verbena *(yerba Luisa)* 209, *237*
Leonotis nepetifolia (See *botón de cadete, molinillo* or lion's ear.)
Lepianthes peltatum (See *baquiña cerrada* or monkey's hand.)
lice (head) 202, 210
life plant *(bruja, yerba bruja)* 180, 195, *237*
lignum vitae *(guayacán)* 214, *237*
limón (lemon) 175, 176, 177, 179, 189, 190, 191, 194, 195, 200, 215, *224*
limoncillo (lemon grass) 194, 198, 200, 214, *224*

linden *(tilo)* 179, 186, *237*
lion's ear *(botón de cadete)* 199, *237*
Lippia dulcis (See *yerba dulce* or sweet verbena.)
Lippia micromera (See *orégano chiquito* or Puerto Rican oregano.)
Lippia stoechadifolia (See *poleo.)*
llantén (plantain) 176, 179, 186, 197, 198, 199, 203, 207, 208, 213, 224
love vine *(alfilerillo)* 140, *237*
Ludwigia octovalvis (See *yerba cangá* or primrose willow.)
lung congestion & asmtha 177-180
Lycopersicon lycopersicum (See *tomate* or tomato.)

Madagascar periwinkle *(playera)* 162, *238*
Madeira vine *(suelda consuelda)* 184-185, 193, *238*
maga (maga wood) 180, *224*
Magnolia splendens 162
maíz (corn) 192, 210, *224*
malá blanca (stipti) 148, 178, 193, 203, 215, *224*
malagueta (bay rum) 16, 28, 176, 177, 182, *224*
malanga (dasheen, taro) 4, 115, 167, *225*
malaria 167
mallow *(malva)* 184, 188, 191, 192, 208, 216, *238*
malva (mallow) 184, 188, 191, 192, 208, 216, *225*
Malachra capitata (See *malva* or mallow.)
maná canelón 200
Mangifera indica (See *mangó* or mango.)
mango *(mangó)* 181, 182, 204, *238*
Manihot esculenta (See *yuca* or cassava.)
manure 197, 198
manzanilla (chamomile or feverfew) 179, 186, 199, 200, 204, 205, 207, *225*
maracuyá, parcha (passion fruit) 163, 204, *225*
maranta (arrowroot) 205, 211, *225*
Maranta arundinaceae (See *maranta* or arrowroot.)
marjoram *(mejorana)* 177, 180, 182, 196, 217, *238*
mata (de) gallina, yerba mora (black nightshade) 176, 194, 199, 204, 208, 213, 216, *225*
Matricaria recutita (See *manzanilla* or chamomile.)
maya (wild pineapple) 189, *225*

mejorana (marjoram) 177, 180, 182, 196, 217, *225*

melisa, toronjil (lemon balm) 180, 204, 205, *225*

Melisa officinalis (See *melisa, toronjil* or lemon balm.)

menorativa, menjunje, menjurio 173

menstrual irregularities 209

menta (peppermint) 180, *225*

Mentha nemorosa (See *yerba buena* or Caribbean spearmint.)

Mentha piperata (See *menta* or peppermint.)

Mexican yam (*ñame*) 44, *238*

midwives 21-31, 124, 125

miel de abejas (honey) 178, 179, 180, 189, 190, 192, 213, 217

migraine 202-203

Mikania spp. (See *guaco.*)

milk 189, 195, 197, 217

Mimosa pudica (See *morivivī* or sensitive plant.)

mind, clear 189

molinillo, botón de cadete (lion's ear) 199, *225*

Momordica charantia (See *cundeamor* or wild balsam apple.)

monkey's hand (*baquiña cerrada*) 163, 208, *238*

Montezuma grandiflora (See *maga* or maga wood.)

moon xvi, 201

moon plant (*campano*) 182, 216, *238*

moquillo (fowl's pip) 200

morera (mulberry) 193, 200, *225*

morivivī (sensitive plant) 214, *225*

morphine 165

Morus nigra (See *morera* or mulberry.)

mosquitos 167

moths 210

mugwort, Caribbean (*altamisa*) 181, 182, 183, *233*

mulberry (*morera*) 193, 200, *238*

mumps & swollen glands 213

Musa spp. (See *guineo* or banana.)

muscle cramps and spasms 188, 209-210

music xii, 159, 246, 247

Myristica fragrans (See *nuez moscada, nemoscá* or nutmeg.)

Myroxylon balsamum (See *tolú* or balsam, tolú.)

ñame (Mexican yam) 44, *226*

naranjo (sour orange leaves) 175, 181, 182, 183, 186, 190, 198, 200, 203, 204, 205, 206, *226*

<u>*Nasturtium officinale*</u> (See *berro* or watercress.)

nemoscá, nuez moscada (nutmeg) 187, *226*

nerves, calming 186

nettle, giant tropical stinging *(ortiga)* 175, 186, 194, 201, 212, *238*

new physics 165

Newtonian science 164-165

<u>*Nicotiana tabacum*</u> (See *tabaco* or tobacco.)

nourishing, cooling drinks 192

nourishment x-xii, xv, xvi, 159

Numoticina 178

Núñez Meléndez, Esteban, Ph.D. xv, 163

nutmeg *(nuez moscada, nemoscá)* 28, 187, *238*

nuez moscada, nemoscá (nutmeg) 28, 187, *226*

ocean 183

<u>*Ocimum basilicum*</u> (See *albahaca* or basil.)

<u>*Ocotea moschata*</u> (See *nuez moscada* or nutmeg.)

ointment recipe 208-209

onion *(cebolla)* 213, *238*

<u>*Opuntia ficus-indica*</u> (See *tuna* or spineless tuna cactus.)

orange *(china)* 200, *238*

orange leaves, sour *(naranjo)* 175, 181, 182, 183, 186, 190, 198, 200, 203, 204, 205, 206, *238*

oregano, Puerto Rican *(orégano chiquito)* 194, *238*

<u>*Origanum marjorana*</u> (See *mejorana* or marjoram.)

orishas 57-58, 69, 70, 71

ortiga brava (tropical stinging nettle) 175, 186, 194, 201, 212, *216*

<u>*Oryza sativa*</u> (See *arroz* or rice.)

oyster plant *(sanguinaria)* 185, *238*

pacholí (vetiver) 210, *226*

pajuil (cashew) 194, *226*

paletaria, prenetaria (ice'n glass) 175, 179, 192, 200, 205, 208, 211, 216, *226*

paloma (dove or pigeon) 197

palma Christi, castor bean plant *(higuereta, ricino)* 181, 188, 190, 206, 211, 215, 216, *239 palma de coco, cocotero* (coconut palm)   159, 178, 191, 200, 202, 205, 208, *226*

palma real (Puerto Rican royal palm)   200, *226*

palo mayombe, palo monte   60, 75

pana, panapén (breadfruit)   115, 159, 185, 187, 246, *226*

Panama tree *(anacagüita)*   189, *239*

Panicum maximum   (See *yerba de guinea* or Guinea grass.)

paños (poultices) 173

papa (potato)   185, 198, 202, *226*

papaya *(lechosa)*   8, 180, 200, 207, *226*

paraffin   209

parasites, intestinal   207

parcha (passion fruit)   163, 204, *227*

pascua (poinsettia)   217, *227*

Passiflora edulis   (See *parcha* or passion fruit.)

passion fruit *(parcha)*   163, 204, *239*

pasteles   xi, 248

pata de perro, cadillo de fibra (bur)   177, *227*

patents for pharamaceutical products   164

pazote (wormseed)   182, 207, *227*

peace of mind   210

Pedilanthus tithymaloides   (See *ipecacuana* or slipper plant.)

Pelargonium odoratissium   (See *geranio oloroso* or fragrant geranium.)

Peperomia pellucida   (See *paletaria, prenetaria* or ice'n glass.)

peppermint *(menta)*   180, *239*

periwinkle, Madagascar *(playera)*   162, *239*

Persea americana   (See *aguacate* or avocado.)

pesticides   x

pests   210

Petiveria alliacea   (See *anamú* or garlic weed.)

phlegm   178

Phyllanthus niruri   (See *quinino del pobre* or gale of the wind.)

Physalis spp. (See *sacabuche* or ground cherry.)

physic nut *(tártago)*   182, 186, 190, 191, 194, 205, *239*

pigeon or dove *(paloma)*   197

pigeon pea *(gandul)*   159, 176, 194, 214, *239*

Pimenta racemosa   (See *malagueta* or bay rum.)

pimienta Angola, dragón (shell plant) 180, *227*

Pimpinella anisum   (See *anís de grano* or anise.)

Pimpinella anisum (See *anís de grano* or anise.)
Piper marginatum (See *higuillo oloroso* or jointwood.)
pitirre 159, 248
Plantago major (See *llantén* or common plantain.)
plantain, common *(llantén)* 176, 179, 186, 197, 198, 199, 203, 207, 208, 213, 239
plants, hot and cooling xv
playera (Madagascar periwinkle) 162, 227
plena 150, 246
Pluchea symphytifolia (See *salvia* or sweet scent.)
poinsettia *(pascua)* 217, 239
poleo 177, 178, 179, 182, 183, 190, 198, 199, 204, 205, 210, 227
Polianthes tuberosa (See *azucena antillana* or tuberose.)
pollution 159, 160
Portulaca oleracea (See *verdolaga* or purslane.)
potato *(papa)* 185, 198, 202, 239
poultices 173
prenetaria, paletaria (ice'n glass) 175, 179, 192, 200, 205, 208, 211, 216, 227
primrose willow *(yerba cangá)* 193, 239
pringamoza (stinging vine) 196, 227
Psidium guajava (See *guayabo* or guava.)
psillium seed 162 (Also, see *llantén* or common plantain.)
Puerto Rican oregano *(orégano chiquito)* 194, 239
Puerto Rican royal palm *(palma real)* 200, 240
pumpkin, squash *(calabaza)* 212, 240
purging cassia *(caña fístula)* 191, 200, 240
purslane *(verdolaga)* 176, 192, 197, 207, 240

quinine 167
quinino del pobre (gale of the wind) 199, 227

rábano cimarrón (dumb cane) 212, 227
rain forests 161, 164
rash 211-212
recao, culantro del monte (broadleaf coriander) xvi, 194, 203, 203, 209, 227
red mint , Caribbean spearmint *(yerba buena)* 179, 180, 182, 183, 188, 195, 199, 200, 204, 205, 240

red sage *(cariaquillo)*   182, 183, 189, *240*

relaxation   171-172

rheumatism *&* arthritis   176-177

Rhoeo spathacea   (See *sanguinaria* or oyster plant.)

rice *(arroz)* 159, 191, 194, *240*

ricino, higuereta (castor bean plant, palma Christi)   181, 188, 190, 206, 211, 215, 216, *228*

Ricinis comunis   (See *ricino, higuereta,* castor bean or palma Christi.)

ringworm   212

ringworm tree *(talantro)*   212, *240*

roble amarillo, saúco amarillo (yellow trumpet)   177, 189, 198, *228*

romero (rosemary)   177, 180, 182, 201, *228*

rompecota (sawgrass)   181, *228*

rompe zaragüey, santa María (bitter bush)   181, 183, *228*

Rosa centifolia   (See *rosa cienhojas* or fairy rose.)

rosa cienhojas (fairy rose)   197, *228*

rose, fairy *(rosa cienhojas)*   197, *240*

Rosmarinus officinalis   (See *romero* or rosemary.)

rosemary *(romero)*   177, 180, 182, 201, *240*

Roystonea borinquena   (See *palma real* or Puerto Rican royal palm.)

ruda (rue)   x, xv, 197, 209, 216, *228*

rue *(ruda)*   x, xv, 197, 209, 216, *240*

rum *(ron)*   178, 179, 190, 197

Ruta chalepensis   (See *ruda* or rue.)

sábila (aloe)   xv, 163, 178, 179, 180, 182, 183, 186, 191, 192, 200, 201, 202, 211, 214, *228*

sacabuche (ground cherry)   181, *228*

Saccharum officinarum   (See *caña de azúcar* or sugar cane.)

saints   57, 63, 68, 69, 70, 76, 159

sal de Eno   194

salsa   159, 246

salt   177, 180, 185, 190, 193, 198, 203, 212, 214, 215

salvia (sweet scent)   182, 199, 202, 209, 214, 215, *228*

Sambucus mexicana   (See *saúco* or elder.)

sanguinaria (oyster plant)   185, *228*

Sansevieria metallica   (See *chucho* or snake plant.)

santa María, rompe zaragüey (bitter bush)   181, 183, *228*

santiguo   ix, 28, 62, 67, 151, 248

saúco blanco (elder) 177, 190, 217, *228*
sawgrass *(rompecota)* 181, *240*
Scleria spp. (See *rompecota* or sawgrass.)
seaweed 175, 186
sebo Flandes (tallow) 179, 198, 199, 211, 213
Senecio aizoides (See *malá* or stipti.)
Senna alata (See *talantro* or ringworm tree.)
Senna occidentalis (See *hidionda chiquita* or coffee senna.)
sensitive plant *(morivivi)* 214, *240*
sesame *(ajonjolí)* 163, 175, 186, *241*
Sesamum indicum (See *ajonjolí* or sesame.)
shell plant *(pimienta Angola, dragón)* 180, *241*
Sida spp. (See *escobilla* or soap bush.)
skin 191, 211-212
slipper plant *(ipecacuana)* 178, 180, *241*
snake plant *(chucho)* 178, *241*
Solanum americanum (See *yerba mora, mata de gallina* or black
     nightshade.)
Solanum torvum (See *berenjena cimarrona* or wild eggplant.)
Solanum tuberosum (See *papa* or potato.)
soap bush *(escobilla)* 211, *241*
sores, cuts & wounds 193
sour orange leaves *(naranjo)* 175, 181, 182, 183, 186, 190, 198, 200,
     203, 204, 205, 206, *241*
soursop *(guanábana)* 159, 196, 204, 205, *241*
Spanish elm *(vara prieta)* 182, *241*
spearmint (Caribbean), red mint *(yerba buena)* 179, 180, 182, 183,
     188, 195, 199, 200, 204, 205, *242*
Spondias dulcis (See *jobo* or yellow mombin.)
sprains & broken bones 184-185
Stachytarpheta jamaicensis (See *verbena* or vervain.)
star anise *(anís estrellado)* 178, 187, 190, 207, *242*
star apple *(caimito)* 194, *242*
Sterculia apetala (See *anacagüita* or Panama tree.)
stipti *(malá)* 178, 193, 203, *242*
stomach (digestion) 195, 204-205
stomach ulcers 213
stinging tropical nettle *(ortiga)* 175, 186, 194, 201, 212, *242*
stinging vine *(pringamoza)* 196, *242*

suelda consuelda (Madeira vine) 184-185, 193, *228*

sugar, sugar cane *(caña de azúcar)* 185, 197, 198, 215, 217

sunburn 211

sweet scent *(salvia)* 182, 199, 202, 209, 214, 215

sweet verbena *(yerba dulce)* 194

swollen glands & mumps 213

Symphytum officinalis (See *consuelda mayor* or comfrey.)

Syzygium aromaticum (See *clavo dulce* or clove.)

tabaco (tobacco) 30, 192, *228*

Tacoma stans (See *saúco amarillo* or yellow trumpet.)

Taíno 68

talantro (ringworm tree) 212, *229*

tallow (sebo Flandes) 179, 198, 199, 211, 213

tamarind *(tamarindo)* 191, 196, *242*

Tamarindus indica (See *tamarindo* or tamarind.)

tanier (yautía) 115, *242*

Tanacetum parthenium (See *manzanilla* or feverfew.)

tártago (physic nut) 182, 186, 190, 191, 194, 205, *229*

taro, dasheen *(malanga)* 4, 115, 167, *242*

tautúa (wild physic nut) 184, 204, 213, 214, *229*

tea *(guarapo)* 172, 173

Tecoma stans (See *saúco amarillo* or yellow trumpet.)

teeth & gums 214-215

Terminalia catappa (See *almendro* or tropical almond.)

throat problems 215

ticks 210

tide 201

Tilia spp. (See *tilo* or linden.)

tilo (linden) 179, 186, *229*

tisane *(tisana)* 173

tobacco *(tabaco)* 30, 192, *242*

tolú (balsam) 178, *229*

tomato *(tomate)* 86, *242*

toronjil, melisa (lemon balm) 180, 204, 205, *229*

traditional medicine, healers ix, xi-xvi, 159-160, 166, 168- 169

Tragia volubilis (See *pringamoza* or stinging vine.)

Triaca 187

tropical almond leaves *(almendro)* 194, *243*

tropical almond leaves *(almendro)*   194, *243*
túatúa (belly ache bush)   184, 204, 213, 214, *229*
tuberose *(azucena antillana)*   184, 186, 217, *243*
tuna cactus, spineless   175, 179, 192, 199, 200, 208, 216, *243*

udder balm *(unguento de ubres)*   193
udder congestion   215
ulcers   213
unguento de ubres (udder balm)   193
<u>*Urena*</u> <u>*lobata*</u>   (See *cadillo de fibra* or bur.)
<u>*Urera*</u> <u>*baccifera*</u>   (See *ortiga brava* or nettle.)
urinary tract   216
urine   176, 199, 210
uterine inflammation   216

valerian *(valeriana)*   186, *243*
<u>*Valeriana*</u> <u>*scandens*</u>   (See *valeriana* or valerian.)
vara prieta (Spanish elm)   182, *229*
Vaseline   208-209
verbena (vervain)   181, 182, 194, 198, 199, 201, 205, *229*
verdolaga (purslane)   176, 192, 197, 207, *230*
vervain (verbena)   181, 182, 194, 198, 199, 201, 205, *243*
vetiver *(pacholí)*   210, *243*
<u>*Vetiveria*</u> <u>*zizanioides*</u>   (See *pacholí* or vetiver.)
Vicks   189, 203
vinegar   215

warming pleasure drinks   217
warts   217
watercress *(berro)*   179, *243*
weakness & fatigue   197
Weil, Andrew, M.D.   166-167
white amaranth, calaloo *(blero, espinaca criolla)*   176, 208, *243*
wild balsam apple *(cundeamor)*   xv, 163, 186, 194, 202, 211, 212, *243*
wild eggplant *(berenjena cimarrona)*   193, 216, *243*
wild lettuce *(achicoria)*   178, 199, *243*
wild physic nut *(tautúa)*   184, 204, 213, 214, *243*
wild pineapple *(maya)*   189, *243*
wild plants   x-xi

wild zinnia *(escopetón)*   180, *244*

witch hazel *(hamamelis, Agua Maravilla)*   178, 179, 180, 183, 189, 202, *244*

wood ashes   193, 203, 204

wormseed *(pazote)*   182, 207, *244*

wounds, cuts & sores   193

Xanthosoma sagittifolium   (See *yautía* or tanier.)

yapaná, curía panacea (japana)   190, *230*

yautía (tanier)   115, *230*

yellow allamanda *(canario amarillo)*   134, *244*

yellow elder, yellow trumpet *(roble amarillo)*   177, 189, 198, *244*

yellow mombin *(jobo)*   189, *244*

yellow trumpet *(saúco amarillo)*   177, 189, 198, *244*

yerba bruja, bruja (life plant)   180, 195, *230*

yerba buena (red mint, Caribbean spearmint)   179, 180, 182, 183, 188, 195, 199, 200, 204, 205, *230,*

yerba cangá (primrose willow)   193, *230*

yerba dulce (sweet verbena)   194, *230*

yerba de Guinea (Guinea grass)   148, *230*

yerba Luisa (lemon verbena)   209, *230*

yerba mora, mata (de) gallina (black nightshade)   176, 194, 199, 204, 208, 213, 216, *230*

Yoruba   *58, 68*

yuca (cassava)   109, 115, 201, *230*

zábila, sábila (aloe)   *xv,* 163, 178, 179, 180, 182, 183, 186, 191, 192, 200, 201, 202, 211, 214, *230*

zanahoria (carrot)   200, *230*

Zea mays   (See *maíz* or corn.)

Zingiber officinale   (See *jengibre dulce* or ginger)

Zingiber zerumbet   (See *jengibre amargo* or bitter ginger)

zinnia, wild *(escopetón)*   180, *244*

Zinnia peruviana   (See *escopetón* or zinnia.)